The
CampusLife
Guide to
Christian Colleges
& Universities

The
CampusLife
Guide to
Christian Colleges
& Universities

answering more than 100 of your
college questions about:

- *the search-and-application process*
- *financial aid*
- *college life and academics*
- *your spiritual life on campus*

PLUS: A special chapter just for homeschoolers

from the editorial team of
Campus Life magazine

Mark Moring
General Editor

also featuring helpful hints from students
and
the hilarious cartoons of John McPherson

ISBN 0–0854–9038–8

Library of Congress Card Catalog Number: 97–32978

Library of Congress Cataloging-in-Publication Data

The Campus life guide to Christian colleges and universities / Mark
Moring, general editor.
p. cm.
   ISBN 0–0854–9038–8
   1. College choice—United States—Miscellanea. 2. Church colleges—United States—Miscellanea. 3. Church colleges—United
States—Directories. I. Moring, Mark. II. Campus life.
LB2350.5.C361998
378.1'98—dc21   97–32978
                                                                       CIP

Printed in the United States of America

1 2 3 4 5 6   03 02 01 00 99 98

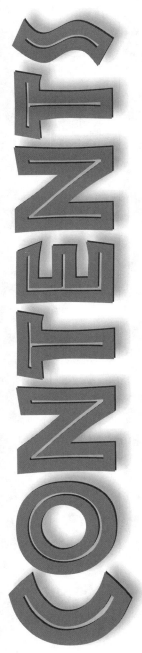

Chapter 2:
First Steps in the Christian College Search   page 19

PLUS: Admissions Officers

Chapter 3:
The Campus Visit   page 35

PLUS: Checking It Out

Chapter 4:

The Application Process   page 47

PLUS: Admissions Essays

Chapter 5:

Getting the Money You Need   page 63

PLUS: Fun With Finances

Chapter 6:

Making the Best College Choice   page 81

Chapter 7:

Living on Campus   page 91

Chapter 8:
Hittin' the Books page 117

***PLUS:* Excuses, Excuses**

Chapter 9:
Your Spiritual Life page 141

***PLUS:* Going To Church**

Chapter 10:
Just for Homeschoolers   page 153

Afterword:
"Dear Nick" page 161
by Ruth Senter

Countdown to College:
A calendar checklist   page 165
What you need to do, and when you need to do it.

Appendix:
Colleges & Universities   page 169
Important information about more than 200 schools

Photo Credits:

p. v, Houghton College; p. xi, Paul Talley/Carson-Newman College; p. 1, Larry Lawfer/ Gordon College; p. 5, Houghton College; p. 19, Greenville College; p. 35, Anderson University; p. 47, Grace College; p. 63, Dordt College; p. 81, Houghton College; p. 91, Greenville College; p. 117, Dordt College; p. 141, Paul Talley/Carson-Newman College; p. 153, Larry Lawfer/Gordon College; p. 161, Paul Talley/Carson-Newman College; p. 166, Anderson University; p. 169, John Corriveau/Calvin College

Acknowledgments

When I was asked to be the general editor for this book, I jumped at the opportunity. Why? Mainly because I want to see students make wise, informed, prayerful decisions when it comes to choosing a college or university.

I had a great college experience. I learned a lot, made some terrific lifelong friends (a dozen Christian guys who call each other Shmoos, which is almost a book in itself, so don't even ask), and really started growing in my faith. Which is kind of ironic, because I really didn't pray about my college decision very much, nor did I put much thought or energy into the process. Looking back now, it's a bit disconcerting to think how little I applied myself when searching for just the right school. Fortunately, God honored my decision, because I can't imagine having a better time in college than I had.

It's my prayer that every reader of this book can eventually say the same thing about his or her college experience. And I hope this book helps you get off to a good start as you begin your college search, as you take your campus visits, as you apply for admission and financial aid, as you make your final choice, and, ultimately, as you move into the dorm to begin what might well be the time of your life.

This book answers more than 100 questions that you and your parents will probably ask at some time during the college search. As you turn the pages, you'll also read helpful hints from students, as well as enjoy the hilarious cartoons of John McPherson, a long-time contributor to *Campus Life*.

Of course, this book wouldn't be possible without the help of many, and I'd like to thank them all:

My Redeemer, who gave me the passion to see high school students grow in their faith and make good choices, and who gave me a pretty cool gift — the ability to write well.

My wife Nina and my sons Peter and Paul, who've been so loving, patient and understanding as I've worked on this book. You guys are the best!

My wild and wacky (and talented!) colleagues at Campus Life magazine, who not only helped with the editing and offered a ton of great suggestions, but were a real encouragement to me as I plugged away at this project. Thanks, *Harold Smith, Chris Lutes, Carla Barnhill, Doug Johnson, Jennifer Ridenour, and Marilyn Roe.* Special thanks to *Marilyn,* who compiled all the information for the list of colleges and universities at the back of the book, a huge task.

The trio of consultants who offered their advice and ideas as I worked: *Dan Crabtree,* Director of Admissions at Wheaton (IL) College; *Ed Hollinger,* Director of Guidance Services at Lancaster (PA) Mennonite High School; and *Mark Seymour,* Executive Director for Enrollment Management at Eastern College in Saint Davids, PA.

Steve Bond at Broadman & Holman Publishers, whose gentle guidance has been much appreciated. And book designer *Karen Baucom,* who has been a joy to work with.

College-bound students everywhere, because this book is just for you and your parents.

Campus Life magazine has been a friend to students and parents for more than half a century. And our thrice-a-year College Guides have long been invaluable in helping students and parents in the college search. Much of what you'll read in this book is built upon that reputation and information.

I hope and pray that as you turn these pages, you'll learn the things you'll need to know to make a great college choice!

Mark Moring
General Editor

Introduction:

Why a Christian College?

by Jim Long

Something remarkable happened to me half-way through my senior year of high school.

You've heard of the domino theory? Something transpires that sets in motion a chain reaction? That was my experience. A series of changes began that eventually affected everything about me, even my educational plans. Funny thing is, I'm not sure I can reconstruct precisely what started it all.

I entered my senior year not with my eyes on the future, but scanning the present, trying to make sense out of it. Like most people, I sometimes found life frustrating; I could write paragraphs about that, I suppose. But as the year unfolded, I was beginning to dwell on the negatives a whole lot less as I met a few people, just a few, who were truly different. They were not immune to hardship, but they were not embittered by it either. They seemed to have a sense of purpose to their lives which I admired. And I noticed these people had something else in common: They loved God and they cared about me.

Faced with authentic faith, I started paying closer attention. I began reading and asking questions, and somewhere in the middle of this whole process that year, I took Jesus seriously, probably for the first time. The dominoes began falling. Change swept through my life. I became more of a positive person, I put bitterness behind me, I started to care more deeply about people other than myself. I woke up one day to the realization that I was on the other side of a chain-reaction. I now fully believed. And if Jesus was who he claimed to be, he deserved my total commitment.

I mention all this here, because that encounter changed almost everything about me, including what I was looking for in a college education. If God had a claim on my life, I wanted to use my energies to advance his purposes in the world. To do that, I reasoned, I would need to understand him better. I would need experience in ministry. I would need the foundation of a caring Christian community. I would need a Christian perspective on all my studies. By the end of my senior year of sweeping change, I had concluded that the best way to meet my new goals was through Christian higher education.

Here, then, is what I was looking for and what I found in my Christian college experience:

A Christian college education gave me the opportunity to study the Bible in depth.

I was not raised as a Christian, but I had hung around the church enough to know that Moses broke the Ten Commandments in more ways than one; that David brought down Goliath with a slingshot, and himself with lust; that Thomas finally figured out that believing is seeing, not the other way around. But now that I felt captured by Jesus Christ, I felt captivated by Scripture. My interest was deep. I found it exciting that I could study the Bible in the same sense at the collegiate level — just as I would study sociology, psychology, history, or science.

I felt motivated. I took classes in personal evangelism, missions, theology, and biblical studies. Before, I had studied Spanish, with mixed reviews. Now I eagerly tackled New Testament Greek.

It was my Christian college that opened up these educational opportunities I would not otherwise have had.

A Christian college education opened my world to unprecedented ministry opportunities.

I began to see the world with different eyes. My Christian college put me in touch with opportunities to share my faith on the beach, in parks, on the streets of Los Angeles and Hollywood. I took week-long missions trips to Mexico. I counseled at camps for underprivileged kids. I shared the Good News at rescue missions. I directed junior church. I taught Sunday school to kids not much younger than I and directed a youth program. I even took some classes at a local community college which gave me some unique opportunities to share my faith with other college students there.

My horizons were broadened because of my Christian college education. I heard about needs and opportunities worldwide. I met and carried on conversations with people who were making a difference all around the world.

A Christian college education put me in a caring family of faith.

As I mentioned, I was not raised a Christian. In fact, we had some pretty significant struggles in my home. As much as I loved my mom, dad, brother and sister, I think it's interesting that God gave me the opportunity to broaden my family. In college, I met fellow students who became like brothers and sisters to me. I was introduced to a dimension of friendship I had not previously experienced. What was it? That we all understood a deeper purpose in life? That through faith we shared something in common that was beyond us all? That we were all beginning to understand love and acceptance in a way we hadn't before? Whatever it was, I found it in my Christian college experience.

It was also during those years that I discovered that the idea of a caring faculty was more than just an advertising gimmick. I wasn't close to all my profs; I could not honestly say I enjoyed every last one. What I did find were several I could only describe as friends. I do not doubt that they prayed for me, and when they asked me how things were going, I knew they cared; it was not just perfunctory.

A Christian college education offered a Bible-centered perspective on all my studies.

It would be silly to have a paranoid fear of every subject other than the Bible, or to think we had to slink away from the ideas of people who do not share our faith. On the other hand, Christians do view life from a different perspective. We study science, and see the hand of a creating and sustaining God, not a chance-convergence of energy and matter. We trace the movements of history, not as the panorama of fatalistic circumstance, but with a sense of agenda, moving toward time's final destination in Christ. We examine the sociology of family dynamics and radically shifting roles, knowing that God has spoken to the needs, fears and aspirations we all bring to such relationships.

A Christian college education is nothing if not a reference point for every subject, a context for every discipline. And to a large degree, that's what it was for me.

Just the beginning.

I entered college relatively new to faith, with my Christian ideas formative and largely untested. But as I studied, my foundations grew more firm. As I shared my faith, I learned to articulate it to skeptics and honest seekers alike. As I related Scripture to all areas of study, a view of the world began to emerge that hung together and made sense; it provided the framework for a lifetime of further study.

I entered college looking for friendship, and found a dimension of it I had never before experienced. I was, in fact, embraced by something more than mere friendship; I found a deeper sense of family.

I entered college, I confess, somewhat self-centered, but trying to break out of my selfishness, looking for ways to touch the world for Christ. In those years I came to see more clearly what life is all about—what it means to waste it, or what it can mean to redeem it, through service.

I entered college feeling that it was the result of sweeping changes that took place in my senior year of high school. I suppose I thought Christian college was the last of all those dominoes to fall — the last stage in a chain-reaction of faith.

I now know it was only the beginning.

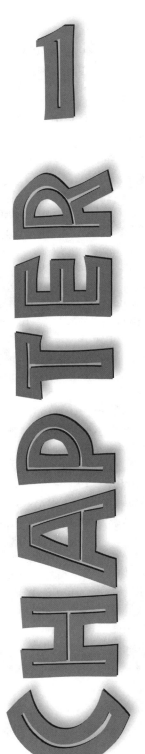

Preparing for College

Q **I want to make sure I'm doing all I can NOW to get into a good college. I make good grades, but do colleges look at more than just grades?**

A Good grades are a great start. But colleges do look at more than just grades when considering your application. They want a much bigger picture of you.

For starters, colleges aren't impressed by good grades alone; they'll want to see that you've taken challenging classes. So, don't just take easy classes (like "The History of the No. 2 Pencil"), where good grades don't mean as much. Take hard classes too (like "Electromagnetic Biomedical Physics in Southeastern Nebraska"). These tougher classes will not only look better on a college application; they will better prepare you for college.

Colleges are also interested in how well you've done on the SAT and/or the ACT. (We'll talk more about these tests later in this chapter.)

But colleges are interested in much more than academic performance and test scores. They're interested in

6 • **Chapter I**

your co-curricular and extracurricular activities, community service, church involvement, spiritual development, job experience, internships, even your family life—essentially anything that's played a vital role in shaping who you are and what makes you tick.

Leadership is also critical. Involvement in activities is good, but taking a leadership role in at least one of them is even better. A leadership role shows colleges that you are someone who stands out in a group, someone other people can look to for guidance. And a leadership role tells colleges that you're willing to commit your time and energy to something you care about.

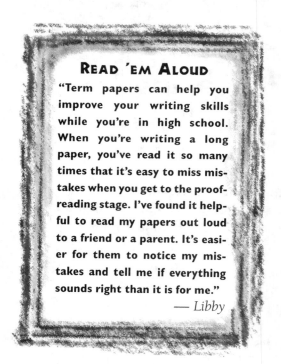

READ 'EM ALOUD

"Term papers can help you improve your writing skills while you're in high school. When you're writing a long paper, you've read it so many times that it's easy to miss mistakes when you get to the proofreading stage. I've found it helpful to read my papers out loud to a friend or a parent. It's easier for them to notice my mistakes and tell me if everything sounds right than it is for me."

— *Libby*

Finally, colleges are interested in what others have to say about you. When you apply to colleges, you'll probably have to submit two or more letters of recommendation from adults who know you well—like a guidance counselor, a teacher, or a pastor.

If you need more advice on what classes to take and what types of activities to pursue to better prepare you for college, talk to your guidance counselor. He or she is your best resource for preparing for college.

We could put the previous paragraph at the end of almost every answer in this book. We're big fans of your guidance counselor, and we strongly encourage you to consult him or her any time you have questions about preparing for college.

Note: If you're homeschooled, there's a special section near the back of the book just for you. But as you read all the references to guidance counselors in this book, you might consider asking your local public school's guidance counselor for help, too. They're great resources!

Q What kinds of courses should I be taking in high school?

A   In a nutshell, college prep courses, classes that are academically challenging. Take your school's "honors classes," or courses with titles preceded by
the words "Advanced Placement." (Note: Some "AP" classes will even earn you
college credit!) Your high school probably has a number of course programs
geared toward college-bound students. Look into them.

Even if you're a senior and you've already met your minimum graduation
requirements, resist the urge to take all easy classes. They might make your
senior year easier, but the lack of intellectual challenge won't help you adjust
to the rigors of college. Keep those brain cells in gear.

Remember, too, that many colleges have minimum entrance requirements
in math, English, science, foreign language, etc. Ask your guidance counselor
and/or the colleges you're considering about these requirements.

While you've got to take a certain number of "core" curriculum classes to
get into college, don't get so caught up in those that you forget about valuable
electives, especially in the arts — chorus, band, orchestra, art, drama, etc. Also,
consider taking a technology or computer course. These types of electives will
make you a more well-rounded student.

Q Should I take challenging courses even if I risk getting lower grades?

A   Yes. Getting a "B" in a college prep course looks better on your
record than an "A" in a piece-of-cake class. Giving your best effort in more
difficult classes shows colleges you're serious about facing and meeting
academic challenges.

Many high schools reward you for taking challenging classes by giving them
more "weight" when computing your grade-point average. For instance, an "A"
in a regular English class might earn you four points on a 4-point scale, but an
"A" in an AP English class might be worth 4.5 points.

One college admissions counselor told us he's "more impressed with a student who took challenging courses and has a 2.5 GPA than one who ends up
with a 3.5 but padded their curriculum with easy classes."

Another counselor said that his college is "interested in the kinds of classes
you've taken. A lot of times students hesitate to take the tougher classes
because they think any grade less than an 'A' will hurt their chances of getting
scholarships or being accepted. But we want students to challenge themselves
as much as possible."

Q **What types of co-curricular and/or extracurricular activities should I be involved in?**

A For the most part, get involved in stuff you like to do. In other words, don't sign up for The Arctic Barefoot Marathon Running Club just because you think it might look good on your resumé. If you're gonna hate it, don't do it.

Get involved in a variety of activities that challenge you in different ways—intellectually (the debate club, an academic team, etc.), physically (sports, intramurals, etc.), artistically (drama, music, etc.), spiritually (Bible club, service organizations, etc.).

And yet don't spread yourself too thin, especially to the point that your grades suffer. It's better to do a few things well than a bunch of things badly. A college isn't as impressed with *how many* clubs you joined as it is by *what* you did in those clubs, how *well* you did, and what you *learned* from those experiences.

One college admissions official advises, "It's smart to have a major activity and several minor ones. In other words, get involved in depth in one area, but participate in others, too."

Q **Why are colleges so interested in my church activities and community involvement?**

A Because these types of things help shape your spiritual development, a dimension of your character that Christian colleges especially want to know about. This information gives admissions officials at Christian schools a better "feel" for who you are and how you'll fit on their campus.

When you start filling out college applications, you'll come across questions that not only ask about your faith, but about the experiences and activities that have had an impact on your spiritual life.

Look for activities that not only help you grow personally, but force you to reach out to others — like volunteering at a local food bank, teaching a children's Sunday school class, or taking a short-term missions trip.

Q **Should I take the SAT or the ACT?**

A It depends on the colleges you're applying to and what they require. Most colleges will accept scores from either test, but some colleges want only one or the other. Ask the colleges you're considering which test they require.

Most schools in the Coalition for Christian Colleges & Universities (CCCU) require *either* the SAT or the ACT. A handful require the ACT only. Several others simply *recommend*, but don't require, taking one test or the other.

(*Note:* All references to "SAT" in this book refer to the SAT I Reasoning Test, the general standardized test that many college-bound students take.)

If you're considering colleges that accept both tests, it might be a good idea to take both. Often, students do better on one than the other. Colleges that accept both tests usually consider the better of the two scores.

It's impossible to predict which test you'll score higher on. Generally, about one-third of students who take both tests score higher on the ACT, one-third higher on the SAT, and one-third about the same on each. (If you've taken the preliminary versions of both tests—the PSAT and the PLAN—you may have a better feel for which of the "real" versions you prefer.)

It's a good idea to take the SAT and/or the ACT twice, since your scores are likely to improve the second time around. One high-school counselor, who advises students to take both the ACT and SAT, said 80 percent of his students raised either their math or verbal score on the SAT by taking it a second time, and 54 percent raised their overall ACT score by taking it a second time.

Q   What are the differences between the SAT and ACT?

A   The main difference is that the SAT is generally considered an "aptitude" test, designed to evaluate your ability to do college-level work, while the ACT is more of an achievement test, evaluating the skills you've already mastered.

Here are a few other differences between the two tests:

• The ACT has a science reasoning test; the SAT doesn't.
• The ACT math includes some trigonometry; the SAT doesn't.
• The ACT is entirely multiple choice; the SAT isn't.
• The SAT penalizes you for wrong guesses; the ACT doesn't.
• The ACT lasts 2 hours and 55 minutes; the SAT lasts 3-1/2 hours.
• The ACT is divided into four sections: English (45 minutes), math (60), reading (35), and science reasoning (35). The SAT is divided into seven sections: two 30-minute and one 15-minute verbal sections, two 30-minute and one 15-minute math section, and one 30-minute experimental section (either math or verbal), which is not scored.
• The ACT score is an average of the scores on each section, with a maximum of 36 points per section; the highest score possible is 36. The SAT is broken down into two scores, a math score and a verbal score, each on a scale from 200 to 800; the highest possible total score is 1,600.

Both tests cost around $20 to take, and both tests allow you to use a calculator.

You can take sample SAT and ACT tests to get a better feel for both types. If your guidance counselor doesn't have sample tests, your local bookstore probably will.

Q What's the best way to prepare for the SAT or ACT?

A The *best way* is for you to have been a good student all along. Your success on these tests will depend a lot on what you've learned through all your school years. So, in some ways, these tests are a gauge of your cumulative knowledge.

Does that mean you can't study for these tests? Of course not. You can study, and there are all kinds of services that are willing to help you do it — some at a pretty hefty cost. Some test-preparation courses charge as much as $700, all but "guaranteeing" they'll boost your test score. These prep courses can't make you magically learn things you haven't been learning all along, but they might be able to help you improve your test-taking skills, teach you tricks and techniques of answering questions, and make you feel more comfortable about what can be an intimidating test. Are these services worth it? That's debatable. Some admissions officers question the value of these services, saying that if you're already a pretty good test-taker, they're probably a waste of time and money.

You can spend much less money by browsing through your local bookstore's reference section, looking for books on taking these tests. There are many helpful books on the shelves, many of them including sample tests.

But the most cost-effective way to prepare for these tests is by asking your guidance counselor for free books and sample tests that will help you prepare.

Taking the sample tests — under timed conditions and in a quiet place — is probably the best way to prepare. Though you probably won't see the same questions on the real tests (sample tests are just old versions of the SAT and ACT), you'll get a great feel for what the tests are like.

Q How can a part-time job in high school help me prepare for college?

A First you should ask yourself if you should get a job. The answer depends on your situation. If you've got a full academic load, you're the captain of the soccer team, you've got the lead role in the school play, you're the chief soloist in your church choir and the vice president of your youth group, *and* you're responsible for watching your little brother and cooking dinner every night, the answer's a no-brainer: You just don't have time for a part-time job.

Here's a good rule of thumb: If taking a part-time job is going to affect your performance in other vital areas of your life — like your studies, your spiritual life, your important activities, or the amount of sleep you're getting — it's probably a good idea to avoid the extra work. If you do take on a part-time job, start slowly: Start at 10 hours a week and if that's working out, ask your boss to gradually increase your hours. But don't work more than 20 hours a week; your studies will likely suffer if you do.

If possible, find a job that fits your career goals. For example, if you want to go into medicine, try to work in a hospital or doctor's office.

A part-time job can be an asset when you're applying to colleges, especially if it applies to your academic and/or career interests. If you want to study forestry, for example, it'll look great on your application if you've worked part-time at a national park.

But even if your job doesn't directly apply to your future interests, the experience can still be helpful. If nothing else, a part-time job can demonstrate that you're responsible enough to handle many demands at once—like academics, extracurricular activities, and so on, in addition to your job. Colleges like people who can handle busy schedules.

EVEN THOUGH JIM SCHAAD COULD BURP THE ENTIRE STAR TREK THEME SONG, IT WASN'T GOING TO BE MUCH HELP WHEN COLLEGES STARTED ASKING ABOUT HIS SPECIAL GIFTS AND TALENTS.

Q I'm thinking about taking a year off between high school and college. Is that a good idea?

A It really depends on what you're planning to do in that year off. If you're just planning on hanging out at the beach in search of the perfect tan and the perfect wave, well. . . . Well, if you can get *paid* while doing that, please let us know, because we'll gladly join you!

Seriously, you have to ask yourself what you mean by a year "off." Such a year has the potential to be quite productive — educationally, spiritually, emotionally, financially.

If you've got a chance to spend a year as a volunteer at a missions hospital in Ghana, we'd probably say, "Go for it!" If you've been studying Russian and have the opportunity to stay with a Christian family while working in Moscow, we'd likely say, "You're there!" If you can travel around Europe for six months, visiting museums and cathedrals and castles, we'd tell you it's a once-in-a-lifetime opportunity.

> **PLAY JEOPARDY**
>
> "A great way to study for exams is to get together with some friends and play High School Jeopardy, like the TV show Jeopardy. The categories are your different classes: chemistry, English, physics, history, foreign language, etc. Each person could bring a set number of questions from one class. Questions should be written on one side of an index card, with answers on the back. Come up with your own system of scoring and prizes. And remember: The host student gets to be Alex Trebek!"
>
> —*Jennifer*

But your "year off" options don't have to include international travel to be considered "legitimate." Perhaps money is really tight, and you'd like to work a year to help finance your college education. Or maybe you've experienced tremendous stress, depression, or a loss in the family, or maybe you or a family member has been seriously ill, and you simply need some recovery time. Maybe you're just not convinced you want to go to college yet, and you need more time to consider such a big decision.

If you're not completely certain you want to go to college right out of high school, it's certainly worth thinking about holding off on that decision, rather than committing as much as $20,000 to something you're not sure you want to do.

Another option to consider is something called "deferred enrollment." After you apply and are accepted, some colleges will allow you to wait a semester or even a whole year before you actually enroll at the college. If you're interested in pursuing this option, ask the colleges you're considering if they offer it.

The bottom line: Colleges won't hold it against you if you choose to take a year off. But they *will* want to know what you did with that year, and how it helped you to grow intellectually, spiritually, academically.

In other words, that year on the beach probably won't help you get into a good school.

Q **How important is it to know what major I want before I start college?**

A It's not that important. Colleges don't ask you to choose a major before they'll accept you, though they might ask what fields of study you're *interested* in. Most colleges don't require you to declare a major until at least your sophomore year.

One college official says, "It's definitely OK to come to college not knowing what you're going to do with the rest of your life. College is a time for exploration."

At the same time, it's good to have at least some idea about what you might want to study. What are your interests? If you think it might be cool to be an engineer, you probably don't want to apply to schools that don't offer an engineering major.

Bottom line: Don't get too caught up in deciding on a major now. You might end up crossing colleges off your list prematurely. Keep your options open.

Take the advice of one college student who told us, "When I started looking for a college, I put all my emphasis on finding a school with a major I wanted. I was looking for a major that would lead to a 'good' career. After praying for God's guidance, I realized I was seeking a career that would 'impress' others—and not necessarily one that would allow me to serve God. So I decided to explore other majors and career possibilities. This really opened me up to look into other schools I never would have considered."

A Goofy Look at the SAT!

by John McPherson

The Scholastic Assessment Test, as most of you know, was created by a national panel of educational experts for the purpose of torturing high-school students. To this aim the test has been a complete success. Teachers and parents have assisted the panel of experts by bombarding students with remarks like, "This is the most important test you will ever take!" or "Your performance on the SAT will decide the direction of your entire life!" As a result of these words of encouragement, hundreds of thousands of students lie awake on the eve of the SAT, convinced that tomorrow will determine whether they graduate with a Ph.D. in nuclear physics, or spend the next 40 years standing in line at the unemployment office.

The Actual Test

The SAT consists of seven parts: three math sections, three verbal sections, and one "experimental" section. It is this last part that has always concerned me the most and is probably the reason I started losing my hair at age 17. The panel of experts uses the experimental section to test their newest and most excruciating questions. They do this by watching students carefully as they work through the section. The questions that evoke the most screaming, fainting, and/or drooling are promoted to the regular portion of the exam. I drooled most of the time while taking the experimental section.

The Scoring

One of the things that bothers me most about the SAT is that the scores don't make any sense. All our lives we're taught to strive for that elusive 100 on tests. Then along comes this exam where if you scored 100 the school psychologist would begin comparing your IQ to that of an amoeba. (On the SAT, 800 is a perfect score. Go figure.)

To make matters worse, some twisted individual decided it would be a good idea to give students negative points when they missed a question. One guy in our class got a -120 on the math section. (I think he was drooling when he took that part.)

The only benefit of the weird scoring system is that parents don't understand it at all.

"What'd you get on those STPs, son?"

"SAT, Dad. I got a 220 on the math and a 260 on the verbal."

If you say this with enough excitement, your father will probably give you a reward.

SAT PRESSURES FINALLY PUSHED TED SCHUSTER
OVER THE EDGE.

The Testing Environment

The SAT is usually held in a large, barren room, such as the school gym or a prison cafeteria. (Mine was given in the gym the day after a donkey basketball game. When I got home, my mother wanted to know why I smelled like a sweaty horse.)

To make matters worse, they fill the designated SAT room with chairs that have those wimpy little mutant desks attached to them. Inevitably, you wind up with a desk into which someone has taken a chain saw and carved "Bubba-n-Darla 4-ever!" When I took the test, I had the added pleasure of getting a desk with one leg shorter than the others, causing me to rock back and forth whenever I was nervous: Clack! Clack! Clack! Clack! One of the proctors (see below) accused me of broadcasting my answers in Morse code. I defended myself by proving that I didn't know any of the answers.

The Proctors

A proctor is, supposedly, just someone who supervises a test. But the proctors at the SAT have been specially trained to terrify students. Most of them are former prison guards. If you do anything out of the ordinary, such as glance at your watch or swallow, a proctor will immediately give you a look that makes you feel like you just got caught beating up a kindergartner.

Perhaps the most important task of the proctors is to escort you to the bathroom when necessary. This is a process which is equivalent in humiliation to running a track meet in your underwear. Generally, it goes something like this: You raise your hand. A proctor walks slowly but loudly to your desk. You then whisper your request. The proctor responds, "The bathroom?!?! Follow me!" You then slither out of the room as 500 of your peers look on, including most of the people you ever wanted to date.

The Results

When you are finally finished with the test, you must wait at least two months to get your results. This gives you ample time to discuss the test with your friends, rehash every question, and begin filling out applications — maybe even to become a proctor for a future pack of terrified SAT test-takers.

Ah, revenge!

SAT SAMPLE TEST

By John McPherson

The following questions are taken from SAT tests given over the past five years. WARNING: Persons attempting to complete this test using anything other than a No. 2 pencil will be dragged from the test room and forced to eat liver.

SECTION 1: VERBAL

A. **Antonyms: Choose the word or group of words that is most nearly opposite to the word in capital letters.**

1. SLENDER:
   (a) red
   (b) banjo
   (c) cattle drive
   (d) Meat Loaf
   (e) sinus headache

2. PLEASANT:
   (a) root canal
   (b) organic chemistry
   (c) poison sumac
   (d) the SAT
   (e) tapeworm

37. Rhinoceros is to Clarinet as Valet Parking is to:
   a. Hula Hoop
   b. Nostril
   c. Regis Philbin
   d. Chia Pet
   e. Ranch Dressing
   f. '67 Chevy
   g. Bon Jovi
   H. Norway

BOB THOUGHT HE HAD PREPARED FOR ANY POSSIBLE QUESTION ON THE SAT. OBVIOUSLY, HE HAD ONLY BEEN KIDDING HIMSELF.

B. **Analogies: Choose the answer which best completes the phrase.**

1. WOODCHUCK is to OIL TANKER as ACNE is to:
   (a) the Magna Carta
   (b) static cling
   (c) the Big Bang
   (d) K-mart
   (e) *Dumb and Dumber*

2. MOSQUITO is to HOT FUDGE as ESOPHAGUS is to:
   (a) wind chime
   (b) Western Samoa
   (c) 37
   (d) Grandma Moses
   (e) violin lessons

C. Sentence Completion: Choose the word or group of words that best completes the sentence.

1. When Lorraine found that she had received a _____ on the math final, she filled the teacher's new car with _____.

  (a) 14 . . . money
  (b) 98 . . . sardines
  (c) blister . . . the Monroe Doctrine
  (d) 21 . . . reinforced concrete
  (e) waffle iron . . . wolverines

2. After Lloyd accidentally stepped on his date's _____, she told all her friends he was a _____.

  (a) foot . . . trapezoid
  (b) biology project . . . nuclear physicist
  (c) steak dinner . . . goat roper
  (d) father . . . prince
  (e) brand new $275 dress, ripping it to shreds . . . real jerk

SECTION 2: MATH

A. Quantitative Comparisons: Compare the quantity in column A with the quantity in column B and choose the appropriate answer.

  (a) if the quantity in column A is larger
  (b) if the quantity in column B is larger
  (c) if both quantities are equal
  (d) if you don't care which is larger

Column A

1. $\sqrt{\dfrac{(41\pi\cos 72°)}{(-413.3)^{\frac{1}{3}}(.017)}}$

2. maximum number of times a pro athlete has said "you know" in a one-minute interview

3. percentage of hearing loss caused by listening to a Soundgarden tape at full volume in the back of a Ford Mustang

Column B

1. $7.2\int_{0}^{\circ}(147x)^{\frac{1}{3}}(72x^2)^{-.07}$

2. number of people over the age of 14 who believe that pro wrestling is real

3. percentage of girls who will say no to a guy who asks them to dance if the guy is wearing bowling shoes

B. Problem Solving: Select the best answer.

1. If Romney goes to the school cafeteria and buys six servings of Spam on a bun for $1.75 each, four side orders of lima beans for $.90 each, six bags of Cheese Doodles for $.60 each, four bowls of chocolate pudding for $.50 each, five cartons of milk for $.40 each, and four Ring Dings for $.45 each, how much time will Romney's friends have to carry him to the nurse's office before Romney loses his lunch? (Show your work.)

  (a) 35 seconds
  (b) 17 seconds
  (c) 11 seconds
  (d) 6 seconds
  (e) they'll never make it

From *Campus Life* College Guide, October 1995. Used by permission.

2
CHAPTER

First Steps in the Christian College Search

Q   **Why should I go to college?**

A   There are *tons* of good reasons for going to college. Here, in no particular order, are a few:

• *Education.* You've got the potential to learn more stuff in four years at college than you learned in elementary, middle, and high school combined. They say we're living in the Information Age and that the amount of information in the world doubles every few years or so. There's way more stuff out there than you could ever learn, even if you lived a thousand years. College is a great chance to learn at least some of this stuff. Learning is exciting. Your brain will love you for it.

• *Money.* Right now, you're probably worried about how you're gonna pay for college. But we'll talk about that later in the book. For now, it's important to know that a college degree will give you more earning power when you start your career. According to one study, the average college graduate earns at least $500,000 more over the course of a lifetime than someone who didn't go to college. That's big bucks.

• *Friendships.* Years from now, the thing you'll most remember about college won't be the classes you took, but the people you met and the friends you made. You'll meet people from other parts of the country and probably other parts of the world, thus learning about other cultures. And you'll make great friends. One *Campus Life* editor thought he'd always stay in touch with his high-school buddies; five years later, he'd lost all contact with them. But he made friends in college that are now his best friends — friends for a lifetime.

• *Character.* You'll grow up a lot in college, making the transition from teenager to full-fledged adult. You'll learn a lot about who you are, what makes you tick, and what you want to do with the rest of your life. One college student told us, "A college will develop your character. In some ways, you will become like the things you learn and the people you meet at college."

• *Spiritual growth.* This is really just another part of your character, discussed in the last paragraph. But it's probably the most important part of your character. In college, your faith will probably become your own. It won't just be the faith you grew up with any more, the faith that was automatically yours because you went to church every Sunday with your family. It'll become personal, with your name on it. That will happen as you begin to really ask questions about your faith: Why do I believe what I believe? You'll read more about your spiritual growth on campus in chapter 10.

Q   How do I know if I'm ready for college?

A   Start by asking your parents. They know you better than anyone. They know your character, your level of maturity and responsibility, your ability to handle new situations, and so on. You'll need these things in college, and your parents certainly know whether or not you've got them.

Talk to your guidance counselor (are we repeating this advice enough?). Your counselor will certainly have a good handle on whether you're academically ready, just by looking at your grades and your SAT or ACT scores. If you're on the verge of flunking out of high school, you're obviously not ready for college. Hopefully, your counselor knows you as a person, too — your character, your maturity. All these factors will help your counselor help you determine if you're ready.

Talk to other adults who know you well — like your youth pastor, coaches, teachers, neighbors.

Talk to friends who either are in college or have just recently finished college. The experience is fresh for them; they know what it takes. Get their feedback.

Talk to God. Seek his will. He will direct you. Proverbs 3:5–6 says, "Trust in the Lord with all your heart and lean not on your own understanding; in all your ways acknowledge him, and *he will make your paths straight* (italics added)."

Finally, don't forget to talk to *yourself.* Do you want to go to college? You have to want it to make it work.

Q   When and where do I start the college search process?

A   Many experts advise starting during your sophomore year in high school — certainly no sooner than that — or early in your junior year at the latest. Don't wait till your senior year. You can still get in at many colleges, but you'll end up rushing your decision.

Where do you start? With God. Choosing a college is one of the most important decisions you'll ever make, and you'll certainly want to consult the Wisest One in the Universe. So pray, pray, and pray some more, asking God to lead you every step of the way.

Your guidance counselor is a vital part of this whole process. Consult with him or her from the very beginning, all the way through till the day you receive that piece of mail that says, "Congratulations! You've been accepted!"

Before you start looking through those thick college directories, ask yourself: What do I want out of a college? Make a list: Do you want to go to a big school or a small one? Do you want a college in an urban setting? Or suburban or rural? Near your home or

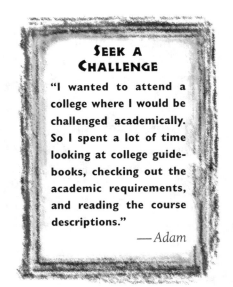

SEEK A CHALLENGE

"I wanted to attend a college where I would be challenged academically. So I spent a lot of time looking at college guidebooks, checking out the academic requirements, and reading the course descriptions."

—*Adam*

far away? Do you know what you want to major in? And so on. (Check out the question later in this chapter, *"What are some things to consider when looking at colleges?"*)

You might not be exactly sure what you do want in a college, but you may be sure of some things you don't want. That's good, because that'll help you eliminate many schools from your list. If, for instance, you're absolutely positive you don't want to go to college on Venus, you can comfortably cross out any and all Venutian institutions of higher learning. (See how easy this is?)

But don't rule out colleges that seem too expensive. Not yet, anyway. There's plenty of financial aid out there, and you might just get enough to go anywhere, no matter the cost. (For more on this topic, see chapter 5.)

As for college resources, well, you've got your hands on a pretty good one now. Check out the college listings at the back of the book. If you live in Virginia and you're sure you don't want to go to the other side of the continent, then put a big X through the schools on the West Coast. There, you're that much closer to making a decision.

Another good resource is *Peterson's Choose a Christian College*. While not all-inclusive, it does include complete descriptions of about 100 Christian schools. If your guidance counselor doesn't have it, or you can't find it in the bookstore, call Petersons at 1-800-338-3282 to order a copy.

There are tons of other college directories available, but save your money. Ask your guidance counselor or check in your local library. (Note: If the editions are more than a few years old, the information might be badly outdated.)

Your computer can help, too. There are plenty of CD-ROMs available (ask your guidance counselor), and there's a ton of college information on the Internet. Many colleges have their own Web sites too. Just go to your favorite Net search engine, and start surfin'.

Q How can my guidance counselor help me?

A A better question might be, "How *can't* my guidance counselor help me?" We've said from the beginning that your guidance counselor is probably your best resource for walking you through this whole process. Your counselor probably went to graduate school just for this reason: To help you make big decisions like this. Guidance counselors want to help you. That's what they get paid for.

Even if you're the smartest student in your school and the president of every club, you still need your guidance counselor's advice. (We heard about one guy who assumed his 3.9 GPA would get him into the college of his choice, so he applied to only one school — and got turned down. Now he wishes he'd consulted with his guidance counselor.)

Think of your guidance counselor's office as sort of a tangible Web site; it's a data bank of information collected for the purpose of helping you not only make the college choice, but other decisions too — like what classes to take in high school, whether to take the SAT or ACT, and so on.

Your counselor's office is a great resource, and it's right down the hall. But it can't help you if you don't drop by for a visit. So, as they say, use it . . . or lose it.

Q **Where else can I turn for advice and information?**

A We've partly answered this question with some of the previous answers. You should talk to your parents, coaches, teachers, friends in college, youth pastor, and others whose advice and opinion you trust.

Another good people source of information is college admissions officers. Like your high-school guidance counselor, college admissions officers are there *for you*. They get paid to help you, to answer your questions.

We know one student who was intimidated by the idea of calling admissions officers for information. She wondered, *Aren't they the people who will read my application essays and determine if I'm accepted into their college or not? What if they don't like me?*

But she put her worries aside and made a few calls. An hour later, she said to herself, "That wasn't so bad after all. The secretaries and admissions officers were friendly and polite — even fun to chat with. They seem genuinely interested in helping me in my search for college. They truly care about the students they meet."

If you'd rather not get into a conversation with an admissions officer, that's fine, too. They can still help. Just call their office and say, "I'm considering your college. Please send me any information." And a few days later, you'll be getting a package in the mail.

Q **What's a college fair, and how can it help me?**

A College fairs are like dating services. Well, sort of. College fairs are events where colleges looking for students and students looking for colleges can meet one another.

There are several kinds of college fairs. The simplest is usually called a "college night," sponsored by a local high school or group of schools. Area colleges send representatives to these events to talk with you and your parents — and to answer your questions.

There are also national and regional fairs organized by the National Association of College Admission Counselors, often with booths representing hundreds of colleges around the country. These fairs are often held in convention centers or big hotels in major cities. *Note:* Sometimes Christian colleges aren't well-represented at these fairs, so you might want to get a listing of the colleges before you decide to go.

And then there are fairs that include just Christian colleges. The National Association of Christian College Admissions Personnel (NACCAP) sponsors about 65 fairs nationwide, in most major metropolitan areas. To find out if and when one will be in your area, call toll-free 1-888-4CFAIRS (1-888-423-2477).

At a college fair, you can just wander around and pick up as many freebies as you can find — brochures, pamphlets, videos, maybe even a CD-ROM if you're lucky. This stuff is nice, but it's not the best way to take advantage of the event.

Go to a college fair armed with a notebook and a list of questions. But do your homework first. If possible, get some info from the colleges you're considering before the fair, think about any questions you have and find as many answers to your questions as you can. Then take the rest of your questions to the fair.

Just remember: The people at the college booths are there to answer your questions. Even if none of the colleges you're interested in are represented at the fair, go and ask questions anyway. Just talking with college officials can help you with your college search process.

Q **What should I do with all the mail colleges send me?**

A Decorate your walls. Make paper airplanes. Build a bonfire and roast marshmallows over it.

Just kidding. Seriously, the best way to look at all that mail is to think of it as yet another means of helping you along in the process. And welcome it as a sign that colleges are interested in you.

Don't throw any of it away without at least opening it and glancing at it first. Even if it's from a school you know you're not interested in, something might jump out at you that you'd never thought of before. You might see a picture of a student playing volleyball, which might trigger you to think, *I want to go to a school that has a strong intramural sports program.* Little things like that can happen as you sort through this stuff.

When stuff comes from colleges you might be interested in, keep it on file — which doesn't mean throw it under the bed with all the other ones. Be organized about it. Buy a cardboard storage box and some file folders, and develop your own filing system. When you start asking yourself, "Now, does Judson offer a major in archaeology or not?" you'll know right where to look.

Colleges won't keep sending you mail if you don't want them to. You'll hear from a lot of colleges only once. That first mailing should include a card you can return if you want to know more. If you don't reply, they'll take you off their mailing list. After all, they don't want their stuff to end up in a bonfire.

Q What's the difference between colleges, universities and Bible schools?

A A "college" is usually a four-year, accredited school where you can earn an undergraduate degree — either a Bachelor of Arts (BA) or Bachelor of Science (BS). A college's main focus is on its undergraduate education. (The category of "colleges" also includes two-year schools and community colleges; we'll discuss them later.)

A "university," meanwhile, usually means the school includes graduate study programs — like a master's degree or a doctoral degree. Universities are also known for their emphasis on research and discovery of new knowledge.

A "Bible college" is generally designed for students who want to go into church ministry or missions, but even that definition is a bit too narrow. Here's the official definition from the Accrediting Association of Bible Colleges (AABC): "A Bible college is an institution of higher education in which the Bible is central and the development of Christian life and ministry is essential. A Bible college education requires of all students a substantial core of biblical studies, general studies, and Christian service experiences, and integrates a biblical worldview with life and learning. It offers curricula that fulfill its overriding purpose: to equip all students for ministry in and for the church and the world."

NORV THOUGHT A SPEED-READING COURSE WOULD HELP HIM GET INTO A GOOD COLLEGE, BUT HE'D OBVIOUSLY GONE A LITTLE OVERBOARD.

Another term you'll encounter is "liberal arts." No, "Christian" and "liberal arts" are not contradictory terms; the word "liberal" here has nothing to do with theologies or politics. A liberal arts college is one where the main focus is on the education of the whole person. The liberal arts and sciences include literature, language, philosophy, history, art, music, sociology, chemistry, biology, psychology, and so on. If you enjoy learning and have diverse interests, you'll enjoy a liberal arts school, where you can take a variety of courses in different subject areas. At liberal arts schools, you usually won't begin concentrating on your major area of study until your junior year.

Q   **What's a two-year college, and why would I go to one?**

A   Nearly 40 percent of all college students are at two-year colleges. These schools provide 1) occupational training, from agriculture to welding; 2) a general liberal arts education, which you can then transfer to a four-year college or university; and 3) remedial programs for students who didn't do well enough academically in high school to be admitted to a four-year school, which generally has tougher admissions standards. At the successful completion of two years of study, a student will receive an associate's degree.

Most two-year college options are at secular schools. There are three main types of two-year colleges:

• *Community colleges* are low-cost, government-supported colleges within commuting distance of a certain community. They have no on-campus housing. Community colleges, which generally have no minimum standards for admission, have been called a cross between high school, college, and a vocational school. Students who aren't academically ready for a four-year college or university can benefit from a community college, which provides such academic preparation. Community college is also a good alternative financially;

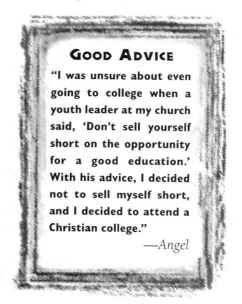

GOOD ADVICE

"I was unsure about even going to college when a youth leader at my church said, 'Don't sell yourself short on the opportunity for a good education.' With his advice, I decided not to sell myself short, and I decided to attend a Christian college."

—*Angel*

it's much more affordable than most four-year schools, and you can save still more money by living at home. Finally, community colleges often have excellent vocational programs, if you want to prepare immediately for a career in a technical field.

• *Technical colleges* are just what their name implies: Schools that prepare you for a career in technology. Some examples include civil engineering technology, electrical engineering technology, and computer technology. Students also take other courses for a more well-rounded education, so that after two years, they can either take a job in their specialty or transfer to a four-year college. The technical college option might be good for students who want to explore technology without the commitment to a four-year program.

• *Junior colleges* are very similar to community colleges, except they're usually not government-funded and they offer on-campus housing. A junior college is essentially a scaled-down version of life at a four-year college or university.

Why would you go to a two-year college? You might go if you didn't do very well academically in high school, because a two-year school's admissions standards usually aren't very demanding. You might go if finances are extremely tight, because they're generally cheaper than four-year schools. You might go if you're sure you're headed for a particular career, and the skills needed are taught at a two-year school. Or you may want to go because you're not completely convinced you're ready for a four-year college, but you do know you want more than just a high-school diploma.

If you want to know more about the two-year college option and whether it's the right one for you, talk to your guidance counselor.

Q **What are some things to consider when looking at colleges?**

A If you're a guy, you're going to want to find a school with a girl-to-guy ratio of at least 8-to-1; if you're a girl, just the opposite.

Just kidding, of course. Seriously, there are plenty of factors to consider. As you read through the following, you'll see some things that are important to you and others that aren't. For instance, you may not care about the size (number of students) of the school, but you may care about how close it is to home. Keep these things in mind as you scan this list:

• *Distance.* How far are you willing to travel? Do you want to stay as close to home as possible, or are you willing to go far away? (If you go a really long way, consider that you may not get to see your family except at Thanksgiving, Christmas, and spring break.) Or do you want something in between? One of the *Campus Life* editors went to college 3-1/2 hours away from home, and felt that was just right: Far enough away that he wouldn't be tempted to go home every weekend, and far enough that he felt like he could start off on that road to independence. And yet it was close enough that he could get home whenever the homesick bug bit—or whenever he had a really big pile of laundry, whichever came first.

• *Location.* Do you like big cities, or do you prefer a rural environment? Or something in between, like a suburban setting? And what about a drastic change in climate? If you've lived in Florida all your life and are considering a college in Minnesota, well, you're gonna need something warmer than a sweat-shirt with your high-school logo on it.

• *Size.* Some Christian colleges have thousands of students. Some only have a few hundred. (One, the Montana Wilderness School of the Bible, had an enrollment of just 52 in a recent school year!) Would you like knowing most of your classmates, or would you rather blend into a larger campus? Where would you best fit in?

• *Admissions requirements.* Colleges vary greatly in their standards for admission. Some schools are quite difficult to get into, others are much easier, and there are many in between the two extremes. If you're a C-plus student who scored 980 on the SAT and you're not in the top 40 percent of your grad-uating class, you might think twice about applying to schools that typically accept students with 3.8 GPAs, 1400 SATs, and top-10 percent standings. If you're not sure whether you should consider a school because of its academic requirements, consult with — you guessed it—your guidance counselor.

• *Majors.* If you know what you want to study in college, this is a key fac-tor. For instance, if you want to study to be an astrophysicist, you can safely rule out something like the Northwestern Manitoba School of Extremely Cool Modern Dance. If you want to be a doctor, you're going to want a college with biology and/or chemistry programs. But if you're not sure what you want to major in, or if you just don't have a clue yet, that's OK, too. You're hardly alone. You don't have to know while you're still in high school; you usually don't have to declare a major until you've finished almost two years of college. Half of all students end up changing their majors, anyway. So, if you're not sure what you want to major in, just pick a school that offers a wide variety of major programs.

• *Cost.* This should go near the bottom of your list of factors. Cost will eventually be a factor, but when you're still very early in the decision-making process, it's not a huge concern. Yes, college can be expensive, and some col-leges are extremely expensive. But keep in mind that you'll rarely pay the full sticker price at a college. Financial aid from the government, private sources, and the colleges themselves is available to cut the costs. When it comes time to apply to your top colleges, you'll get financial-aid packages that will give you a better feel for what you and your family can—and can't—afford. Till then, don't sweat it too much.

• *Denominational affiliation.* Many Christian colleges are officially related to a particular church denomination. Is that important to you? If so, that information can go a long way toward helping you narrow your list.

• *Spiritual climate.* Since you're reading this book, you're obviously strongly considering a Christian college. That means the spiritual life on campus—and opportunities for your faith to grow—will likely be strong. Still, ask about these opportunities when you begin investigating schools. Ask about student fellowships, the campus chapel, nearby churches (you will want to plug into a local church), and service and missions opportunities. Also, most Christian schools have a statement of faith, a statement of what its faculty and administration believe about God, Jesus Christ, the Holy Spirit, the Bible, salvation, and other important issues of faith. Study this statement carefully and ask yourself if you agree with it. It might be OK to disagree with minor details in the statement, but many items will be non-negotiable—things like the fact that Jesus was resurrected and other vital Christian doctrines. Another thing to consider is the college's "code of conduct agreement," which spells out certain behavior expectations at the school. Most codes include regulations regarding sexual activity and the use of alcohol and illicit drugs. Many codes also include regulations regarding social dancing; some have rules about playing cards. Read these codes carefully. If you have any questions about them, talk to your pastor and/or an admissions official at that school. If you read anything in the code that you feel you can't abide by, then cross that school off your list.

These are the main factors. You may come up with more of your own.

You might have noticed that factors like "national rankings" aren't in the above list. That's because rankings usually reflect *other* people's opinions, not yours. Your opinion counts the most in this process. The opinions of alleged "experts" make good reading, but they shouldn't have much influence on your decision.

At the same time, a college might have a reputation for certain strengths—like the Massachusetts Institute of Technology's reputation for producing great engineers. A reputation like this can be objectively measured; a list of NASA astronauts confirms MIT's success.

So, when you're considering a school's "reputation," make sure it's a reasonably objective measurement, and not just the opinion of a so-called "expert."

Q **How do I narrow down the possible choices to a select handful?**

A This is a process you'll want to go through during your junior year of high school. Start by asking yourself a question you've already asked yourself:

"Why do I want to go to college?" Many months may have elapsed since you first asked yourself that question, and your answer may have changed. But now's a good time to define your answer as clearly as possible and write it down. Knowing exactly *why* you want to go to college will help you choose what type of school you're looking for.

Now look over the factors listed in the previous question. Which of those factors are important to you, and which ones aren't? Throw out the ones that aren't, and you're left with a list of your own personal criteria. You've identified the difference between information you need and info you don't need.

Look at your list of criteria—distance, size, majors, etc. Weigh each of the factors by its importance, on a scale of 1-5, with 1 being not very important and 5 being non-negotiable. Then visit your guidance counselor or the local library and look at either (1) a good college directory that includes statistical profiles of all accredited colleges, or (2) computer software with the same information. The profiles will tell you which colleges match your personal criteria.

Computer software can be a huge help at this point. You can usually type in certain criteria, and the program will spit out the names of colleges that meet those criteria—and at the same time weed out the hundreds of schools that don't. For instance, if you know you want to major in journalism, you can do a search on all schools that offer it as a major. And just like that, you've narrowed your list down significantly.

But here's a caution about using computer software: While you can narrow down your list quickly, you can also eliminate some schools you might otherwise consider. If you're only *considering* a journalism major, for instance, the

EVER SINCE MRS. LIMPKIN REVAMPED THE LIBRARY'S BOOK CLASSIFYING SYSTEM, NOBODY COULD FIND THE COLLEGE REFERENCE MATERIALS.

previous example would eliminate hundreds of colleges that might be a very good fit for you in many other ways. So, don't let a computer program take too many shortcuts for you.

Continue using your criteria to narrow your list down more and more until you've got a list of maybe 10–12 colleges, 20 at the most, where you believe you'd be happiest. Don't think in terms of getting your list down to "The One" at this point; besides, there's no such thing. There are at least several, if not dozens, of colleges that will fit you — and where you will fit — just fine, and any of them would be a "right" decision.

By the time you're into the second semester of your junior year, you'll want to cut this list way down to the five or so colleges where you'll most likely apply (see chapter 4) and where you'll want to make campus visits (see chapter 3). At this point, don't just go back to directories, software, and the stuff you're getting in the mail. You've studied all of that thoroughly. Now the process becomes much more subjective. Start listening to opinions, advice, and even your own intuitions; maybe you've got a "certain feeling" about a particular school or schools. That's good; sometimes that's just how God speaks to us.

Now it's time to pick a team of "consultants"—a best friend or two, your parents, and at least a couple of other adults. Pick people whose wisdom and advice you trust. Pick people who are willing to first be your "sounding board," people who will just listen to you brainstorm without being too anxious to offer their own opinions — yet. At this stage, you're just trying to sort through your maze of thoughts and questions. The process of bringing all that stuff out of your brain and into the open will help a lot.

Once you've said everything you've got to say, *then* it's time for you to listen up — to the advice your "team" has to offer. They know you best, they've been listening to your thoughts and concerns, and they've earned the right to let you know how they feel. Their advice is vital. You might get some conflicting advice, but that's OK; at least you're getting advice.

All along, of course, keep praying about your choice. Trust God to lead you each step of the way.

Ultimately, there comes a point where the choice is yours. No one else can help you. God will guide you, of course, but he's not likely to open one of those big college directories to page 734 and say, "This is where I want you, my beloved child."

But if you've been prayerfully following all the steps listed here, you *will* end up with just the right list.

What If They Don't Like Me?

by Christy Simon

The thermostat read only 67 degrees, but the temperature inside the house felt more like 107. My palms were sweaty, my stomach hurt like it does right before final exams, and my mouth felt like sandpaper. Taking a big gulp of Dr. Pepper, I breathed deeply and stared at the long list in front of me.

It was the summer before my junior year in high school. My mom had been helping me make a list of colleges we thought I'd be interested in. Now, it was my job to call the schools and request more information.

I was terrified. Aren't college admissions officers the ones who read your application essays and determine if you're accepted into the college or not? What if they don't like me? What if they try to pressure me into coming to their school?

Forty-five minutes and many phone calls later, I breathed a huge sigh of relief. That wasn't so bad after all. The secretaries and admissions staffers I had talked to were friendly and polite—even fun to chat with. They seemed genuinely interested in helping me in my search for a college. Several even asked me about things not related to college—like my family. And not one person pushed his or her college on me or even mentioned how great the school was or how much I'd like it there.

The next month, as my family traveled across the Midwest visiting the colleges I was most interested in, I was no longer afraid of talking with admissions counselors. As I sat in their offices, I realized they were human beings just like me. Their desks were decorated with pictures of their families and friends and they drank Diet Coke and snacked on potato chips. More importantly, they seemed to care more about me as a person than about my test scores, grade-point average, and class rank.

I know it's sometimes hard to believe that real people are behind this whole college search. But trust me: Colleges do employ real people. I know, because I've met some of them—in person, over the phone, and through written correspondence. And they truly care about the students they meet.

Sure, choosing a college is time-consuming and occasionally frustrating. Nothing can change that. But knowing someone actually cared about helping me find the right school meant a lot and made my college search less stressful.

And less scary, too.

From *Campus Life* magazine, October 1996. Used by permission.

The Campus Visit

Q **How important is it to visit the colleges I'm interested in?**

A Would you marry someone you've never met?

OK, so going to college isn't exactly like getting married—though you just might meet your future spouse there! But the analogy isn't ridiculous, either.

No, you won't spend the rest of your life "married to" a college, like you will your spouse. But you will spend the next four or five years there. And that's about 25 percent of your life, up to now. That's a pretty significant chunk of time.

So, it's vital that you get to know the place first, and its "personality." Yes, colleges, like people, have personalities. And it takes a little time to get a feel for that personality.

Like people, it's not fair to judge a college by your first impression. You've met people who wowed you at first, only to learn later that they weren't so cool after all. You've also met people who may not have initially impressed you, but later became your good friends.

Same goes with colleges. Slick brochures, hi-tech videos, and upbeat mail may give you a great first impression, but you might find something completely different when you visit. On the other hand, you shouldn't rule out a college because it doesn't send you a fancy piece of mail every week; that school may be investing its money elsewhere, like toward raising faculty salaries or improving college facilities.

We've heard of colleges that spend as much as $3,000 per *freshman* in the recruiting process—just trying to convince you that their school is your best choice. Much of that money goes toward a slick mailing campaign. Is it worth all that expense? Sometimes yes, sometimes no. The bottom line: Don't completely judge a college by the quality of the free stuff they're sending you.

One college admissions officer told us, "I always advise students to visit the college or colleges they're considering. Look for evidence that the college you visit is the right place for you. How's the fit? If the fit feels right, you will most likely be happy at that college."

Another admissions officer said, "Visiting a campus is the best way to get a gut-level feeling about a college. Ask yourself, 'Can I picture myself here?' Only a campus visit can answer that important question."

Q How many colleges should I visit?

A   This probably depends on how much time and money you and your parents are willing to spend. The schools you're considering aren't likely to be in your hometown. Chances are, you'll have to do some traveling, perhaps even overnight.

If you're considering a college that's far away, the cost of airline travel will probably drive the cost of your visit way up. Still, if you're seriously considering the school, it's probably worth the cost. One admissions officer says, "It's scary for me to think that the first time a student would step on campus would be with suitcase in hand at the start of freshman year. The cost of visiting is a small investment compared to the price you'll pay if the school is not a good fit for you. There is nothing to substitute for that gut level feeling of being there."

So, if at all possible, try visiting all of the schools on your final "short list" of about five colleges—the ones you're thinking about applying to. And keep in mind that your "short list" may very well change after your visits: You might discover something on a visit that would cause you to cross a particular school off your list.

Q **How do I line up a college visit?**

A Simply call the admissions office and tell them you're planning a visit. Call at least two weeks in advance so they can plan for your arrival. They'll bend over backward to accommodate you.

When you visit, you'll definitely want to meet with someone in admissions. You may also want to arrange meetings with someone in financial aid, and, if you've decided on a major, a professor in that department. These people will appreciate it if you've scheduled an appointment, rather than just "dropping in." And you'll make a better first impression.

If you show up at a campus unannounced, you may get to see these people, but they may not have the time to answer your questions thoroughly. So definitely plan ahead.

Q **When is the best time to visit a college campus?**

A The best time to visit colleges might seem to be during summer vacation, because you're out of school and more likely to be free of other responsibilities. Unfortunately, summer is also one of the worst times to visit colleges, because they're often practically "shut down" at that time of year. School's out, except for maybe a few classes, and there are probably only a few students and profs on campus. A summer visit will certainly yield a nice stroll around the campus, but you won't get a very good feel for the college's "personality."

Many experts say the spring of your junior year is a great time to visit. Again, you'll want to visit when the college is in session, so don't schedule a visit during the school's spring break. Note: You might visit during *your* spring break, though, because high school spring breaks and college spring breaks often don't occur at the same time. Check with the colleges you're considering to find out when their spring breaks take place.

If you can't get to all the colleges you're considering in the spring of your junior year, wait till the fall of your senior year to make the visits. If you have to visit in the summer, those visits are much better than no visits at all.

Q **What should I do while I'm there?**

A Start with the admissions office. They're pros at making you feel comfortable, telling you all about their school, and giving campus tours. They'll ask you all kinds of questions about yourself. They'll expect you to ask all kinds of questions about their school, so come prepared with a list of questions. (We've listed some of these questions in the next item.)

But the admissions office is only the beginning. As already mentioned, you might want to talk with a financial-aid officer, and perhaps a professor in the field of study you'd like to pursue.

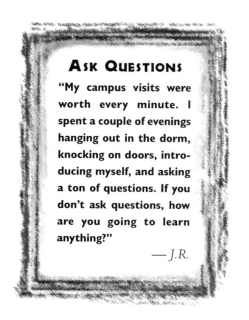

ASK QUESTIONS

"My campus visits were worth every minute. I spent a couple of evenings hanging out in the dorm, knocking on doors, introducing myself, and asking a ton of questions. If you don't ask questions, how are you going to learn anything?"

— *J.R.*

Meeting with these people is a great start to your visit, but the best way to get a "feel" for the college is from the students themselves. If you know a student at the college, ask him or her to set aside a day—and, preferably, a night—to show you around. Follow your friend around everywhere—to class, to the library, to the chapel service, to the cafeteria, to his or her afternoon assignment for the college newspaper, to a sporting event, to Bible study, to a downtown jaunt for a movie and pizza. And don't be shy. Ask lots of questions, not only of your friend, but of his or her friends too.

Additionally, you'll want to stay in the dorm. If your friend is of the same sex, no problem. If your friend is of the opposite sex, ask him or her to find someone of the same sex for you to stay with in the dorm. If you don't have a friend on campus, ask the admissions department to set you up with someone who can show you around.

Why stay in the dorm during your college visit? Because you'll spend about one-third of your college life in a dorm, including all of your sleeping hours. Dorm life is unlike anything you've ever experienced before, or will ever experience again. And we mean that in a good way. So it's a good idea to hang overnight in a dorm during your visit, if at all possible. (If your parents are with you, they can stay off-campus in a hotel or motel. Some schools might even have an agreement with a local hotel or motel for a special rate for these situations, so be sure to ask.) If you can't spend the night in a dorm, try to at least spend a couple of hours there in the evening. That'll give you a better feel for dorm life. Checking out a dorm at 11:00 a.m. on a weekday won't tell you as much; it'll be pretty empty because most of the students will be in class. (You can read more about what to expect from dorm life in chapter 7.)

And try to eat at least one meal in the campus cafeteria. No matter what kind of meal plan you have once you get to college, you'll probably eat a few meals a week on campus. And while colleges are not known for their gourmet cuisine, some schools do a good job of offering students tasty choices, like a salad and sandwich bar, low-fat entrees, and good desserts.

Check out the campus as thoroughly as you can, but don't stop there. Check out the town, too. What's it like? College towns can range anywhere from huge, like Chicago and Los Angeles, to tiny, rural villages in the middle of nowhere. There are advantages and disadvantages to both; for instance, a big city might offer plenty of exciting things to do (museums, concerts, pro sporting events, etc.), but it might also come with higher crime rates. On the other hand, small towns usually offer peace and quiet, a slower, relaxed pace, and a warm, "down-home" feeling. And yet some students complain that small towns are "boring," that there's "nothing to do." You have to decide what type of town is best for you. That's your call.

While you're looking at the town, see what it offers. Is there a good selection of churches nearby? A good grocery store? A place to pick up odds and ends—like a Wal-Mart, Target or Kmart? A movie theater? A park? Or even, um, a mall?

Q **What questions should I ask during a campus visit?**

A Generally, you should ask any questions you can think of. There's no such thing as a stupid question. Well, maybe you shouldn't ask if you can keep your pet rhino in the dorm. But seriously, you should feel free to ask almost anything of the people—admissions and financial-aid officers, profs, students—you meet on your campus visit.

Don't just wing it when you get there. Take a list of questions with you, and ask the same questions of everyone you talk to. If you get conflicting answers to the same question, that might be reason to raise a red flag—or at least to ask more questions to clarify something. And don't just stick to your list; feel free to ask any new questions that might come up as you get involved in conversations.

You've probably already got a bunch of questions about admissions and financial aid. You'll want to ask those questions on your college visit, too.

But what other questions should you ask? Here are some suggestions:

• *What kind of extracurricular activities are there?* Find out about clubs, organizations, and volunteer service opportunities. Ask about sports and intramurals. These non-academic activities will be important to your overall college experience.

• *What do students do for fun on weekends?* What kind of stuff is there to do in the community? What activities are offered on campus? Where do students hang out? Do most students even stick around on weekends, or do a lot of them head somewhere else?

• *What are the dorms like?* Can you get a light bulb when you need one? Are the bathrooms well stocked with supplies? Are there study areas in the dorms? How are the laundry facilities? Do you need to bring rat poison or roach killer?

• *How much time do students spend studying?* This is a good indicator of the kind of free time you can expect. Sure, the answer will be different for everyone, but you can at least get an idea of how busy you'll be.

• *Where can I go for privacy?* There will be times when you want to be alone, whether it's to study, read your Bible, or just think. Ask where you can go when you need some time to yourself.

• *How safe is the campus?* No matter what size town the school is in, crime will likely be a factor. Do students feel safe walking alone at night? Do they lock the dorms after a certain hour? Are walkways well-lit? Is there on-campus security?

• *Where do students go to church?* Ask students about the churches they attend and how they went about choosing those churches.

• *How accessible is the faculty?* It's one thing to say a school has a low student/professor ratio.

AND HERE'S OUR FRESHMAN DORM! I'D TAKE YOU THROUGH IT, BUT THEY'RE, UH, REFINISHING THE SOLID OAK FLOORS.

It's another to say that faculty members make themselves available to students. Find out if profs are willing to go that extra mile.

• *What opportunities are there to help me grow spiritually?* It's easy for your spiritual life to suffer when you've got tons to do. Finding a fellowship group or Bible study could be a great way to stay on track.

• *How's the food?* You may eat more than 2,000 meals in the campus dining hall over the course of four years, so it's a good idea to ask about the eats. Find out what options are available (salad bars, sandwich stuff, a snack shop) that will give variety to your meal plan.

Whom do you ask? Certainly, ask these types of questions of admissions officials. They'll give you honest answers, but they might be a bit "canned." The best source for the answers to these and all your questions is the students themselves.

During your visit, think of yourself as a reporter. Crank up your observation powers full throttle. Be inquisitive, even skeptical. If you see or hear something that strikes you as odd or a little out-of-place, don't just let it slide. Ask questions; get answers. You're there to observe, to learn, to get as many answers as you can, so that you can make the best decision possible.

Q How do I cut through the PR "salesmanship" and see the college as it really is?

A Again, by talking to students. Admissions officials will be honest with you, but for the most part, they aren't going to volunteer negative information about their schools. Admissions officials often wear at least two hats: Not only do they make decisions about what students do and don't get admitted to their colleges, but they're also kind of advertisers and marketers for their schools. They generally want you to come to their colleges, and they're expected to present their colleges in a positive light. (After all, if they spoke negatively about their schools, they wouldn't keep their jobs very long, would they?)

So, we repeat: Get the scoop from students. Why did they choose this school? What do they like most and least about it? Are they there for academics, certain majors, athletics? Are their reasons for being there similar to your reasons for considering this school?

If you don't know a student at a school you're visiting, the admissions department can set you up with a student tour guide. But that student has likely been trained by the admissions department to say all the right things. So it's best if you know a student at the school who'll be honest with you. Even if you don't know anyone at the school, you may know someone who does. Ask your guidance counselor if any graduates from your high school are at that college. Ask your parents if they know anyone whose son or daughter is at that school. With a little digging, you might be able to find someone at the school.

If you can't arrange in advance to spend some time with a student during your visit, you can still get honest student opinions while you're there. You just can't afford to be shy. While you're walking around campus, walk up to a student and introduce yourself. Tell them you're considering coming to this college, and ask if they'd be willing to answer a few questions. Unless they're running late for class, most students will be more than happy to spend at least a few minutes, and maybe more, with you, answering your questions and showing you around.

Q **What role should my parents play on my campus visits?**

A If one or both of your parents can go with you on your campus visits, they should. They'll play a vital role, especially when you're meeting with officials from the admissions and financial-aid departments. Your parents will have a ton of questions for those people, too, and they'll think of questions you never even thought of asking.

You'll probably want your parents to take the official tour of the campus with you, too. Think of it this way: If you tour the campus alone, that's just one set of eyes and ears taking it all in. But when you add Mom and Dad, that's six eyes and ears observing. They'll see things you didn't see. They'll pick up on things you missed. And they'll usually be more objective than you; that incredibly cute student standing by the statue of the founder of the college isn't going to sway Mom and Dad's opinion one bit. Later, you and your parents can talk about all of your observations, which will give you a better overall picture of the whole visit.

You probably won't want your parents with you the whole time during your college visit, though. If you're spending the night in the dorm, they can stay in a hotel or motel in town. But even if you're not spending the night, ask Mom and Dad to go explore the countryside or something while you take at least a few hours to check out the campus on your own.

When you visit a college with your parents, you all need to remember who's supposed to take the lead—you, the student. *You,* not Mom or Dad, should say to the admissions official, "Hello, we're here for our visit." You should take the lead in asking and answering questions. Your parents should certainly take part, because they'll think of things you wouldn't think of. So don't roll your eyes if you think Dad's asking something silly; he's just showing his love and concern for you by taking an active role in this process.

When you're back in the car or on the plane on the way home, talk to your parents about everything, and get their valuable feedback and advice. Welcome their opinions, and consider them seriously. But in the end, the decision about whether or not you will fit at a particular college is yours to make, because you'll be the one spending the next four or five years there.

Q **What if I can't visit a certain college or colleges?**

A If you absolutely cannot visit a certain college, there are alternatives to the campus visit.

It starts with the information they're sending you—the brochures, the catalogs, the promotional videos, everything. Study all of this stuff, but study it critically and with a bit of skepticism. Again, most of these things are marketing tools meant to give the college the best spin possible. As one admissions officer told us, "You need to know that college video tours are a lot like sports highlights films. You're only going to see the good plays."

Also, most colleges have Web sites on the Internet, many including "virtual tours" of their campus and other interactive stuff. These are worth your while.

As you study the brochures, catalogs, videos, and other stuff, make a list of questions; you might include the list suggested earlier in this chapter.

And then get on the phone. Arrange interviews with admissions people, financial-aid officers, profs, and students. Tell them right up front, "I can't make it for a college visit, but can we schedule a time when I can ask you a bunch of questions?" They'll be more than happy to help.

Find some local alumni of the colleges you're interested in, and talk to them. Note: It might be fun to talk to someone who graduated from the school in '72, but you won't necessarily get an accurate picture of what that school is like *today*. Time and sentimental feelings may skew their memories. Try to find relatively recent graduates of the college.

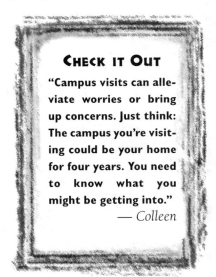

CHECK IT OUT

"Campus visits can alleviate worries or bring up concerns. Just think: The campus you're visiting could be your home for four years. You need to know what you might be getting into."

— *Colleen*

A Ton of Questions

by Christy Simon

What if I don't like my roommate? I muttered as I overheard two students talk about an annoying roommate.

How will I survive without seeing my friends, family, and pets for several months at a time? I wondered as my eye caught a glimpse of a bulletin board plastered with snapshots of home. Will the food taste as bad as high-school cafeteria food? What if I can't figure out how to do the laundry? Will I find friends?

Questions, concerns, and "what ifs" raced non-stop through my head. I was spending the night on the campus of a Christian college, hoping to decide through first-hand experience if the school was right for me.

As I took in the college close-up, I thought a lot about whether this school was the one. I also kept thinking about all the fears I had about college.

As I walked down the sidewalk past total strangers, I worried a lot about leaving my friends and family behind. Sure, I'd survived without my family for one week during summer camp. But living without them for months at a time suddenly felt impossible. And what if I lost contact with my high-school friends? Would they forget me when they formed new friendships at college? And I wondered if I'd forget them after graduation.

How will my new friends, teachers, and environment change my personality? Will I graduate from college a completely different person than I am now? What if I don't like the person I become?

Before I visited this campus, I'd talked with some college grads and current students about my fears. And those talks helped me see that I'm not alone in my fears. Everyone I talked to was at least a little hesitant about college, if not downright scared.

I'd also read books about college life. I particularly enjoyed Letters from the College Front (Baker Book House), which comes in separate editions for girls and guys. While I checked out classrooms and watched people interact in the student union, I thought about the advice and insights these books offered. Doing so helped me feel a little less fearful.

And then there were those student newspapers I'd read from various colleges. Somehow, reading student-written articles and seeing pictures of kids in jeans and T-shirts made my own brief on-campus visit not so scary. It helped me realize that college students are just regular people, like me, who have decided to take their education a step farther.

As I flew back home, I knew I still had some fears about college. Many of those fears won't actually go away until I'm a college freshman and have adjusted to college life. So why spend so much time worrying about them? Besides, I needed to concentrate a bit more energy on worries that weren't several months away—like Tuesday's big physics test!

From *Campus Life* College Guide, March 1996. Used by permission.

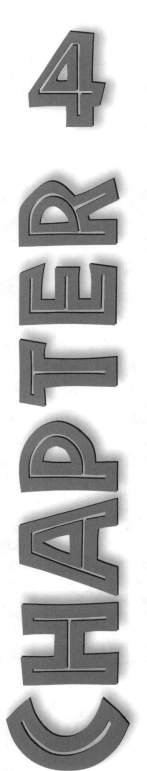

The Application Process

Q **What kind of timeline should I follow in the application process?**

A By the fall of your senior year, you'll want to have narrowed your list of potential colleges down to around five. These are the schools you'll actually apply to.

If you haven't gotten the applications from those schools by the fall of your senior year, contact each of them and ask for an application.

When are applications due? It varies from college to college. When you ask for applications, be sure to ask about deadlines, too.

For regular admission, most college applications are due by March 1 of your senior year. Some colleges will take your application as late as August after you graduate from high school, though it's not recommended that you wait that late.

Some colleges also offer "early admission" or "early decision" options. Those applications are usually due in November or December of your senior year. (Read more about these options later in this chapter.)

Hint: It's a good idea to at least read the applications when you get them, even if they're not due for six months. If they're not due till March 1, *don't* wait till the last week of February to look at them. For the most part, applications are relatively easy forms to fill out. But some of the questions take time, thought, and a little research to answer. Plus, most applications require you to pass along two or more recommendation forms to be filled out by others. So don't wait till the last second.

Q How many schools should I apply to?

A Most experts and publications recommend around five or six. Certainly no less than two, and probably no more than seven or eight.

You definitely don't want to make the mistake of just applying to one college and assuming you'll "definitely" get in, just because you've got good grades and a high SAT score. Don't take anything for granted.

At the same time, you don't want to apply to too many schools. It's tempting to think, "I'm having trouble narrowing my list down to five. I'll just apply to 10 or 12 or 15 and see which ones accept me. *Then* I'll make my decision." That can get costly. Many colleges require an application fee of about $25; applying to a dozen could cost you (or your parents) $300 or more.

By the spring of your junior year, get your list down to five or so. Then, also during your junior year, visit as many of those five as you can. You might learn something on your visits that will make you want to adjust your list, and there's still plenty of time to do that. (Read more about campus visits in chapter 3).

Finally, keep in mind that different colleges often have different admissions standards: Some colleges are difficult to get into, some are quite easy, and many fall between these extremes. It's OK to "aim high" and apply to a couple of schools that might be especially difficult to get into. But don't count on anything, even if you're going to graduate at the top of your class. At the same time, it's a good idea to apply to at least one "safety" school, where the admission standards aren't terribly difficult, so you'll be all but assured of getting into at least one school.

Q How do I apply, and how much does it cost?

A The most conventional way to apply is simply to ask the colleges you're considering to send you an application. They send you some forms to fill out, and you complete the information and return them by a certain deadline. Simple as that. But now there are other options, too.

One option might be to apply digitally. Many colleges will not only send you their application on paper, but on a computer diskette. You just pop the disk into your computer, fill out the information, and return the disk (and sometimes the printout, too). Check with the schools you're considering to see if they offer this option.

Another option is to apply on the Internet. Some schools have made it possible for you to call up their Web site, click your way to the application, and send it, via modem, directly to the admissions office. Again, check with the schools you're considering.

Still another option is the Common Application, a standardized form created by the National Association of Secondary School Principals (NASSP). They figured that since many college applications ask essentially the same questions, why not create a form that students only have to fill out once, sending it to all the colleges they're applying to? If you're interested, ask your guidance counselor for a hard copy or a computer disk of the Common Application. If he or she doesn't have one, you can write for one at NASSP, 1904 Association Drive, Reston, VA 22091. Note: Not all colleges accept the Common Application, so be sure to check with the schools you're considering.

Applying to college costs anywhere from free to about 50 bucks, but the average is about $25, plus a postage stamp, if you're using snail mail.

Usually, the application fee is non-refundable. If your family is struggling financially, a college may reduce or even waive the fee. If it will be difficult to pay the application fee, contact the college and ask if any other arrangements can be made. Or ask your guidance counselor for suggestions on how you might have the application fee waived.

Q   What's "early application" mean?

A   Generally, "early application" means you can apply to a college—usually the top school on your list—early in the admissions process. This is done in the fall or early winter of your senior year, rather than waiting till late winter or spring, when most students apply. If you go through the early application process, you'll get a response from the college sooner than you would via the regular process.

There are two main types of early application options—"early action" and "early decision." "Early action" is "non-binding," meaning that if you are accepted by the college, you can still go to another school. "Early decision," meanwhile, is "binding," meaning that if you're accepted, then you're obligated to attend that college. A binding agreement also means you might have to withdraw all applications to other colleges.

Colleges sometimes admit only the best students through early application options. So don't get discouraged if you don't get into your first choice early; you'll still be considered when they look at all the applications for regular admission.

If you're interested in applying early, talk to your guidance counselor and/or the colleges you're considering.

Not many Christian colleges offer early application options. Of the 90 schools in the Coalition for Christian Colleges & Universities (CCCU) in 1996-97, only 11 offered early application.

"Early decision" and "early action" are only two admissions terms worth knowing. Here are a few others:

• *Regular decision.* This means just what it implies. It's the regular process colleges use to decide which applicants they'll admit to their schools. It comes after the early decision and early action deadlines.

• *Rolling admission.* This means that the college evaluates its applications on a first-come, first-served basis. There still might be a deadline date for receiving applications, but you shouldn't wait that late. The sooner you apply, the better, because they'll stop accepting applications when they fill their incoming freshman class. So, if you apply via rolling admission, do it before early spring of your senior year, and preferably sooner.

• *Deferred admission.* This is an option for the student who wants to take a year "off" after high school before going to college. You still apply during your senior year, but you clearly indicate on your application that you don't intend to come to college until the following year. Again, check with your guidance counselor or the colleges themselves to see if this is the right option for you.

• *Wait list.* This happens when an admissions department considers your application and decides to wait on making a decision. If you're "wait-listed," you have neither been accepted nor denied, just delayed. If you get a wait-list letter from the school, it will also say when you can expect a final decision.

Q What kind of questions do they ask on a college application?

A We looked at 54 applications from Christian colleges, and we found that most of the questions fall into two categories:

• *No-brainer questions.* These are the types of questions you can answer while you're watching TV. They'll ask your name, address, birthday, phone number, Social Security number, and other facts. They'll ask about your academic progress and achievements, and your extracurricular activities. They'll ask

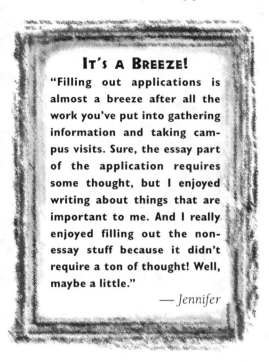

IT'S A BREEZE!

"Filling out applications is almost a breeze after all the work you've put into gathering information and taking campus visits. Sure, the essay part of the application requires some thought, but I enjoyed writing about things that are important to me. And I really enjoyed filling out the non-essay stuff because it didn't require a ton of thought! Well, maybe a little."

— Jennifer

about community service, leadership awards, honors, and such. They may ask about your church denomination and your involvement in the church. They might ask what you want to study in college and what extracurricular activities you plan to participate in. They might ask about your race and ethnic background, but you don't have to answer those questions; they want this information for statistical purposes only, and it will not affect their decision whether or not to admit you. They might ask about your physical and emotional health, and whether you have any special needs; again, this info has no bearing on their decision.

• *Essay questions.* Now it's time to turn off the TV. This is the part of the application where you've gotta use your brain. Colleges are looking for thinkers, and the essay question is the best place to show them how well you can think and express yourself. It's also your chance to tell the college more about yourself and what's important to you. There's at least one essay question on most applications, and some contain two or more. We read four types of essay questions on the applications we reviewed:

Spiritual. Christian colleges want to know about your Christian experience. They want to know if you're a Christian (though a few say that's not a determining factor on whether or not they'll admit you), and they want to know how your faith has affected your lifestyle and the way you view the world. Some examples: "What does having a relationship with God mean to you?" "Relate briefly your salvation experience (include Scripture references)." "What in your life indicates that you are walking with the Lord?" It's a good idea to start thinking about how you'd answer these types of questions before you even get your college applications.

Academic/achievement. This is where they ask what you've done in your school and community, and how those experiences have made you a more well-rounded person. Some examples: "Please write a well-thought-out essay to discuss your ideas, your experiences, interests and achievements." "Summarize your school experiences in both academic and extracurricular activities. . . . You may also want to discuss which of your talents, interests, or school activities means the most to you and why." "Why are you interested in attending [name of college]?" Be especially prepared to answer that last question, whether it appears on the application or not. If you plan to apply to a certain college, you ought to have well-defined reasons for doing so.

Goal-oriented. Colleges want to know what you want to do with your life, and why you think their school will help you reach those goals. So, does that mean you have to know, before you even turn 18, what you'll major in, what company you'll want to work for after college, what position you'll want to hold, whom you want to marry, and what you'll name your children? Of course not. If your goals aren't clearly defined yet, that's fine. Just don't invent

SHEILA GIVES A DEMONSTRATION OF HOW NOT TO HANDLE
YOURSELF AT THE CAMPUS INTERVIEW.

lofty goals to impress the admissions people; don't tell them you want to be the CEO of IBM, or that you want to be the next Billy Graham, if it's not true. Be honest, and say that you hope the college experience will help you define your goals. But don't be completely vague. Some of your goals are obvious: You want to keep growing in your faith. You want to get a good education. You want to get a good job after college. Some examples of the questions you might see: "Discuss how your system of values would help you succeed as a student at [name of college] and throughout your lifetime." "Please specify your personal ministry goals and how you perceive an education at [name of college] will assist you in meeting them."

Open-ended. These are essay questions that don't really fit into any of the other three categories. It's almost "anything goes" with these questions. Some examples: "Write about something that is important to you. Describe what it is, and tell why it is important." "Describe one of your most significant experiences and how it has affected your life." "What is the most interesting book you've ever read, and how did it impact you?" "Share any additional information about yourself that might be helpful to the Committee on Admissions in the selection process."

Bottom line: Expect to answer just about anything when you get to the essay questions on your college application. Many of the questions will require very little thought, but some will require quite a bit.

Q **How important is the essay, and how do I write one?**

A The essay questions are important stuff, the kind of stuff that could make or break a college's decision whether or not to admit you. Even if you've got a 3.9 GPA, a 1450 SAT and a .486 batting average with 17 home runs, those things won't matter much if you can't put your thoughts down on paper, logically and intelligently.

Colleges want thinking people on their campuses, people who can express themselves—preferably in complete sentences. That's why the essay questions are critical. Take them seriously.

How do you write one? Enough students have asked that question that publishers have actually printed entire books on the topic. (We especially liked *Peterson's Practically Painless Guide to Writing a Winning College Essay*. If you can't find it in your bookstore or guidance counselor's office, call 1-800-338-3282 to order a copy.)

Start by being prepared. Re-read the above question ("What kind of questions do they ask on a college application?"), and be sure to give these issues some thought even before you get your applications.

For some more tips on writing a good essay, read "Give the Write Impression" at the end of this chapter.

Q How much information about myself should I share with colleges?

A That's your call. But keep in mind that the colleges want to get to know the true you when they're considering your application. Colleges don't expect perfection; if colleges only admitted perfect people, there would be a lot of empty campuses.

It's OK to tell admissions people about your mistakes. In fact, they'll probably like it—as long as you can tell them what you learned from your mistakes. They may read your essay and think, *This applicant learned a valuable lesson through their mistake. This is the kind of person we want at our school.*

Some college applications will come right out and ask you about mistakes. They'll ask if you've ever used alcohol, tobacco, or drugs. They'll ask if you've ever been kicked out of school, arrested, or even convicted of a crime. The best way to answer these questions is to be honest and then to follow up with what you've learned and how you've changed since then.

> **ONE MORE STEP**
>
> "College applications can tell you things about yourself and things about the college that you may not have known or considered before. Think of the application as one more step in the process of narrowing down your list of potential colleges."
>
> — *Mark*

At the same time, use your discretion. Don't share all the graphic details just to make an impression. One college admissions official advises, "Don't try to appear edgy. Discretion and maturity are factors that we look for. Don't write in a way that will be offensive or shocking."

King David certainly made his share of mistakes, adultery and murder among them. But he went down in history as a man "after God's own heart." Why? Because he was repentant and he was honest.

David even wrote a song about honesty (Psalm 15), concluding by saying that people who are honest "will never be shaken." That's a fact.

Q **How important are letters of recommendation?**

A They're also called "reference letters," and they're important enough that most colleges ask for them. In making the decision whether or not to admit you, colleges want to know what other people think of you. These people are your "references."

Obviously, what other people have to say about you is vital. If you think you're the smartest, coolest, most spiritual person on the planet, you might think you can get into any college you want. But if your guidance counselor writes a reference that says you have poor study habits and that you're too immature for college, the admissions people won't be as impressed with all the nice things you said about yourself.

Letters of recommendation help you create a more well-rounded picture of yourself for college admissions officials. Recommendations turn your application into more than just a data- and fact-filled document; it gives a more complete picture of you as a person.

Q **Who should I use for references?**

A In some cases, you won't have a choice. Some college application packets include exactly two forms to pass on to references, and they tell you whom to give them to—your guidance counselor and your pastor.

Often, though, colleges will ask you to have others write letters of recommendation for you. Note: If the college doesn't ask you to do this, they'll often accept them anyway. Ask the colleges you're considering if they'll accept any unsolicited letters of recommendation.

Who should you ask to write these letters?

You might be thinking, *Hey, I'll just ask Mom to tell 'em all about me. She thinks I'm the best thing on the planet.*

Sorry, but that won't work. Mom's opinion doesn't count. Colleges don't want to hear from your relatives; they're too biased. You already know that most Christian colleges will want to hear from your guidance counselor and your pastor (or youth pastor). Some colleges will also want to hear from other people who know you well, preferably adults. Teachers and coaches are good choices. And if you know someone who attended or is currently attending the college you're applying to, it's a good idea to ask that person to be a reference.

Many colleges will send you forms, with the application, to pass along to your references. The forms include a handful of questions about you, and they essentially ask the person if they think you would be a good fit at that particular college.

The people you choose as references will fill out the forms and, in many cases, mail them directly to the college—or return them to you in a sealed envelope. That's right: Sometimes you won't get a chance to read what they wrote. So, when you have a choice, give your reference forms to people who actually like you! (Hint: If you borrowed some of Jennifer's favorite CDs six months ago and you *still* haven't returned them, don't use Jennifer as a reference!)

When you select your references, remind them of some of your accomplishments. They can't share this information with the colleges if they don't have it. You might even give your references a brief list of some of the things you've accomplished.

Q   What are some mistakes students make in filling out applications?

A   The most common mistakes usually result from laziness—spelling errors, grammar problems, sloppiness, incomplete information, and so on. Other mistakes include missed deadlines (don't ever be late with your application) and forgotten fees (don't forget to write the check!).

Here are three more things you must avoid:

• Don't use those goopy white correction fluids. An ugly glob of that gunk points to sloppiness, which really stands out when compared to other neatly-completed applications.

• Don't write in cursive or longhand. If you don't use a typewriter or a computer, then print neatly in ink. Or, ask someone else to type it for you.

• Don't leave any question blank, unless it's clearly marked "optional."

And those are just the objective mistakes. Another common mistake is simply not investing enough time into filling out the application. Applications take thought and creativity, and thought and creativity take time.

Most applications include a checklist of steps to cover before sending in your application. Take these checklists seriously; if you skip a step, especially missing a deadline, the process will bog down at the college, possibly causing your elimination from consideration. And you don't want that to happen.

Again, it's always a good idea to ask your English teacher to look at your completed application, checking for errors.

The last thing you want to do is submit an application with mistakes. Think of your application as a reflection of you as a person. Do it right, do it well, do it thoroughly.

Q **I've heard that some colleges require an interview. What's that all about?**

A By the time you've submitted your application, your essays, your transcripts, and other paperwork, you might be wondering if there's anything else the college could *possibly* want from you.

Well, yes, there could be. They might want to interview you, too. Why? It's just one more step that some admissions departments like to take when they consider your application.

"It's a way for us to really get to know our students," one admissions director tells us. "We want students to have a clear picture of what our college is about and what's expected of our students."

Says another, "Sometimes we need to find out the facts more thoroughly. We just want to make sure that the student and our college are on the same wavelength."

Not all colleges require or even recommend an interview. Of the 90 colleges in the Coalition for Christian Colleges and Universities, only four *require* an interview. Another 31 schools "recommend" an interview, while 47 others say it is "required for some." Contact the colleges you're considering and ask what their policy is concerning interviews.

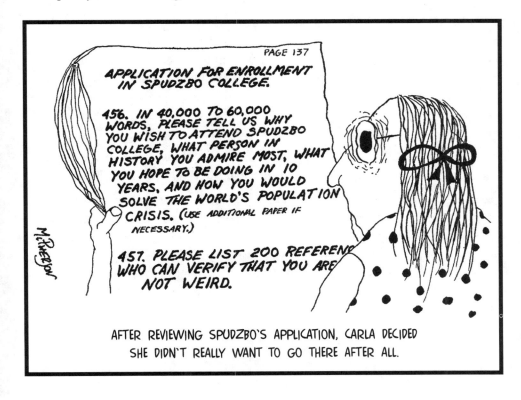

PAGE 137

APPLICATION FOR ENROLLMENT IN SPUDZBO COLLEGE.

456. IN 40,000 TO 60,000 WORDS, PLEASE TELL US WHY YOU WISH TO ATTEND SPUDZBO COLLEGE, WHAT PERSON IN HISTORY YOU ADMIRE MOST, WHAT YOU HOPE TO BE DOING IN 10 YEARS, AND HOW YOU WOULD SOLVE THE WORLD'S POPULATION CRISIS. (USE ADDITIONAL PAPER IF NECESSARY.)

457. PLEASE LIST 200 REFERENC WHO CAN VERIFY THAT YOU ARE NOT WEIRD.

AFTER REVIEWING SPUDZBO'S APPLICATION, CARLA DECIDED SHE DIDN'T REALLY WANT TO GO THERE AFTER ALL.

There's no reason to be afraid of an interview. Instead, you should see it as an additional opportunity to show your strengths, interests, and maturity.

"The college doesn't want to intimidate you," says one guidance counselor. "They will make the interview as positive and easygoing as possible. The word 'interview' sounds a little more formal than what really occurs. It's usually just a conversation about you and what you want out of a college education."

If you do have an interview, just be yourself. Don't try to make yourself sound better than you are; that will be obvious. Take the interview seriously, but not so seriously that you get over-stressed.

Most colleges prefer an in-person interview. It's to your advantage—and the college's—to have the meeting face-to-face, rather than over the phone.

Often, the interview is held on campus. But sometimes admissions officials will set up interviews when they're traveling through your area. Some colleges also ask local alumni to interview high school students.

At many schools, the interview is just "recommended," making it sound optional. In that case, should you go for it?

"I encourage you to take every chance to promote yourself to the college," says one guidance counselor. "They've been looking at you on paper—grades, test scores, a list of activities, letters of recommendation. The interview gives you an opportunity to bring yourself to life, to showcase yourself in a positive, real way that is not just a list of facts and numbers."

When you have an interview, remember that everything about you sends a message. Don't be like the student who showed up for an interview at one college while wearing a T-shirt, torn jeans, and a backward baseball cap. "We tried to give him every benefit of the doubt, but he didn't help himself," says the admissions official who interviewed him. "It was easy for us to make our decision." They didn't accept him.

Q   **Some applications have a "code of conduct agreement." What's that?**

A   The "code of conduct agreement" spells out certain behavior expectations at the school, and it sometimes includes specific doctrinal beliefs.

Colleges will ask you to read their code and to sign your name, agreeing to abide by that code if you're accepted at that particular school.

Most codes include regulations regarding sexual activity and the use of alcohol and illegal drugs. Some codes include regulations regarding social dancing as well.

Here's an example of the code of conduct at one school, which we'll call College X:

> "College X respects your integrity as an individual. At the same time, your life is expected to be consistent with the ideals and purposes of a Christian community. It is the position of the college that such things as alcoholic beverages, tobacco, habituating drugs, profane language, and improper behavior or attire cannot be a part of the College X experience. Therefore, students are held to this position. When College X students show respect for order, honesty, courtesy, and a high standard of morality, they are interacting in a manner that promotes the college ideals. Worship is also important at College X. The college provides chapel programs three times per week and attendance at these services is required."

Read the codes and the doctrinal beliefs carefully. If you have questions about the doctrinal positions of a particular school, talk to your pastor and/or an admissions official at that school.

If you read anything in the code of conduct or doctrinal statement that you disagree with or feel you can't abide by, then don't apply to that college.

Q   When will colleges let me know if I've been accepted?

A   The answer varies from college to college, but often depends on when you apply. If you've done "early application" at a particular college, you might hear from that school before Christmas of your senior year in high school, and certainly sometime well before the winter is over.

If you've applied for "regular" admission, you'll probably hear sometime in the spring of your senior year, most likely between March and May.

As mentioned before, many colleges have "rolling admissions," which means they fill their freshman classes on more of a first-come, first-served basis. These same colleges also often use something called "continuous notification," meaning they'll let you know their decision as soon as possible.

Check with the colleges you're considering to see when they notify applicants of their decision.

Give the Write Impression

by Ruth Senter

So you've never written a college application essay before. Neither have most high-school seniors. You might be surprised to find that the job is not as difficult as it may seem.

You might be asking, "Why do I have to write an admissions essay, anyway? Don't I get enough of that in English class? Besides, what can 1,500 words on a piece of paper really tell anybody about me?"

Plenty. Especially if you've written the right words. You see, admissions people want to know you. They want to know what kinds of experiences you've had. Your opinions. Who you admire. What you dream of doing someday.

True, they can get that information if they interview you. And they can learn some things about you from your "fill-in-the-blank" answers on the application. But an essay gives them a picture of you they'd have a hard time getting any other way. An essay shows the admissions staff how you think. Writing 1,500 words on "The Person I Most Admire and Why" calls for a little more mental effort than listing the activities you were involved in during your senior year in high school. Even the way you write the essay—how you organize yourself and your words—tells the admissions people something about you.

Yep, your application essay is a pretty important part of the whole application process. It's also a pretty exciting part. After all, this is where you really get the chance to shine, to bring your true personality into the process. So you'll want to take the essay seriously, and you'll want to do it right.

To make your application essay the best it can be, you've got to be organized. And that means focusing on a topic. As you look at an application, read the essay question carefully. If the application asks you to respond to a particular question, the focus has been given to you. However, if you're free to choose your own topic, make sure it's narrow enough. You might want to write about a significant event in your life, but you don't have to build up to it with your entire life story. Remember, you're writing an essay, not a book. Admissions officers want to know what you're passionate about, what makes you tick. So whatever you choose to write about, make sure you write about something that excites you.

Once you've chosen your topic, spend some time brainstorming. Jot down whatever comes to mind about your topic. Then, corral those stray elements into some semblance of order—most often called an "outline." Once you have a rough outline, it's time to start writing a first draft. Unplug the dam and let the words flow—keeping in mind your focus, of course. Forget about spelling, grammar, syntax—for the moment. Just concentrate on getting words on paper in some orderly stream.

Now read what you've got, keeping a few things in mind. It's tempting to try to tell the admissions committee everything about yourself in one essay. But if you tell them too much, they won't remember anything. So keep your essay clear and focused. Ask yourself, "What's the main point of my essay? Is that point clear?" Remember, you're selling yourself. You want the committee to accept you into their school. You want to stand out from all the other people seeking admission. A clear essay will help you do that.

Sometimes an essay can stand out because it's so well written. The action and descriptions are in the verbs and nouns. The essay avoids long strings of descriptive adjectives. Sentences are short. The introduction is a "grabber"—it clearly tells the reader where the author is going and makes the reader want to come along. Transitions are strong. Paragraphs contain one thought only. The conclusion clearly "draws the net" by summarizing and giving the "so what" of the piece.

Sometimes an essay can stand out because of its unique style. But remember: Make sure the style you use is your style. If you're not a humor writer, don't try to be funny on your application essay. But if you're known on the school newspaper staff for your humorous style, you might consider lightening up your essay with a little fun. If humor is used well, the application people will most likely thank you for making their job more enjoyable.

Sometimes an essay will stand out for its honesty. It's OK to tell admissions people about your mistakes. In fact, they'll probably like it—as long as you can tell them what you've learned from your mistakes. They may read your essay and think: This person is a better person because of what they've been through. This is the kind of person we want at our school.

Above all, make sure your essay is uniquely "you." Don't try to impress. A committee will know if you're just filling space. Don't try to sound like your parents—but you would be wise to let your parents read your essay. They may catch mistakes or see something you've overlooked. But don't let your parents put words in your mouth. After all, the admissions committee is considering you—not your mom or dad.

Above all, be positive and personal. Write as though you're having a conversation with someone. When the admissions counselor finishes your essay, they should feel like they know you.

Once you've drained your reservoir of brilliant thoughts and said what you want to say, it's time for the tedious work of editing. Read, re-read, and re-read some more. Edit. Edit. Edit. Look for flow, sense, focus, spelling, grammar. And don't rely on your spell-checker to catch all your mistakes. Polish off your piece until you feel confident you've said what needs to be said. After you're convinced you've done your best, ask your English teacher to read your essay, not necessarily for style or content, but more for construction and flow.

And don't forget: How your essay looks is also important. Make sure you have set proper margins, double spaced, and used a printer with enough toner (or a typewriter with a well-inked ribbon). If you're asked to write your essay in "the space provided below," make sure you stay in the allotted space and that someone doesn't go blind trying to make out your handwriting. Care for the "little things" will tell the admissions committee something about the kind of student you will be. (So will when you turn in your essay. Admissions people can spot procrastinators from afar.)

So, take courage. With a well-organized plan, some creative thought, careful writing, and genuine warmth, you should be able to represent yourself favorably to any admissions committee.

From *Campus Life* magazine, October 1996. Used by permission.

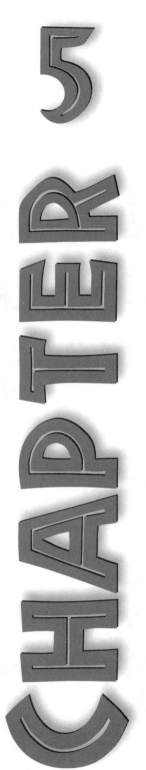

Getting the Money You Need

Q **Paying for college seems overwhelming. Where do I start?**

A Here we go again: Start with your guidance counselor. He or she will have plenty of resources available to help you get started. If you're homeschooled, or if you go to a small private school with limited resources, take advantage of the services of your local public-school guidance counselor.

Ask your guidance counselor about the two broad categories of financial aid: need-based and merit-based. Need-based aid is granted to students who would otherwise have trouble meeting college costs. Merit-based aid is based on a student's high-school performance—academic and otherwise. Ask your counselor any questions you or your parents have about the differences between these two types of aid, and how you go about getting them.

Also, talk to someone in the financial-aid office at one of the colleges you're considering. Take advantage of their wisdom. They'll be glad to help.

Familiarize yourself with financial-aid terminology. Many of these terms are defined throughout this chapter. As you talk to the experts, you'll have a better understanding of what they're talking about as they mention things like FAFSA forms and Pell Grants and FSEOGs. (Whew!)

There are tons of excellent books on the subject of financial aid. Here are a few we'd recommend: *Peterson's College Money Handbook '98* (Peterson's), *Paying for College* (College Entrance Exam Board), *You Can Afford College* (Doubleday), and *USA Today's Financial Aid for College* (Peterson's). There's even a book that rates many of the books on the market: *The Best Resources for College Financial Aid* (Resource Pathways).

The federal government is a good source, too. Get a copy of *The Student Guide,* a free book all about financial aid, by calling the Federal Student Aid Information Center at 1-800-4-FED-AID (1-800-433-3243).

And don't forget the Internet. Do a search on "college financial aid," and you'll be amazed at the volume of information you'll find. Here are two especially helpful Web sites:

• *FinAid (http://www.FinAid.org)* You can find almost everything you need to know here: scholarship databases that take your survey answers and hook you up with potential cash, loan-payment schedules to print out so you don't miss payments, sources of aid including grants and special contests, and something called a "forecasting calculator" to determine what you'll need and when you'll need it.

• *fastWEB (http://www.fastweb.com)* A helpful cousin to the FinAid site, fastWEB searches a huge database of scholarships to connect you with free money. It takes a few minutes to fill out the extensive online survey, but the results are worth it. There are hundreds of scholarships that never get used because students don't realize they're available; fastWEB does, and can help you find them.

That's where to start for *information.* But where do you start for money? By saving. Starting now. Whether college is just a year away, or several years, it's always a good time for both you and your parents to save whatever money you can for college. Even if you end up getting a full scholarship, with tuition and room and board completely paid for, you'll still have plenty of expenses. So start saving!

Just remember that getting any kind of financial aid requires work. Financial aid will *not* come looking for you. But by working with your guidance counselor and other sources, you can learn more than enough about getting the money you need.

Another thought: Don't rule out a college because its "sticker cost" seems too high. Private colleges in particular have a lot of aid available, which can make the school affordable. One financial-aid officer says many students tell her, "I'd love to come to your college, but we just can't afford it." But after working out a financial-aid plan that fits their needs, those same students say, "I can't believe it! I *can* come here!"

More than *$40 billion* in financial aid is awarded to college undergraduates every year. More than half of all students qualify for some type of assistance. Rarely do students pay the full "sticker price." Never rule out a college until after financial aid is considered.

Q **What's the difference between scholarships, grants, and loans?**

A Scholarships and grants are gifts toward your college education; you don't have to pay them back. But you do have to pay back loans, usually with interest.

Scholarships are monies usually awarded for some special achievement or talent. Scholarships are also sometimes awarded based on a student's financial need.

Grants are usually awarded according to financial need only; earning a grant has nothing to do with performance or skill.

Sometimes scholarships and grants are referred to as "gift aid." Gift aid can come from many places—the federal government, state governments, the colleges and universities themselves, and tons of private sources, sometimes as local as your own church! We'll talk more about *how* to track down this money later in the chapter.

While scholarships and grants qualify as "gift aid," loans and work-study programs (discussed later in this chapter) are called "self-help aid," because you have to do something to get the money—either pay it back (loans) or work for it (work-study).

Q **What's FAFSA, and how does it work?**

A FAFSA is the Free Application for Federal Student Aid. But it's more than just an application for federal aid. It's an application for federal, state, *and* college financial aid. This form, which you and your parents fill out as soon as possible after January 1 of your senior year, gathers information about your family's income and financial situation—information the government uses to determine how much aid you're eligible for.

You'll want to pick up a FAFSA at the beginning of January of your senior year. You can get a FAFSA from your guidance counselor's office, from one of the colleges you're considering, or by calling the Federal Student Aid Information Center at 1-800-4-FED-ID (1-800-433-3243).

Another option is to file the *FAFSA Express,* the electronic version of the FAFSA form. Your guidance counselor may already have the software, or you can get it for free by calling 1-800-801-0576. You can also download it from the Internet at http://www.ed.gov/offices/OPE. Filing electronically with *FAFSA Express* is the fastest, easiest way to apply. Note: If you file electronically, you'll still have to mail in signatures. The *FAFSA Express* instructions tell you how to do this.

Fill out the FAFSA or *FAFSA Express* as soon after January 1 of your senior year as possible. You'll need a Social Security number. You'll have to report both your and your parents' financial information, so you'll need your current tax returns. If you and/or your parents haven't filled out your tax returns by late January, go ahead and fill out the FAFSA anyway, estimating your answers. You will be able to correct them later.

When you file the FAFSA, keep a copy of it, as well as copies of all tax and financial forms. You may need them later in the process.

On the FAFSA, you can list schools you're interested in attending, and those schools will get the results of your FAFSA after it's been processed. You aren't required to list colleges on the FAFSA, but doing so speeds up the financial-aid process.

About four weeks after you file the FAFSA, or one week after filing *FAFSA Express,* you'll receive a Student Aid Report (SAR) from the government. The SAR will repeat the information you provided on the FAFSA form. Check the SAR carefully for mistakes; this is your chance to correct them by sending in a response form. If you don't receive your SAR within four weeks, call the processing center at 1-319-337-5665; this is not a free call.

If the information you provided on the FAFSA was complete (i.e., no estimates), your SAR will also

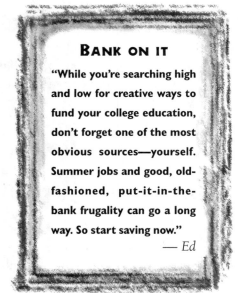

BANK ON IT

"While you're searching high and low for creative ways to fund your college education, don't forget one of the most obvious sources—yourself. Summer jobs and good, old-fashioned, put-it-in-the-bank frugality can go a long way. So start saving now."

— Ed

include your Expected Family Contribution (EFC). The EFC, determined by a formula established by law, is exactly what it implies: a dollar amount the federal government says you and your family will be expected to pay for your freshman year at college. Colleges use the EFC to determine the amount of your federal grant, loan, or work-study, if you are eligible. Colleges also use this information to determine the make-up of your entire financial-aid package, which is discussed later in the chapter.

Also, the EFC doesn't necessarily tell you the *entire* amount your family will have to pay; the college just uses it as a guideline to determine financial aid. Often, your family will have to pay more than the EFC.

Note: Your FAFSA application is good for one year only, *not* for your entire college stay. So you'll have to fill out a new FAFSA, called a Renewal FAFSA, every year you're in college.

Q **What kinds of federal financial aid are available?**

A The federal government provides about 75 percent of the $45 billion in college financial aid awarded every year.

There are two federal grant programs—the Federal Pell Grant and the Federal Supplemental Educational Opportunity Grant (FSEOG); three loan programs—the Federal Perkins Loan, the Federal Direct Loan and the Federal Stafford Loan; and a work program that helps colleges provide jobs for students—the Federal Work-Study program. There is also a parental loan (PLUS) available.

Here's a closer look at each:

• *Federal Pell Grant.* This is the largest grant program, with more than 5 million students receiving Pell Grants every year. Pell Grants are the starting points of assistance for lower-income families. The amount of a Pell Grant depends on your EFC, the cost of the college, and other factors. The maximum Pell Grant for 1997-98 was $2,700.

• *Federal Supplemental Educational Opportunity Grant (FSEOG).* The FSEOG provides additional money to especially needy students. The maximum is $4,000 per year, and the amount depends on the college's policy, the availability of FSEOG funds, the total cost of education, and the amount of other aid awarded.

• *Federal Work-Study.* This program provides jobs for students who need help paying for college. The salary is paid by funds from the federal government and the college. (Read more about work-study, and similar cooperative education programs, later in this chapter.)

• *Federal Perkins Loans.* A low-interest (5 percent) loan for students with exceptional financial need, Perkins Loans are made through the college's financial-aid office. Students may borrow up to $3,000 per year for up to five years. You can take up to 10 years to repay the loan, beginning nine months after you graduate, leave school, or drop below half-time status. A Perkins Loan does not accrue interest while you're in college.

• *Federal Stafford Loans.* These loans can be borrowed from two sources— either from the federal government through the Direct Loan Program, or from a commercial lender (bank, credit union) that participates in the Federal Family Education Loan Program. Interest rates vary, up to a maximum of 8.25 percent, and the 1997-98 rate was 8.25 percent. There are two types of Stafford Loans. With a subsidized loan, which is given based on financial need, the government pays the interest while you're in college. With an unsubsidized loan, which is not based on need, you'll have to pay interest while you're in school. The maximum amount dependent students (still financially dependent on their parents) may borrow is $2,625 for freshmen, $3,500 for sophomores, and

HARD AS SHE TRIED, EDITH JUST COULD NOT CONVINCE A SINGLE COLLEGE TO OFFER HER A FULL SCHOLARSHIP FOR YODELING.

$5,500 for juniors and seniors, with a maximum of $23,000 for the total under-graduate program. You'll have to start paying back your Stafford Loan six months after you graduate, leave school, or drop below half-time enrollment.

• *Federal PLUS Loans.* These loans are for your parents. Your parents don't have to demonstrate a financial need to qualify for these loans, just a good credit history. Your parents can borrow up to the cost of your education, minus other financial aid received. The variable interest rate cannot exceed 9 percent, and the 1997-98 rate was 8.98 percent. Your parents must begin repaying PLUS Loans within 60 days, meaning they'll be paying off the loans while you're still in college.

Again, for more information on federal financial aid, get a free copy of *The Student Guide* by calling the Federal Student Aid Information Center at 1-800-4-FED-AID (1-800-433-3243).

Q Please tell me more about work-study. What's that all about?

A When you fill out the FAFSA, you'll eventually receive a "financial-aid package" (discussed later in this chapter), detailing the types of aid you've been awarded. One of those types might be Federal Work-Study.

In this program, students work on an hourly basis at jobs on-campus, getting paid at least the federal minimum wage—earning a maximum of the amount noted in the financial-aid package. You won't get the money you're awarded "up front." You must work for it, and you'll get a piece of it every pay period.

What should you do with that money when you get it? Well, it's supposed to be used for "funding your education." Now, that can mean a lot of things. There are costs outside of tuition, room and board, fees, and books. There are also personal expenses like transportation—which, technically, is needed to get a college education.

Colleges don't have a lot of control over how much you take from your work-study paycheck and actually apply toward your student bill. But here's the bottom line: If you're awarded $1,000 in a work-study program and you never apply the first dollar toward the cost of your education, you'll come up $1,000 short at the end of the year when the bill arrives from the college.

One cool thing about work-study is that it doesn't count as income on next year's financial-aid application.

Another program, similar to Federal Work-Study, is called "cooperative education," or co-op programs. These programs have nothing to do with the Federal Work-Study program, but are offered by the colleges themselves. Co-op programs are usually set up as a formal arrangement between the college and off-campus employers, not only to give you a chance to earn money but also to gain experience related to your degree or major.

Co-op programs are either "alternating" (work and study in alternating school terms) or "parallel" (work and study scheduled within the same term).

Don't be intimidated by the prospect of working a part-time job *and* making the adjustment to college life. Studies have shown that college students with part-time jobs make better grades than those who don't work. One financial-aid official told us that he worked about 20 hours a week in college, adding, "I got the best grades I'd ever gotten because I didn't have time to goof around. A job can teach you a lot about responsibility—and the lessons carry over into other areas."

Working on campus is especially beneficial. You'll get a chance to know more students, professors, and administrators. You'll get to know your college better. Plus, on-campus employers recognize the fact that you're a student first and an employee second, so they're willing to work with you at crunch time, like during final exams.

Q What's the Financial Aid PROFILE?

A   The PROFILE is used by about 400 private colleges and universities to award their own private funds—money you can't get by filling out the FAFSA form. The PROFILE is filled out *in addition to* the FAFSA form. Ask the colleges you're considering if they take part in the PROFILE program.

You can register for the PROFILE with the College Scholarship Service (CSS), a service of The College Board. CSS sends you an application, which you fill out and return to CSS, which forwards the information to the colleges of your choice.

The PROFILE service uses slightly different methods than FAFSA in determining the amount of financial aid to be awarded. PROFILE tends to be more thorough in the data it collects than FAFSA. The PROFILE service also tends to allow for more consideration of special circumstances (like medical expenses and private secondary school costs) than FAFSA.

While FAFSA is free, there is a charge for the PROFILE service. The $5 registration fee covers the cost of preparing and mailing the application packet to you. It'll cost another $14.50 for *each* college you choose to receive your PROFILE information.

To register for the PROFILE, or to get more information about the service, call toll-free 1-800-778-6888.

Q **Are there any other financial-aid forms I might have to fill out?**

A That depends on the college(s) you're applying to. Many colleges require you to fill out additional forms when applying for financial aid. Some colleges will use the PROFILE, while some will use their own forms. It's best to check with each college to see which supplemental forms, if any, are required.

And if you decide to pursue certain scholarships (see the question on scholarships later in this chapter), there will be still *more* forms to fill out.

Yes, you might have to fill out a lot of paperwork—the FAFSA, maybe the PROFILE, and maybe others, too—to get financial aid. But before you start thinking, *What a drag!,* remember *why* you're filling out these forms: You're applying for money—often *free* money—to help pay for your college education. So it's more than worth the effort.

Q **What's a "financial-aid package"?**

A It's the combination of grants, loans, scholarships, work-study, and possible discounts that a college offers you. This package is detailed in a letter from the college, telling you what types of aid you are eligible to receive. The aid comes from a variety of sources—federal, state, college, and/or private.

When you get your aid package, usually in the spring of your senior year, study it carefully. How much of it is "gift aid," money you won't have to earn or pay back? How much of it is "self-help aid," in the form of loans or work-study? If there is a loan involved, what's the interest rate, when will you have to start paying it off, and how many years will it take to pay it off? If there's work-study involved, how many hours a week will you have to work? The package should include an explanation of all these details; if not, be sure to call the financial-aid office and ask for more information.

Here's something to consider: If part of your aid package includes a loan, and you're trying to avoid debt as much as possible, you can decline all or part of the loan. You can ask the financial-aid office if it's possible to have some of the loan changed to Federal Work-Study. If that's not possible, you can find your own part-time job at college; many colleges have an employment office that will help you find work.

What if the package doesn't provide as much financial aid as you had hoped? Most colleges are willing to talk to you and your parents about it, so feel free to call and ask. Sometimes, colleges will grant more aid if you have extenuating circumstances—or if your family's financial situation has changed (through job loss, divorce, medical expenses, or other situations) since you filled out the FAFSA and other applications. But most often, the aid package represents the best offer the college can make; they're not going to "hold back" and make you beg for more. Still, it can't hurt to ask a college if it can possibly find a way to help even more.

Sometimes, students take a financial-aid package from one college and use it as leverage to "negotiate" with other colleges, matching one offer against another. Some colleges don't mind this practice, but many frown on it. If you're thinking about using your aid packages to bargain with schools, be careful, because you just might offend some financial-aid officers.

> ## WORK FOR THE FUTURE
>
> "Talk to financial-aid people about a school's work-study program. Don't look at it as just a way to help pay for school. Work-study can help you prepare for or try out a future career. It also can be a lot of fun—like working in the cafeteria with a bunch of your friends."
>
> — *Angela*

Here's something else to consider when you get your financial-aid package: Many of those dollar figures may apply to your *freshman year only*. Read the package carefully. Call the financial-aid department and ask questions like, "How long is this award good for?" "Is it only for my freshman year, or is it renewable?" "Is it based on some sort of criteria, like keeping a certain grade-point average or staying on the basketball team?"

Also, ask about something called "stacking." This means the school will "stack" one scholarship on top of another. For example, let's say you have a 4.0 grade-point average in high school. And the college awards scholarships for both a 3.5 and a 4.0 GPA. Well, some schools will "stack" one scholarship on another, awarding you two scholarships—one for your 3.5 GPA, and one for your 4.0.

Once you understand all the information in the financial-aid package, it's time to turn to the "bottom line"—how much you and your parents will have to pay. We address that in the next question.

Q **How can I estimate my college expenses, the portion my parents and I will have to pay?**

A Once you get your financial-aid package, you'd think it'd be easy to figure out how much is left. Just add up the cost of tuition, room and board, and any mandatory fees. Then subtract the total of the aid package, and you'll have to pay the difference. Right?

Well, mostly right. You'll need to figure in other expenses, too—like the cost of books, personal expenses, travel, and so on. How much should you estimate for these things? *Peterson's College Money Handbook* recommends $750 for books and $1,250 for personal expenses per year. Travel costs will vary significantly from student to student. If you live on the West Coast and go to school in the East, you're probably looking at two or three round-trip plane tickets per year. If your college is just a hundred miles from home, your travel expenses will be much less. If you're taking a car to school, you'll have to figure out those expenses as well. You probably won't drive around much on campus, but you might use your car for other reasons. Students at suburban colleges often drive the 10-20 miles into the nearby big city or to the mall or movie theater; these trips can add up.

To determine costs for later college years (sophomore and beyond), the *College Money Handbook* recommends adding a six-percent increase per year to all of your freshman costs—tuition, room and board, books, and so on.

Q **What happens if it looks like we still can't afford the college of my choice?**

A For families that can't afford to pay a large lump sum, many schools offer helpful payment plans. Here's an example: Let's say your financial-aid package is $5,000 short of what you need. For a small initial fee, many colleges will allow you to pay $500 per month for 10 months.

Make sure you ask any and all financial-aid questions—including questions about your payment options—*before* you get to the school. That way there will be no surprises. One financial-aid officer says, "Occasionally, students come into my office with tears running down their faces because they weren't aware of certain costs or of the process of paying their bills. We want students to know the financial facts *beforehand.*"

Finally, if you're willing to take on the added debt, you can always look into taking out additional loans. Check with a financial-aid officer for more information.

Q The thought of going into debt for college seems scary. Should I borrow? And if so, how long will I be in debt?

A You need to think about college as a *long-term financial benefit.* Remember, a college grad makes an average of $500,000 more in the course of a lifetime than someone who doesn't have a degree. So, yes, the debt may well be worth it.

On the other hand, there are plenty of people without college degrees who make a lot more money than people with diplomas. This happens especially often for college grads who choose to go into the ministry or some kind of service-oriented profession, where the pay isn't necessarily that high.

But a college degree is about more than just earning potential. It's about making you a more well-rounded person. College will probably make you a better thinker, and that's a worthwhile investment in itself.

College is definitely an investment for the rest of your life. Fortunately, student loans have low interest rates and deferred payment options, meaning you can often postpone payments until after you graduate from college. Students who decide to use loans must carefully figure out: 1) how much they need, 2) how much debt they feel they can handle, 3) how large a monthly payment they can afford to make when they graduate, and 4) how many years they want to take to repay the loan.

One college's financial-aid official gives this advice: "Apply for all the free money you can, earn money while in school, and conservatively borrow the rest."

Where do you turn for a loan? The college financial-aid package usually gives some suggestions and options. If not, ask the financial-aid officer for some advice.

What can you afford to pay back after college? Much of that depends on what type of job you'll have. Some careers pay better than others. Resource books, such as *The Encyclopedia of Career Choices for the 1990s,* give you a good idea of the average starting salaries in various careers. Once you have a rough estimate of your potential salary, ask your parents or guidance counselor to help you create a sample budget, including all the expenses of living on your own—insurance, taxes, groceries, rent, utilities, clothing, transportation, etc. Again, you won't be working with exact figures, but rough estimates.

Now look at that budget. Would you still be able to survive financially if you added a monthly $100 loan payment? What about $200 a month? What would you have to give up to make these payments? What's the maximum payment you could make? The minimum? Asking yourself these questions will give you an idea of how debt could affect your future lifestyle.

Once you've gone this far, ask a financial-aid counselor to help you take a realistic look at these projected figures and give you a better idea of how much debt you could manage.

What will the loan really cost? You've got to consider the full cost of your education, not just your freshman year. A $5,000 loan for your first year might sound manageable, but that's just your first year. That can easily grow into a $20,000 loan or more if you keep borrowing that much every year you're in college. And that's assuming the rest of your financial situation stays the same. Some of your grants and scholarships may be for your freshman year only, leaving you with a bigger chunk to pay in your remaining years. And college costs rise every year.

Deciding whether or not to take out a student loan isn't easy. For you and your family to feel comfortable about your choice, talk to your pastor, youth pastor, or a trusted family friend who's been through this. Ask that person to pray with you, and for you. And look to God for guidance.

The Bible has plenty to say about making wise decisions. As you and your family explore your options, check out passages like Proverbs 2:2–5; Matthew 25:14–30 and James 4:13–17. You'll find that God is less concerned with the details of your decision than with your willingness to trust and honor Him.

Q **How can I find out what kind of scholarships are available to me?**

A Sorry if this sounds like a recording, but start with your guidance counselor. He or she will have a ton of resources—like books, CD-ROMs, and recommended places on the Internet.

There are thousands upon thousands of private scholarships available, often in your own backyard. Your own church, or at least the denomination to which your church belongs, might even offer scholarships. Local businesses, civic clubs, banks, and organizations often offer scholarships. And often, one or both of your parents' employers might offer a scholarship.

You've just got to start asking around, digging through books, surfing the Internet. There are all kinds of scholarships out there. And some of them are *really* "out there"!

We did some searching and found some of the most unusual scholarships available. Things like:

• A $700 scholarship just for left-handed freshmen at a certain college.

• An award worth $1,200-$2,000 if you can prove one of your ancestors signed the Declaration of Independence.

• A $250 scholarship in memory of Hernesto K. Onexioca. The catch: Your last name must be Onexioca, you can't be related to Hernesto, and your birthday must be January 1.

See? There's no telling what you might find with a little digging.

When you find a scholarship you'd like to apply for, study the requirements carefully. As you can see from the above examples, some scholarships have a very narrow focus.

When you do apply, apply right. Follow the rules and requirements. Be neat and thorough. Don't sell yourself short. And make sure you meet the deadlines.

Scholarships are usually *earned*. Many students often compete for the same scholarship, and it can often only be awarded to one student. You've got to stand out. You've got to be your own public relations firm.

One college student advises: "Without coming across as conceited, be honest and upfront about your strengths. Scholarships are available, and I did my best to get them. I wasn't going to fabricate things, but I wasn't going to hold back on why I thought I deserved a scholarship, either."

Scholarship searching takes a lot of time and effort. But you can streamline the process. Keep copies of every scholarship application you fill out; the next one may be very similar to the last one. If it is, you don't have to re-think everything.

Many students wonder if they should use a scholarship search service. With the amount of information available through your guidance counselor, your local library, your local bookstore, and the Internet, you should think twice before paying someone to do the searching for you. Often, search services say they'll give you a "guaranteed" number of scholarship sources for which you are eligible—but for which you still need to apply. It's not the money they guarantee, it's the *source*. Scholarship search services are often accurate and legitimate, but they also often work with the same databases and resources that are available, for free, in your guidance counselor's office. So, think twice before forking your money over to someone to do the work that you can do for free.

Money-Making Madness!

If you really put your mind to it, you can come up with all kinds of ways to earn a few extra bucks to pay for college.

by John McPherson

TED'S CHANCES OF GETTING A RAISE WEREN'T LOOKING TOO HOT.

"DIDN'T THAT PIZZA DELIVERY GUY USED TO BE OUR PAPERBOY?"

BOB'S NEW BUSINESS VENTURE WASN'T THE GOLD
MINE HE THOUGHT IT WOULD BE.

BUD FOUND A GREAT WAY TO EXPAND ON
HIS SUMMER LAWN JOB.

WELCOME TO BURGER CITY DRIVE-THRU. MAY I TAKE YOUR ORDER?

From *Campus Life* magazine, December 1996. Used by permission.

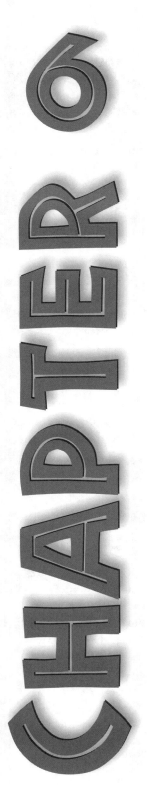

Making the Best College Choice

Q   **How can I sort through all the information I've got and make my final college choice?**

A   When it's time for you to make this choice, you probably won't be short on criteria. Those things have been covered in great detail in previous chapters, especially chapters 3 and 4.

At this stage, you'll more likely be overwhelmed by information overload. You've learned a ton of things about a handful of colleges. To get down to your final choice, you'll use the same criteria you've used all along. Only now you'll go through that criteria with a microscope, instead of merely taking a "big-picture" look at all the information.

If you haven't done it already, now would be a good time to list the "pros" and "cons" for each college on your final list. Get one blank sheet of paper for each college. On each sheet, write the name of the college at the top of the page, then divide the rest of the page into two vertical columns, with the headings "Pros" and "Cons." Then start writing what you like and don't like about that school. Just brainstorm at first; don't avoid writing something down because you think it's too trivial or silly. If one of your colleges is 2,000 miles away and you're concerned about missing your Labrador retriever, write it down. Later, when you compare your lists of pros and cons, mark out the items that are less important.

As you consider the colleges on your final list, ask yourself a few questions about each one:

- "How will this college help me grow as a total person?"
- "How will this place prepare me, not just to get a job, but to face the rest of my life?"
- "How will this school help me grow in my faith?"
- "What signs are there that the professors care about me?"
- "Do the students at this college seem like the kind of people I want to be around?"

Write the answers to these questions on the back of your pros-and-cons sheets.

Keep in mind that part of your decision might be made for you in the admissions and financial-aid process. You might apply to five or six schools, but only be accepted by three or four. Or, once you receive your financial-aid packages from colleges, you might find you and your family still can't afford a particular school. Note: Don't let the "value" of a financial-aid package alone make your decision. For instance, if the package from your first-choice college means your family has to pay $2,000 and the package from your second choice means you have to pay $1,000, don't immediately rule out your first choice just to save the money. Remember that college is an investment for life; finding a way to come up with that extra $1,000—even borrowing it— might well be worth it to attend your first choice.

The bottom line: If you've followed all the suggestions in this book, considering all the factors, you've got the criteria and information you need to make a good decision. You don't need more information at this stage of the process. You just need some time to make up your mind.

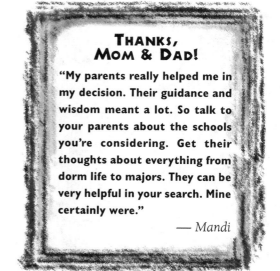

THANKS, MOM & DAD!

"My parents really helped me in my decision. Their guidance and wisdom meant a lot. So talk to your parents about the schools you're considering. Get their thoughts about everything from dorm life to majors. They can be very helpful in your search. Mine certainly were."

— *Mandi*

Q **What role should my parents play in this decision?**

A A vital role. In chapter 3, we talked about the importance of your parents, input on the campus visit. The same principles apply here.

By bringing your parents into the picture—not to *make* your decision, but to *help* you make the decision—you'll have two extra brains to pick in the process. They may think of things you'd never think of.

So think of your parents as valuable resources as you tackle this huge decision. Pick their brains. Ask for their observations. Seek their advice. Get them to help you compile your list of pros and cons of each college. And ask them how they went about making *their* college choices.

When you get to your final list of colleges, your parents might have some clear preferences, even before you do. Feel free to ask about these preferences. Ask why they might want you to go to a certain college or why they'd want you to avoid another.

But *don't* ask them to make the decision for you; ultimately, that's up to you. You're the one who has to spend four or more years on the campus, not your parents.

Q **Who else should I talk to about making my final choice?**

A Pretty much the same people you talked to when you started your college search. Of course, talk to your guidance counselor. Talk to teachers and coaches. Talk to your pastor or youth pastor. Talk to friends who attend the colleges you're considering, and talk to recent alumni of those colleges. Talk to other friends who've recently made the college choice; even if they're at colleges you're not considering, their decision-making advice can still help. Talk to admissions officials, and ask them any questions that come to mind; that's what they're there for, to answer your questions.

Ask all these people for their suggestions and observations, but don't put them on the spot by asking, "What college do you think I should choose?" Remember, the decision is yours; no one else can make it for you. But their advice and feedback can help a ton.

Q **Where does God fit into the decision-making process?**

A Everywhere. God should be in on this process from the very beginning. You should be seeking his wisdom all along, from the very early stages to the final choice.

How do you tap into God's wisdom? Three main ways:

• *Pray.* Just talk to God. Tell him your concerns. Ask him to guide you, to give you discernment and wisdom. Remember what the Bible says: "Trust in the Lord with all your heart . . . and he will make your paths straight" (Prov. 3:5–6).

• *Read.* The Bible is full of great advice and wisdom. Start with Proverbs, maybe Proverbs 2:1–15. This passage promises that if you seek God, "if you call out for insight and cry aloud for understanding, God will enable you to make a wise decision."

• *Talk.* Seek the advice of mature Christians—your parents, your youth pastor, perhaps another adult friend. The Bible says "many advisors make victory sure" (Prov. 11:14).

The process of choosing a college is a great chance to see God at work in your life. You can experience God opening and closing doors as you go along.

One admissions official told us: "God expects you to think carefully about all your decisions, including choosing a college. But he also wants to teach you to wait on him, to experience how the Spirit leads you. You'll see that God uses all those everyday, mundane things to sensitize you to his direction."

Q How critical should I be of a college's "imperfections"?

A No more critical than you'd be about your own imperfections . . . or the imperfections you typically find at church, at school, in a teacher, in a best friend, in your little brother, and so on.

Colleges are like people. They have personalities. They have strengths, and they have weaknesses. You probably listed some of those weaknesses when you made your list of pros and cons.

So, count on finding imperfections. Don't rule out a college because it has a few flaws, especially if it has a ton of things you're excited about. If one school's flaws seem to outnumber its good points, think twice about attending that school. But you're not going to find a flawless college.

Q Is there really a "perfect" school for me?

A No. There is no perfect choice. Sure, some colleges will fit you better than others, but no place is going to meet *all* of your needs.

One admissions official told us, "If you've been doing your homework, praying consistently about the process, and have been open to the leading of the Holy Spirit, then you've taken a lot of the guesswork out of it. God will bless your decision, whatever it is."

So, let go of a little of that pressure. Don't think there's only *one* right choice out there, and that all the others are wrong. Find the schools you're excited about and trust that God will lead you, no matter which one you finally settle on.

Q **What if I'm unhappy with my choice after I get there?**

A First of all, give it some time. Don't decide you hate a place in the first few days or even weeks. Making the jump to college life is a big adjustment, and it takes time. It'll be more difficult academically. You may have a hard time making new friends. You might get pretty homesick. But all these are natural parts of the adjustment process; these things happen at *all* colleges. A difficult transition doesn't mean you've made a bad choice.

THIS IS NOT A GOOD WAY TO CHOOSE A COLLEGE.

Give it at least a semester, and preferably a year. In the meantime, pray about it. Talk to your parents. Talk to a campus chaplain or counselor. If most of your struggles are with the books and your classes, talk to your profs or your academic advisor. College officials want to help you.

If you're still unhappy after a semester or a year, you might consider transferring to another school. That's always a better move than staying at a college where you're miserable for three or four more years. If you do decide to transfer, first finish the semester or term you're already in. Don't drop out in the middle of a term; you'll lose all the work, time, and money you've invested.

If you decide to leave a school, talk to your academic advisor first and ask about withdrawal procedures, and about the possibility of transferring credits you may have earned to your next college.

Transferring is not the end of the world. Many students do it, for one reason or another. It's nothing to be ashamed of or embarrassed about. And it doesn't mean you necessarily made a "bad" decision in the first place. If you trusted God all along, you made the best decision you could make with the information you had at the time.

God always wants what's best for you. Because he loves you, he's not "inflexible" in his plans.

We know of a student named Andrew who decided to go to a college that none of his friends were attending. He thought he needed to branch out from his close high-school friendships, meet new people, and experience a different part of the country.

At the time, Andrew's college decision seemed like the right one. He made new friends, took on new challenges, and gained self-confidence. But then a tragic thing happened during his second year of college: His brother was killed in a car accident.

As the grief set in, Andrew needed to be with his family and with the people who knew him well. He needed their support and comfort. He decided to transfer to a college closer to home.

Andrew's change of mind about college was not made out of weakness. It wasn't made to correct a mistake. Andrew really believes he was where God wanted him to be during his first year of college. But because he needed the comfort of close friends and family, he chose to switch colleges.

If your plans seem to change, it's not because God wants to confuse you or because he's undecided about how he wants to use you. It's because God is in control and wants the very best for you.

THE FINAL CHOICE

"I Can't Decide!"

by Nick Martin as told to Ruth Senter

If I said it once, I said it a hundred times during my senior year in high school: "I can't decide!"

Sometimes I just looked at my mom and dad with a blank stare and said, "How will I ever know which college I'm supposed to go to?" Every college I considered had something I liked about it and something I didn't like. No matter how many college catalogs I'd pored over and how many campuses I'd looked at, I was still confused.

As my senior year began to tick away, more and more of my friends made their choices. Finally, I whittled down my list to the top three colleges. Then two. That made things a little easier, but not much. Now I was stuck: Which of the remaining two should I choose? I'd already been accepted at both schools, but I just couldn't decide which one was right for me.

One day I'd decide it was College A. The next day, I felt certain it was College B. Pressure was mounting. I knew that in just a matter of days, my dad had to write the check to reserve my housing for next year. Both schools were already sending me information for orientation day. And still I was vacillating back and forth like a bouncing tennis ball. I simply could not decide.

"I have an idea," Mom said, sensing my dilemma. "Let's sit down and make a list." So we sat at the kitchen table on Saturday afternoon, three days before D-Day. I divided a sheet of notebook paper into two columns: College A at the head of one column, College B at the head of the other. "List everything you want in a college," my mom said.

I followed her instructions, hoping her idea would lead me somewhere. Yet when I finished, the two columns looked almost identical.

So much for the lists!

Then my mom said something I'd never thought of before: "Nick, if you've done all the right things ahead of time, when the time comes, you will make the right choice." She said it with such certainty that I almost believed her.

I began to think about what Mom had said. I walked myself back over the last two years. One thing was sure: I had done everything I knew to do to make sure my college decision was a good one. As a Christian who believed that God would guide me, it was a given that I prayed about my college choice. I knew my parents were praying about my decision, too.

But I also knew there was much more to choosing a college than just asking God for help in the decision. Looking back now as I approached the zero hour, I began to realize I had done the right things. Attended college fairs. Taken SATs and ACTs. Talked with my guidance counselor. Gotten a computer printout of ten schools that met the requirements I'd set for my college. Visited campuses. Attended a college financial-aid seminar. Filled out forms and more forms.

I did the right things. I got the right responses: Accepted by all three schools!

But getting accepted was the easy part, at least compared to what I was going through at decision time. Now, just days before I had to know for sure where I was going next year, my mom's words made me look at the process in a whole new way.

What my decision came down to, I concluded, was having confidence in my own ability to make good choices. My parents helped me realize that in the past I had made some good choices. When Mom said, "You will make the right choice," she was giving me a vote of confidence. I realized I needed to do the same for myself.

Once I remembered I was capable of making wise choices, I found myself relaxing. That weekend I forgot the big decision that loomed over my head. I just enjoyed my friends.

Monday morning when I woke up, the first thing I thought about was waking up in the dorm of College B. I could picture the dorm; I could see myself rolling out of the bunks and heading down the hall for the shower.

Just like that, I knew what the right decision was. I jumped out of bed and ran downstairs to tell my parents. Typical of my parents, my mom hugged and kissed me, and my dad shook my hand, patted me on the back and said, "Congratulations, Son." (I knew they would have done the same if I'd chosen the other college too.)

I drove to school that morning more relaxed than I'd been in a long time. I was sure my choice was the right one. And I'd made my decision a whole day before my dad had to write out the check reserving space for me in the dorm.

And today, having completed my first year at College B and about to begin my second, I've never been more sure of anything: I did make the right choice. And my mom wasn't off either when she said, "If you do all the right things ahead of time, when the time comes to decide, you will make the right choice."

From *Campus Life* magazine, October 1993. Used by permission.

7

Living on Campus

Q **I'm kinda nervous about making the transition to college, especially those first few days. Will any kind of help be available?**

A Yes, and plenty of it, *especially* during those first few days.

Almost all colleges offer an orientation program for new freshmen. College officials know you're taking a big step and facing some major changes when you step onto their campus, so they try to make the transition as easy for you as possible—academically, socially, and emotionally.

That's what freshman orientation is all about. These programs last anywhere from two days to a week. Sometimes they're held in the few days immediately before classes begin, and sometimes they're held earlier in the summer. Orientation programs are often free, or charge a nominal fee. And they often include your parents.

What happens during the orientation period? Volunteers—everybody from upperclass students to the college president to the town mayor—are available to show you around. Some people will be assigned just to help you move into your dorm and answer your questions during that process.

Once you get all your stuff moved in, a typical orientation program will often include a campus tour, maps and brochures, a review of rules and regulations, academic advice, and social events so you can meet other freshmen right away. There might be seminars just for you, with titles like, "What to Expect the First Year," and there might be sessions just for your parents, with titles like, "The College Transition for Parents." There might be meetings and/or social gatherings with faculty; take advantage of these to start to get to know some profs and ask some questions.

Some colleges offer special "wilderness programs," or at least some sort of outdoor recreational event, for their incoming freshmen. Some colleges include service projects during orientation; this gives you a chance to get to know other freshmen quickly by working side-by-side with them on a special project. Many orientation programs also give you the opportunity to register for your freshman classes.

During orientation, everywhere you turn, there will be plenty of people available to answer any questions you and your parents have.

Often, orientation programs are mandatory. But at some colleges they're optional. Our advice? Even if it's optional, don't skip it. Even if you've visited the college a dozen times, even if your parents and your big brother went there, even if you think you know everything there is to know, *go to the orientation*. It'll make your transition a lot easier, and it'll get your college life off to a great start.

Q What will my dorm room be like?

A Hard to say. It varies from college to college. But you can probably count on it being sort of like a hotel room, with a couple of beds and a few pieces of furniture. It probably won't have a bathroom; you might have to go down the hall for that. And unlike a hotel room, your dorm room may not have climate control. Or cable TV. Or a telephone; that's probably down the hall, too. Or a cleaning service; it'll be up to you and your roommate to keep the place looking spiffy.

Dormitory rooms are hardly the lap of luxury. They're usually fairly small. They might be considered a little-less-than-average-sized bedroom for one person, but you're most likely going to share a dorm room with someone else.

Dorm rooms are usually pretty sparsely furnished, too. In most dorms, you can count on a couple of beds, some kind of desk, and a closet; but after that, the pickings might be pretty slim. You might think, "Hey, no problem! I'll just bring my own bedroom furniture from home!" Think again. There's probably no place to put it. You *might* be able to bring a dresser and/or desk, if those things aren't already furnished.

Really wanna know what your dorm room will look like? Ask the colleges you're considering. Or, if you took a campus visit, you probably already know.

While your dorm room may not quite live up to the Hilton, life in a dorm—or "residence hall," as some colleges call them—is usually a blast. The whole concept behind a dorm is to build a sense of community among students. That's what Thomas Jefferson had in mind when he designed the University of Virginia almost two centuries ago. Jefferson's "academical village" includes rows of side-by-side student rooms, because

CHEAP ENTERTAINMENT

"For me and my friends, a fun, cheap evening is taking in an action movie in town. We'll go to a movie complex with a bunch of screens and low prices. Then on the way back we'll stop someplace for a burger and a Coke."

— *Tyrone*

he wanted the students to interact socially and intellectually when they weren't in class. And colleges have been putting students close together ever since.

Your dorm is more than just a place to sleep, study and store your stuff. You'll spend more time there than anywhere else on campus. You'll live closely with a bunch of people—not only your roommate, but others on your hall or in your suite. You'll get to know them almost like family; you might even find yourselves arguing over who gets dibs on the shower next, just like at home! Through your shared experiences, including your occasional spats and disagreements, you'll make some of the best friends you've ever made, the kind of friends you'll have for the rest of your life.

Your dorm "family" will get together for social events in your dorm, and perhaps for friendly competitions against other dorms. One of the *Campus Life* editors fondly remembers a "Dorm Olympics" showdown with the dorm next door, with corny events such as a pie-eating contest, water balloon fights, sack races, and so on. They tallied points for every event, and at the end of the day, the winning dorm got some sort of silly prize. Corny, yes, but a ton of fun. And the stuff of great memories.

Q **What kind of stuff, and how much of it, can I take?**

A Again, much of the answer depends on the college.

Once you know which college you're going to attend, ask the school for a complete description—including pictures, if possible—of the freshmen dorm rooms. Ask them to include dimensions, too. Ask what's furnished . . . and what isn't. If they furnish a dresser, don't take yours. If they provide a desk, leave yours at home.

And ask about rules and regulations. Ask what is and is not allowed in the dorms, and under what conditions. Some colleges, for example, don't allow any appliances that have to stay plugged in—like a mini-refrigerator or microwave oven—because of potential fire hazards.

Also, if possible, find out in advance who your roommate will be, and what he or she plans to bring, so you don't have many repeat items. You'll each want your own pens and pencils and other stuff, but you probably don't need two stereos in the same room.

When it comes time to move into the dorm, you'll probably be one of hundreds of new students doing so on the same day. So expect chaos! One student told us, "The stairs and halls were jammed with people—especially dads and brothers carrying boxes, bags, and furniture. There was one elevator; it was faster to use the stairs, and I was moving to the third floor! While my dad and

MANY COLLEGES HAVE A DRESS CODE. FORTUNATELY, NONE OF THEM ARE AS HUMILIATING AS THE DRESS CODE AT BLOSSOM STATE.

my brother carried stuff in, Mom and I started putting it away. When our van was finally unloaded, it was almost impossible to walk through my dorm room. Fortunately, my roommate wasn't arriving until the next day. And believe me, it took that long to restore order to the chaos!"

Sounds like fun already, eh?

To keep the chaos to a minimum, make a checklist in advance of items to take with you on moving day. You can find a sample checklist on page 110.

You'll notice that the checklist does not include suggestions for clothing. That depends on you, your preferences, and where you're headed for college. If you're from Minnesota and you're going to college in Florida, you can leave the heavy winter clothes behind. But if you're from Florida and headed to Minnesota, you've got some shopping to do, because your three sweatshirts and a sweater just aren't going to get you through the frigid winter.

Q Do I have to live in a dorm?

A Most colleges require freshmen to live in a dorm.

After your freshman year, though, the rules vary from school to school. You might have the option of living in campus housing throughout your college stay, but many give you the option of living off-campus after your freshman year.

The number of students who continue to live in dorms varies considerably from college to college. For instance, at Abilene Christian University in Texas, 50 percent of all undergraduate students live on campus. At Biola University in California, it's 65 percent. At Messiah in Pennsylvania, it's 90 percent. At Warner Southern College in Florida, it's 23 percent.

Ask the colleges you're considering what their rules are for student housing.

Q Can I choose a roommate? What if I don't get along with him or her?

A Many colleges allow you to choose your own roommate. Just be sure to tell the college of your plans. And be sure your chosen roommate tells the college the same thing! The college has to hear it from both of you to make the necessary arrangements.

A word of caution here: Best friends don't always make the best roommates. Yes, the odds are in your favor, because you know each other so well. But *living* together is much more intense than most close friendships go. One of you might regularly stay up later than the other; how will that affect your relationship? One of you might always eat popcorn without closing your mouth when you chew; anybody can stand that for one evening, but night after night after night? Little things you might overlook in a friendship can explode into minor crises when you're roommates.

So, if you and your best friend want to room together, be sure to have a heart-to-heart conversation first. Be realistic. Understand that there will have to be some give-and-take in a roomie relationship. Discuss *everything* that is important to you. Each of you will have a need for privacy at some time; how will you handle that? Explain why you need a corner of the room that's all yours, or that you like to have a 20-minute quiet time of Bible reading and prayer every morning before breakfast. Even though you're best friends, don't assume anything about each other.

Often, best friends choose not to be roommates because they're afraid the experience of living together in a small room might ruin their friendship. Its a legitimate concern. So, the subject of not rooming together is also worth discussing with your best friend. But only the two of you can decide what's best for you.

If you don't choose a roommate for your freshman year, the college will choose one for you. Yes, it sounds a little scary. You may be wondering, "What kind of person are they gonna pair me up with?" Often, colleges will try to put you with someone you appear to be compatible with. They might ask you to fill out a questionnaire, asking about your personality, living and study habits, preferences, and so on. In other words, if you're the quiet, non-athletic type who likes to study three hours every night while listening to Beethoven before

OBVIOUSLY, KYLE AND DAN NEEDED TO DO SOME MAJOR NEGOTIATING
TO DECIDE WHO GOT WHICH BED.

going to bed at 9:30, they probably won't pair you up with a sports nut who listens to hard rock till midnight, and *then* starts studying before falling asleep about 2 a.m. On paper, that just isn't a very good match.

When the college assigns you a roommate, it's a good idea to contact him or her *before* you move in together. Call or write to get better acquainted. You can start to understand and appreciate each other even before you move in together.

Still, some amount of conflict is almost inevitable. Usually, the conflicts are small and easily resolved: You wanna listen to dc Talk, but your roommate wants the Newsboys. So you talk it out, you find compromises and work out solutions. Often, conflicts revolve around the need for privacy, and the bottom line is that you *both* can't have it at the same time while you're in the same room. It's good to know your roomie's schedule—especially the times he or she is *not* likely to be in the room. When you need time alone, seize the opportunity to be in the room when your roommate is not. Stretch out on the bed and listen to the silence. If you can't be alone in the room, go somewhere else for your privacy—the library, under the big oak tree, the waiting room of the campus health clinic, a nearby open field, even a utility closet! Be creative, and you can always find your own "space."

But what if the conflict escalates to the point that you're both so stressed out you just want to strangle each other? What do you do in those cases?

First, try to talk to your roomie about what's going on. As Christians we're called to be honest with one another, sharing one another's burdens and concerns. We're supposed to apologize when we've wronged someone; if you feel like you're the cause of some of the conflict, say so and apologize. We're called to confess our sins to each other, and to forgive one another. And we're supposed to pray together, asking God to give us the strength and wisdom to overcome our differences and live in harmony. This isn't just Bible talk. This is the epitome of conflict resolution, and you can almost hear Jesus adding, "And, hey, these words of wisdom apply especially to college roommates."

If you've tried all these things and the conflict still remains, you'll want to bring in a third party to help you sort things out. And the first person you'll want to turn to in this case is your R.A., or Resident Advisor. You'll read more about R.A.s in the next question, but for now, suffice it to say that part of an R.A.s job is to help students solve problems and resolve conflicts. If your R.A. can't help you and your roomie work things out, he or she will know someone who can.

Occasionally, things can't be worked out between roommates, no matter how hard you try, and no matter how many people are trying to help. In those rare cases, colleges sometimes will agree to split up roommates—and then match them up with another pair of roomies who aren't getting along. Usually, a change like this is all it takes to solve the problem. If this happens, it doesn't mean you've "failed" as a person; it just means that two people were put together whose personalities simply don't mesh. It doesn't mean you or your roomie is any less "Christian" because of it. Hey, plenty of strong believers have had tiffs before. Even the apostle Paul and one of his best buddies split up because of a clash in personality and a difference of opinion. (See Acts 15:36–40.) So, it happens.

But don't dwell on what *could* go wrong with a roommate; we just offer these suggestions in case there is conflict. Instead, look forward to all the things that will go right. You'll have someone you can talk to about your day—and about the ups and downs of college life. You'll learn a lot about sensitivity, compromise, diplomacy, compassion, and love. You'll learn a lot about one person's likes and dislikes, joys and sorrows, and many needs. In learning to respond in a Christian way, you'll learn to be more like Christ. And roommates often become lifelong friends.

Some students ask if they can choose to live in a room alone. Unless you have special needs, you probably can't—at least not as a freshman. If you feel like you have strong reasons for living alone, discuss those reasons with the college to see what their rules and regulations are.

Q What's an R.A.?

A An R.A. is a "Resident Assistant" (some colleges call them "Resident Advisors"), usually an upperclass student who has a thorough knowledge of the school and its rules, regulations, and other valuable details—like where to find a good pizza at midnight. An R.A. lives with and looks after students in the dorm, helping them make the transition from high school to college life. Often, there's an R.A. assigned to each hall or suite in the dorm.

An R.A. is a mentor, a "den mother" (or father), a problem-solver, a social planner, a mediator, a counselor, an advisor, a listener, a trusted friend. Usually, R.A.s get something in return for what they do—perhaps a break in tuition, free room and board, or a small salary. But mostly, R.A.s do what they do because they care about you. They want to make your transition to college life as easy as possible. They want to help guide you through that first year, and get you off to a great start in your college career. R.A.s can answer most of the typical freshman's questions. And when they can't answer, they'll know somebody who can.

So, take advantage of your R.A.'s services. Don't ever think, *Well, I don't want to bug him, because he's an upperclassman, and he must have more important things to do than talk to me.* R.A.s are there to help you.

At the same time, remember that R.A.s are human. They have stress and struggles, just like you. If you see your R.A. having a hard time, don't assume you can't help him or her just because you're the "underclassman." Offer to be a listener, and offer to pray. Also, remember that R.A.s are students too. Don't just drop by to shoot the breeze if you know your R.A. is cramming for a big exam tomorrow morning. R.A.s have agreed to make many sacrifices to do the job they do, but you also need to respect their privacy when they need it.

LEARNING TO DO YOUR OWN LAUNDRY IS A FUNDAMENTAL PART OF LIFE AS A COLLEGE FRESHMAN.

Q The R.A. sounds like a great source of support. What other ways will a college be a "support system" to me?

A Colleges realize that freshmen usually need more support than older students, who have often made the adjustment to college life and found their "niche" of friends, routines, a major course of study, a fellowship, and a church. They're already "plugged in."

But freshmen typically need a little more attention. That's why the "experts" on a college campus include much more than just the academic faculty—who, by the way, might well be able to help you sort out some of the things you're going through. There are also all kinds of advisors, counselors, tutors, career consultants, coaches, deans, chaplains, and campus security available to help you with any problems or questions. There will be student fellowships where you can feed your faith—and your face! There will be plenty of upperclassmen you can turn to for advice, starting with your R.A., but including other older students you meet along the way. Many colleges even offer a sort of "extended orientation" program for freshmen, often in the form of a course called something like "Freshman Year Experience" or "College 101." These programs usually include a lot of student discussion, rather than a lecture format.

If you're having any kind of problem, you can start with your R.A. If your R.A. can't help you, he or she can probably steer you in the right direction. If you're struggling with academics, you'll have an academic advisor who can help and offer suggestions. If you're struggling with one class in particular, talk with that professor. If you're struggling emotionally, the college probably has an on-campus counseling center. If you're struggling spiritually, you can visit the college chaplain. And if you're struggling physically—in other words, if you get sick—there will also be student health care available. (We'll address health care in more detail in the next question.)

And these are just the people on campus. When you start attending a local church, you'll automatically be a part of yet another support system. At church, you'll probably meet people from the local community—people who aren't even associated with the college—who can be your friends. Often, local families will informally "adopt" college students to give them a home-away-from-home. They might invite you over for Sunday dinner, include you in family events, or send a care package back to the dorm with you. Try to find a church where this is practiced, and you'll be glad you did!

Q What do I do if I get sick?

A   Unfortunately, Mom won't be there to take care of you—but your teddy bear might be! Fortunately, there will be a student health facility nearby, probably right on campus, and probably open 24 hours a day. And though doctors and nurses may be available at all times, it's good to call ahead for an appointment if possible.

Campus health center services vary from college to college. But, a typical health center may include the following services:

- round-the-clock urgent care
- immunizations
- a pharmacy ,
- gynecological care
- nutritional counseling

Most colleges have a supplemental health fee you'll have to pay every year to use the health services. Many colleges will also require you to purchase a supplemental health insurance plan, or show proof that you have an alternate plan; usually you'll be covered by your parents' insurance as long as you're a full-time student. Ask the colleges you're considering about their health services, insurance requirements, and fees, and discuss these with your parents.

Many college students have such full schedules that they think they're too busy to get sick. As a result, students often ignore early signs of sickness and wait until they're very sick before seeing a doctor. You probably don't have to run to the campus clinic every time you have a cold, but if you have any of the following symptoms, you should go to the clinic as soon as possible:

• a fever of at least 101 degrees (yes, you should take a thermometer to school with you)

• vomiting for more than 24 hours, without being able to keep down food or water

• ear pain, especially if accompanied by a fever or sore throat

• a persistent cough that lasts more than a few days

• severe or persistent muscle or joint pain that's not caused by a hard workout at the gym or by menstrual cramps

Because you are living in close quarters, sharing a bathroom with several other people, and most likely getting less sleep than you'd like, your chances of getting sick increase at college. The most likely illnesses are the common cold and the flu. There's not much you can do to prevent catching a cold, but you can take a step toward preventing the flu by getting a flu shot each fall. Studies have shown that flu shots are about 75 percent effective in preventing the flu.

But the best thing you can do to keep your trips to the health clinic to a minimum is to eat well, sleep well, and get plenty of exercise.

Q What about eating at college?

A Almost all colleges offer some sort of meal plan; that's the "board" part of those "room and board" fees. Some colleges even offer you several meal plan options—including the option of not using the meal plan at all. But as a freshman living in a dorm, you won't have a kitchen, meaning you won't be able to cook your own meals, meaning you most likely *will* want some kind of meal plan. Besides, being on a college meal plan is almost always more cost-effective than eating on your own.

Your meal plan options will vary from campus to campus. Sometimes you can get a five-day plan, where you eat in the dining hall Monday through

Friday, but fend for yourself on weekends. Sometimes you can opt for two meals a day (usually lunch and dinner). With most plans, you'll get a card or tickets to admit you to the dining hall and keep track of the number of meals you've used up each day, week, or month. Be sure to understand the details of your college's meal plan; you probably won't be able to step into the cafeteria every time you want a snack. Many plans include allocations—in other words, limits on how often you can eat at the dining hall and sometimes even how much you can eat on a particular visit. For example, a complete meal plan may provide three meals a day, seven days a week. But if you drop by for a fourth meal on Monday and Wednesday, you might come up two meals short on your card at the end of the week. So read the fine print of your meal plan contract when you get it.

Jokes have always been made about cafeteria food, especially on college campuses. But the food is rarely as bad as people say it is.

Still, you're going to have to be nutritionally aware of what you're eating. College food is often high in starches and fat; even the milk is often whole milk. Plus, many meal plans are all-you-can-eat—including all the desserts you want. It's not unusual for college freshmen to pack on 10–15 pounds in their first semester. So, even if you've never had to count calories before, college is a good time to start paying attention to what you eat. And when you have a choice, avoid fat foods; if they're offering fried chicken and broiled chicken, go for the broiled. Even if the main course—whatever the "Chef's Surprise" is that particular day—looks and/or tastes unappealing, you can still fill up with "safe" foods, like fresh fruit, vegetables, and breads. So, load up at the salad bar! Also, drink lots of water, up to eight glasses a day, and avoid soft drinks and coffee as much as possible. Finally, it also might be a good idea to take a multiple vitamin-and-mineral supplement every day to make sure you're getting your essential nutrients.

Also, if you need a special diet, you can often get the college food service to provide it. But you'll need to contact them before school starts and let them know what your needs are.

Q **I'm afraid I'll be homesick. What can I do?**

A First, take comfort in knowing you're not alone. Many college freshmen struggle with homesickness and/or feeling lonely, even if they're only 15 minutes away from home. These feelings have little to do with geographical distance and much more to do with all the changes students are experiencing.

Homesickness isn't just something that happens to little kids at camp. It's a natural reaction for anyone leaving the familiar people and places they love. So, understand that these feelings are quite normal and natural.

What can you do when you're homesick? Perhaps the most obvious thing is to go home, if that's possible, for a weekend. But don't head home your first weekend at college, or even your second. Try to give it at least a month. Going to college is often the first step toward establishing your independence, and you won't take many strides in that process if you go home every weekend. Besides, you'll miss out on cool campus stuff like ballgames, dorm activities, and other events that help you make new friends and feel more at home in your new environment. So, if you can manage it, don't go home more than once before Thanksgiving break.

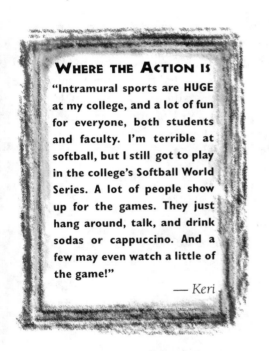

WHERE THE ACTION IS

"Intramural sports are HUGE at my college, and a lot of fun for everyone, both students and faculty. I'm terrible at softball, but I still got to play in the college's Softball World Series. A lot of people show up for the games. They just hang around, talk, and drink sodas or cappuccino. And a few may even watch a little of the game!"

— *Keri*

Another thing you can do when you're homesick is to tell your R.A. Or just grab a friend to talk to. You'll probably find somebody who's feeling the same way or has felt the same way.

It's also helpful to remember home as it really was. One *Campus Life* editor says that when she missed home, she thought of her hometown as the most charming place on the planet. And she remembered her high school friends as the funnest people on earth. But she'd completely forgotten all those boring Friday nights when she sat around with her friends trying to think of *something* to do.

Your freshman year is a time to deliberately start shifting your focus and energy from thoughts of home to making new friends at college. College is a wonderful time to develop quality friendships that are precious long after graduation. Sit down in the dining hall with someone else who's alone. Have lunch with people from your dorm. Participate in campus activities. Join a club, or play intramural sports. Get busy. Stay active.

This doesn't mean you should turn your back on your roots, though. Stay in touch with letters, e-mail, an occasional phone call. Be careful about phone calls, though; your bill can run up really fast.

Here are some other ways to stay in touch with home:

• Get your hometown newspaper. If you don't subscribe, ask your parents to send you occasional copies.

• Make a surprise visit home for a family member's birthday or other special occasion. But let *someone* know first. If not, you might get there when everyone's on their way to visit you!

• Ask a friend to take pictures of you at various "landmarks" on campus. Have fun with crazy poses. On the back of each picture, write something about where the photo was taken. Each time you write home, include one of the pictures.

• Remember special occasions. Send homemade cards on birthdays. Send a friend a buck and ask him or her to buy your little sister's favorite candy bar and then deliver it. Buy a gift certificate to your parents' favorite fast-food restaurant and send it with a note saying, "Hey, you fed me all these years. Have one on me!" Whatever you do, be creative and give it a personal touch.

• Invite your family to join you for on-campus family weekends. If your family can't make it, ask your youth pastor and a group of friends to come and be your "family" for at least part of the weekend.

• Borrow a camcorder from someone and take your family on a video tour of your campus. Point out places of interest. Do brief, candid interviews with students and profs. Keep it light with funny comments throughout.

Finally, if you're homesick, use the time to lean on God more. Take comfort and hope in these words: "Be strong and courageous. Do not be terrified; do not be discouraged, for the LORD your God will be with you wherever you go" (Josh. 1:9). And that includes college!

Q What kinds of extracurricular activities will be available?

A   Tons of stuff. You'll find lots of interesting things to do while you're in college. And they're not just fluff; they're an essential part of your total college experience and education. So, get involved!

First, and most importantly, you'll want to find some kind of Christian fellowship on campus. There will probably be several options available, so ask the colleges you're considering what campus fellowships are offered. Once you get involved in a fellowship, which will probably include weekly large-group meetings, you'll want to join a Bible study, too. The fellowship will be fun, but the Bible study is where your faith will really grow. Ask the fellowship's leader to help you get involved in a Bible study.

You will also find plenty of service opportunities—perhaps even through the fellowship you join. Keep an eye out for these ways to put your faith into action.

There will be a ton of clubs. For every club offered at your high school, there are probably half a dozen or more offered at college. Ask the colleges you're considering for a complete list.

Then there's intramural sports, a great way to hang with friends and get exercise at the same time. And it can be quite competitive. Some of the sports offered might include archery, badminton, basketball, bowling, cross-country, fencing, field hockey, football, golf, gymnastics, ice hockey, racquetball, rugby, skiing (downhill), soccer, softball, swimming and diving, table tennis, tennis, track and field, volleyball, water polo, and weight lifting.

Some other things to do include going to sporting events, working at the student newspaper or college radio station, or joining a musical group or the drama/theater groups. And don't forget campus politics; you can be active in student government, and even run for office.

Q Are Christian colleges more restrictive than secular colleges?

A Depends on what you mean by "restrictive." Do they have more rules and regulations than secular colleges? Often, they do. We reviewed some of these in chapter 4, when we discussed colleges' "code of conduct" agreements.

These codes or agreements spell out certain behavior expectations at the school, and they sometimes include specific doctrinal beliefs. Most codes include regulations regarding an honor code, dorm visitation and hours, sexual activity, and the use of alcohol and illegal drugs. Some codes include regulations regarding social dancing.

But these codes are more than merely lists of "Thou Shalt Nots." They are meant to reflect the Christian commitment at the college.

Restrictive? Again, it depends on your perspective. Many nonbelievers have called the Christian life "restrictive," complaining that it is little more than a list of rules of things we *cannot* do. They cite the Ten Commandments as proof. But Christians know better than this. Christians know that following Christ is hardly "restrictive," but instead it's the most liberating lifestyle one can live. After all, Jesus said, "If you hold to my teaching, you are really my disciples. Then you will know the truth, and the truth will set you free" (John 8:31-32).

And again, as we noted in chapter 4, if there's anything in a particular college's code of conduct that you disagree with or feel you can't abide by, then *don't apply to that college.*

Q What's the best way to handle money while I'm at college?

A Very carefully. You wanna watch every single penny. Let's put it this way: If you make a financial decision that prompts a friend to call you a "cheapskate" or "tightwad," just smile and say, "Thank you very much. I'm trying my hardest!"

Unless your parents are sending you unlimited money every month, you're going to have to learn to live on a very tight budget. Even if your parents are a source of tons of bucks, it'll probably be best for you if they don't send whatever you want, whenever you want it. College is a great time to start developing lifelong spending and savings habits. It's the right time to begin the whole process of becoming independent—including financially.

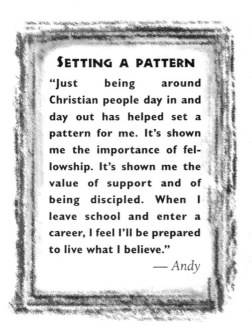

SETTING A PATTERN

"Just being around Christian people day in and day out has helped set a pattern for me. It's shown me the importance of fellowship. It's shown me the value of support and of being discipled. When I leave school and enter a career, I feel I'll be prepared to live what I believe."

— *Andy*

One of the first things you'll want to do is open your own account at a bank near the college. You may want to do this in your first few days on campus, during orientation and before classes begin.

You'll want to open a checking account so you can write checks to pay your bills and to have access to your money. You'll also want a bank that offers a 24-hour teller machine so you can get to your money any time. And never withdraw a lot of money at once; if you have $100 in your wallet, you're more likely to spend it. Withdraw smaller chunks ($10-$20) at a time. For safety's sake, try to use these machines during the daytime. If you need to get money at night, don't go alone; bring a friend.

If you have a job, it'll be easy to deposit your earnings into a local bank. Sometimes it's even possible to arrange for a "direct deposit" plan, which means that on pay day you won't get a check from your employer, but your earnings will go straight into your account. Ask if this is an option.

If your parents are going to put money into your account by sending you checks, keep in mind that some banks "hold" out-of-town checks for a few days before they "release" the money. In other words, if Dad sends you a check for $100 and you deposit it on Tuesday afternoon, don't assume that money is available on Tuesday night. It might not be available till Friday . . . or later. Ask the bank about out-of-town checks and "availability of funds."

There are a few other questions you need to ask about checking accounts, such as: Is there a charge for writing checks? Are there monthly charges? Do I have to keep a minimum balance in my account? If so, how much? What are the penalties if I dip below this balance? What are the penalties if I "bounce" a check? ("Bouncing" a check means you write a check for more money than you have in the account; so, before you write a check or withdraw money at the 24-hour machine, make sure you have enough in your account.)

Keeping a checking account requires discipline. You'll have a little ledger in your checkbook where you need to record *every* transaction—checks written, cash withdrawals made at the automatic machine, deposits made into your account, and any fees and/or penalties. Don't miss anything. For instance, if your bank has a $3-per-month service charge, don't ever forget to enter it. Sure, $3 doesn't sound like much. But let's say you've got $114 in your account, and you've got to pay a bill for $112. You might think, *Well, that leaves $2 in my account.* But if you forgot to enter a $3 service charge, that'll really leave you at minus-one dollar. You might think, *No problem, I'll just give the bank a buck to bring my balance out of the negative numbers.* Nope. If you "overdraw" by going into negative numbers, the bank might charge you a $20 penalty for bouncing a check, and the person you wrote the check to might also charge a penalty. Suddenly, you go from $1 in the hole to $41 (or more) in the hole. And that's if you bounce just *one* check. If you write and bounce several checks during that time, it can literally cost you hundreds of dollars in penalties. So watch that bank book like crazy.

Here are some more tips for managing your money in college:

• Consider keeping a credit card, but use it only for emergencies. If you don't have enough cash (either in your wallet or in your checking account) when you want to buy something, don't buy it. Credit cards can run up big debt in a hurry, even if you're just buying small things.

• Buy as much used stuff as you can—textbooks, a refrigerator for the dorm, small furniture, and clothes (at a thrift store).

• Use the campus meal plan as much as possible. It's much cheaper than eating out, especially visits to the local fast-food joint. That's not only bad for the bank account, but it's not great for your health, either.

• If you want to catch a movie, check out the local dollar theaters or special on-campus screenings, which are dirt cheap. If you've got to see the latest film in the theaters, go to a matinee in the afternoon; you'll save a few bucks over going at night.

• Avoid vending machines. If you feel like you need a Diet Coke every day, buy 'em cheap at the grocery store and keep 'em in your fridge at the dorm. If you can find a 24-pack at the store for $5, they'll cost you about 21 cents a can; at the vending machine, they'll be at least 50 cents, and maybe 75. That adds up fast.

• Keep receipts from everything you buy, especially if you buy new text-books. And don't write in the new books right away; if you decide to drop a class, you'll be able to return them to the bookstore for a full refund. Also, if you buy a product that comes with a warranty, keep the warranty.

• Don't take a car to college unless you absolutely have to. Insurance, gas, and maintenance costs make a car expensive. Take a bike instead, and/or use the campus bus service. (Note: Taking a car might not even be an option for you, because many colleges don't let freshmen have cars on campus.)

• Keep phone calls to a minimum. Write or use e-mail instead.

• If you travel to and from home by plane, make your reservations as far in advance as possible. If you decide on Thursday that you want to drop in on Mom and Dad this weekend, you'll pay a bundle for the flight.

• Finally, keep a budget. Keep a record of every penny you spend for a month. At the end of the month, look it over and determine which expenses were absolutely necessary, which just seemed necessary at the moment, and which ones were just plain frivolous. Next month, cut out all the frivolous expenses, and a few of the things that "seemed necessary at the moment."

Set your financial priorities, and stick to them. Make sacrifices. And hope that somebody *does* call you a tightwad. That means you're doing a great job handling your money.

Q   What about peer pressure while I'm at college?

A   As you know, peer pressure can get pretty intense in junior high and high school. You'd think that as you "mature" into the college years, the effects of peer pressure would diminish—especially if you're at a Christian college.

Well, the good news is that peer pressure usually *does* diminish in college. By the time students are heading off to college, they tend to be more sure of themselves, more secure in their self-image and, often, in their faith.

But the sorta bad news is that peer pressure does *not* disappear in college. (Actually, it *never* disappears.) You won't suddenly find yourself immune to temptation. (And you never will.) And you'll find yourself with more freedom and independence than you've ever had before, meaning you'll have to make more choices on your own.

You don't just arrive on a Christian college campus and say, "Hey, I've *really arrived*. I'm practically at the gates of heaven! I'll grow in my faith. I'll never be tempted. I'm ready to become Super Christian!"

Doesn't work that way. Christian colleges are full of imperfect people, people who tempt and are tempted, people who fall, people who sin. And people who will try to talk you into doing something you know you probably shouldn't do. The rules of the world still apply on a Christian college campus.

No, it won't be like a secular college, where you might expect to find wild fraternity parties, rowdy beer bashes, rampant drug use, and casual sex in many dorm rooms. It's hard to go to a secular college and not be exposed to these things. But don't think that a Christian college is completely immune to these things, either. They're just not as prevalent.

At a secular college, you might see a hundred students drinking beer, unashamed, on the front lawn of a frat house on a Friday night while university officials drive by. Happens all the time. But at a Christian college, students are obviously going to be more discreet about such things, which not only break the college rules, but the "rules" of the Spirit, written on their own hearts.

Additionally, college campuses are rarely "in the middle of nowhere." They're usually in towns or cities. So, most likely, there will be places to buy alcohol, there will be bars, there will be movie theaters showing raunchy flicks.

At a Christian college, you won't be removed from the real world. You'll still be very much a part of it.

We raise these issues not to alarm you, but to help you understand that you *will* face peer pressure and temptations in college. Your fellow students are just as human as you are, just as vulnerable and imperfect as you: "For all have sinned and fall short of the glory of God" (Rom. 3:23).

But, at a Christian college, you stand a much better chance of resisting temptation. You can join a fellowship, a Bible study, an accountability group— the types of things that will build your faith and help you resist temptation and peer pressure. (We'll talk more about your spiritual fitness in chapter 9.)

Peer pressure at a Christian college? Yes, expect it. But expect victory, too. With the help of solid Christian friends, faculty, and advisors—not to mention people who are praying for you—God will give you the strength.

College Checklist

Here's a checklist to help you pack for college. The list doesn't include clothes or personal items, because they vary significantly from person to person.

You probably won't want to take *everything* on this list, but it's a good place to start.

BEDDING/LINENS

- ☐ Mattress pad
- ☐ Comforter
- ☐ Blanket
- ☐ Sheets/pillow cases
- ☐ Pillows
- ☐ Back rest or big floor pillow
- ☐ Towels and wash cloths

FIRST AID

- ☐ Hydrogen peroxide
- ☐ Cotton swabs
- ☐ Cotton balls
- ☐ Antibiotic ointment
- ☐ Adhesive bandages
- ☐ Sunscreen
- ☐ Insect repellent
- ☐ Nail clippers
- ☐ Thermometer
- ☐ Tweezers
- ☐ Pain medicine (for headaches)
- ☐ Medicine for upset stomach
- ☐ Any prescription medicines

APPLIANCES/ELECTRONICS

(Check with college to see what's allowed.)

- ☐ Microwave
- ☐ Mini-refrigerator
- ☐ Computer/printer
- ☐ Surge protector
- ☐ TV/VCR/tapes
- ☐ Clock/radio
- ☐ Answering machine
- ☐ Stereo
- ☐ Coffee maker
- ☐ Lamps
- ☐ Extension cords
- ☐ Popcorn popper

LAUNDRY/CLEANING

- ☐ Laundry detergent
- ☐ Fabric softener
- ☐ Iron/ironing board
- ☐ Laundry basket
- ☐ All-purpose cleaner (like 409)
- ☐ Abrasive cleaner (like Bon Ami)
- ☐ Broom, mop, sponges, bucket
- ☐ Furniture polish/dust rags
- ☐ Paper towels
- ☐ Dishwashing detergent

FOOD

❑ Hot chocolate mix
❑ Instant oatmeal packets
❑ Coffee, filters, mug
❑ Lemonade mix
❑ Snack mix
❑ Granola bars
❑ Pretzels
❑ Peanut butter
❑ Instant soup
❑ Popcorn
❑ Some utensils, including a knife
❑ A few plastic plates and bowls
❑ Plastic storage containers
❑ Plastic wrap
❑ Hand-held can opener

STATIONERY/OFFICE SUPPLIES

❑ Assorted stationery
❑ Stamps
❑ Tape, glue
❑ Stapler/staples
❑ Pens, pencils, sharpener
❑ Colored markers, highlighters
❑ Bookends
❑ Personal planner
❑ Paper clips
❑ Hole punch
❑ Notebooks, paper
❑ Rubber bands
❑ File folders
❑ Scissors
❑ Desk caddie

SPORTS EQUIPMENT

❑ Tennis racket/balls
❑ Other balls (football, basketball)
❑ Baseball/softball glove
❑ In-line skates
❑ Bicycle, pump
❑ Athletic bag
❑ Water bottle

MISCELLANEOUS

❑ Posters/pictures
❑ CDs/cassettes/organizers
❑ Rug(s)
❑ Clothes hangers
❑ Backpack
❑ Sunglasses
❑ Bible
❑ Favorite books
❑ High-school yearbook
❑ Sleeping bag
❑ Photo album
❑ Camera, film
❑ Framed pictures, hangers
❑ Hammer, pliers, screwdriver
❑ Flashlight
❑ Sewing kit
❑ Calendar
❑ Soap dish
❑ Wastebasket
❑ Batteries
❑ Games
❑ Checkbook/cash card
❑ Phone card

compiled by Sarah McManus

Dear Mom and Dad

by Marshall and David Shelley

Going away to college has its advantages, but it also has some problems. And college freshmen soon learn that writing letters to the folks back home is one of those problems.

It's easy at first, but after everything's been said three or four times and your schedule has settled into the old routine, it hardly seems worthwhile to write home about the weather.

Even so, parents deserve some word, and since most freshmen need help with their back-home correspondence, here are some techniques to help fill the menacing empty page as quickly as possible.

The most primitive technique is repeating words, a variation of the old grade-school punishment. Remember having to write "I will not throw spitwads in class" 300 times? Just modify the system.

Dear, dear folks,

I'm really, really busy with my classes. Some of these professors are tough, tough, tough. So I'm working very, very, very hard.

Lots and lots and lots of love,
Kermit

When that gets trite, try adjectival eloquence:

Dearest familial acquaintances,
My short, snotty-nosed roommate is painfully and
terribly noisy, but his expensive, imported Sony stereo
is beautiful. The sound is deep, clear, and undistorted.

Mastering this technique, however, may require a thesaurus. Many students prefer to impress the folks with their scholarship—to sound like a student, to "talk shop," so to speak. Not only can you lift whole sections from class notes to fill space, but you can also get a good review of the material:

Dear Folks,
I'm really gaining insight from my research. In
psychology we learned how Brehm's theory of psycholog-
ical reactance predicts the circumstances under which
people react adversely to perceived attempts to limit their
freedom. I've even observed this phenomenon in the
social groups I encounter at this institution.

If you're the type who tries to save paper by squeezing a lot onto each page, you have another thing to learn: WRITE BIG! Not only does it fill more space, it commands more attention. And another must: Always use question marks and exclamation points—frequently and freely:

Dear Folks,
Guess what?!?!?!? I auditioned for the band!!!!! CAN YOU BELIEVE IT???? I didn't make it, but that's OK because I don't have time anyway!!!!!!!

Notice how another subtle but effective filler showed up in that last letter: the meaningless question (CAN YOU BELIEVE IT????). It can almost double your word count without adding any new thought.

Pre-med students have suggested another technique that anyone can learn with practice: illegible handwriting. It comes in handy when you have nothing to say, and will provide hours of challenging work for your younger brother who's into secret codes:

Before long you'll have them thinking you're studying Greek.

But sometimes the problem with letter-writing is just the opposite; it's not that you have nothing to say, but you have something important to say and don't know how to say it. Subtlety is the key:

Dear Folk$,

How are thing$? OK, I tru$t. I'm fine. You've been $o good to me and I'm thankful to know that I can alway$ count on you for help. You $eem to know what need$ to be done even before I a$k.

When a real crisis arises, however, you have to pull out all the stops. Gimmicks won't make it. Getting it said exactly right is the only way:

```
Dear Mom and Dad,
        Sorry it's been so long since I've
written. The skull fracture and broken leg
I got after I jumped out the window of my
dormitory when it caught fire have almost
healed. I was only in the hospital three
weeks. I can almost see normally again, and
those sick headaches return only once in
awhile. Fortunately, the fire and my jump
were seen by a girl who was hitchhiking on
the street. She called the ambulance and
also visited me every day in the hospital.
We've fallen in love and plan to be mar-
ried. I'm sure you'll like Agnes. She made
it through to the 10th grade before she
dropped out, and she's only been married
once before. Lately, she's been traveling
all over; it's amazing how far you can
travel hitchhiking. I've told her that these
things won't bother my loving, tolerant par-
ents. We haven't settled on a date for the
wedding yet, but I promise to call at least
a week ahead of time.
        Now that I've brought you up to date,
I want to tell you that there was no dormi-
tory fire; I did not have a skull fracture
or broken leg; I was not in the hospital; I
am not engaged (still haven't even kissed a
girl here); and there aren't even any
prospects. I am, however, getting a D in
English and I'm failing psychology, but I
thought you'd like to see it all in per-
spective.

        Your loving son,
        Kermit
```

From *Campus Life* College Guide, March 1996. Used by permission.

Hittin' the Books

Q **Will college academics really be harder than high school?**

A Most college students would tell you that yes, college is harder than high school.

You'll be learning at a faster pace, trying to grasp more information in a shorter amount of time. Subjects are covered in more depth, so you'll need to understand concepts, not just facts and figures. You'll do a lot more reading than you've done in high school. And with more material to cover, you just can't cram it all in the night before an exam. You'll need to pace yourself and commit to doing the work even when you don't want to. And there won't be anyone around to remind you to get your work done. College professors have high expectations of you; they trust you to keep up with your assignments and do the work required of the class, usually without supervision.

Hard work? Yes. But you're learning more than just facts and figures. You're learning how to "do" life. College students say their classes usually help them develop other, non-academic skills as well. Along with teaching you the expected stuff in the course, professors want you to learn to speak, write, and think clearly and thoughtfully, great "life" skills to have long after college graduation.

But until you personally experience college classes and academics, no one can say how hard or how easy it will be for you. Much of it will depend on the kind of study habits (or lack of them!) you've had throughout high school, how well you manage your time, and how motivated you are as a student.

The main thing you'll have to do in college is *keep up* with your assignments. In high school, you might have been able to slack off for a day or a week or even the better part of a month, and then "cram" with an all-nighter and still make good grades. Don't count on using that strategy in college; it just won't work. You've got to keep up and do the work every day.

Q **How many classes will I have to take in college?**

A The answer mostly depends on what type of "term" system the college uses. Colleges usually use one of three types: semesters, quarters (sometimes called trimesters), or the 4-1-4 system.

A semester system is run a lot like your high school. In a college semester system, students typically take an average of five classes per semester. The first semester usually runs from late August till right before Christmas, and the second semester usually runs from mid-January till some time in May.

Some colleges use a quarter system, using three 10- or 11-week quarters—fall, winter, and spring—with breaks between quarters. Students in this type of system typically take three to four classes per quarter.

Other colleges use a "4-1-4" system, meaning there are two 4-month semesters, separated by one 3- or 4-week interim term in January; sometimes this interim is called a "J-term." In this system, students typically take four classes during each semester, and one class during the interim term. The interim class is often either an intensive, in-depth course or an independent research project.

Additionally, many colleges offer summer terms, but there are usually only a few classes offered.

None of these systems are "better" than the others; they're just different styles. In a semester system, you're usually taking more classes in a given term, but you've got longer to learn the information than in the other systems. In a quarter or 4-1-4 system, you're taking fewer classes, but you don't have as long to learn the stuff. So it all evens out.

One thing to note about college classes is that they rarely meet every day. Some classes will meet three times a week, for about an hour each time. Some might meet twice a week, for about 90 minutes each time. Some might meet just once a week, but for three hours.

Different colleges have different graduation requirements, and those requirements will determine how many classes you'll take each term. For example, one *Campus Life* editor went to a university that required 120 "credit hours" to graduate. To graduate in four years, he had to average 30 hours per year, or 15 hours per semester. Since most classes at his school were worth three credit hours, he had to average five classes per semester (5 classes x 3 hours each = 15 hours). Twice, he only took 12 hours, or four classes, in a semester. But that meant he had to take 18 hours, or six classes, in two other semesters to make up the hours and to stay on course for the required 120 to graduate.

Make sense?

FEW THINGS ARE MORE FRUSTRATING THAN HAVING A ROOMMATE WITH AN EASY COURSE LOAD.

If it's still a little confusing, ask your guidance counselor to help. Or ask someone at the colleges you're considering what their academic requirements are, and what you'll have to do to stay "on track" to graduate. Of course, you don't necessarily have to graduate in four years; some students take five years. If you do that, you won't have to take as many classes each term, but you will have another year of college expenses to deal with.

One way to take fewer classes per term and still graduate in four years is to take some classes during the summer. For what it's worth, though, we wouldn't recommend doing that more than one or two summers while you're in college. Take advantage of the long summer vacations while you can. You can earn a little money for the coming year and still have some fun. Remember, once you graduate and get a job in the "real world," there won't be any such thing as summer break any more—unless you're a school teacher!

At many colleges, you'll "pre-register" for your freshman year classes during the summer before you arrive on campus. Some schools send you forms for this process, so you can pre-register by mail. Some schools let you pre-register by phone. And some schools won't let you pre-register until you arrive for freshman orientation.

Ask the schools you're considering what their requirements are for freshman class pre-registration. And while you're at it, ask if you might be able to test out of certain required classes because of high scores on advanced placement exams or exceptional performance in a particular subject. If you've had five years of French, spent a summer in Paris and can *parlez-vous* with the best of 'em, you might be exempted from the foreign-language requirement, if there is one.

Q How much will I have to study every week?

A   That'll depend on how many classes you're taking, and how difficult your classes are. Some courses will require more study time than others; you'll probably have to study more for your biomedical engineering class than for your History of Jelly Beans 101 class.

For the most part, count on spending about two hours studying for every hour you spend in class. So, if you're in class for 15 hours a week, you'll probably study another 25-30 hours. Sounds sorta like a full-time job, doesn't it? Well, in many ways, that's exactly what college is: A full-time job that's a lifetime investment, an investment in your future.

Early in the term, when you're learning easier material, you may be tempted to study less. But take time to study anyway. When the material gets more difficult later in the term, you'll already be in the habit of studying hard, and you won't feel as much of a time crunch when you're writing term papers and preparing for exams.

It's worth mentioning that the word "studying" also includes your reading assignments. Some classes, especially literature classes, require a lot of reading, perhaps 200 or more pages a week. You'll have to block off time to get that reading done. *But,* 200 pages of reading in a literature class may *not* be as time-consuming as 40 pages in a chemistry class. Sometimes it's much easier—and faster—to breeze through a couple hundred pages of a novel than it is to get through a couple dozen pages of a difficult science textbook, which might require reading, re-reading, and re-reading again to get the facts straight.

So, when you're planning your class schedule, it's a good idea not only to know *how much* reading will be required, but *what type* of reading. All of this will figure into the time you'll need to set aside for your studies.

Q Can you give me some tips on how to study more effectively?

A   Perhaps the best place to start is to understand that studying in college is not going to be like studying in high school. Sure, if you've had good study habits all through high school, those good habits will come in quite handy in college, too.

But some of your good habits won't necessarily work well in college. In high school, you've probably been busy most of the day, from about 7:00 in the morning till at least 3:00 in the afternoon. Your typical high-school day probably lasts much later than 3:00 p.m. if you're involved in after-school activities, or if you've got a part-time job. You might not even get home till 9:00 p.m. or later on many nights. And that's when you typically start studying—at night. You put in a couple hours a night, and next thing you know, it's bedtime.

That won't be the case in college. You'll probably have a lot more free time during the day. In high school, you might spend 30 hours or more per week in classes; in college, you'll spend about half that. And one critical key to being a good college student is taking advantage of that daytime free time.

On Mondays, Wednesdays, and Fridays, for example, you might have back-to-back one-hour classes at 9:00 a.m. and 10:00 a.m., and then a three-hour break before your next class begins at 2:00 a.m. That adds up to nine hours a week of those mid-day breaks. Of course, you'll spend about 45 minutes of that time doing lunch. But what about the rest of those two-plus hours? It's a great chance to study. Yes, you'll be tempted to do something else—watch TV, read a magazine, or just veg out in your dorm room. It's OK to do some of those things sometimes, but you won't want to pass up significant time chunks to get some studying done.

Get out of the mindset that studying is something that's only done at night. Look for every opportunity to study during the day, and you won't have to study as much at night. And as a result, your weekends will end up relatively free.

Here are a few more suggestions for developing good study habits:

• Study between classes. We've already talked about this a bit, but it's key to remember. Don't think you need a big 3- or 4-hour gap to study. An hour here and 30 minutes there will help a lot.

• Use your Friday afternoons well. Once the week's last class is over, it's tempting to let down and welcome the weekend. But if your last Friday class ends at 1:00 or 2:00 p.m., take advantage of the rest of the afternoon. Study for a few hours now, and you might not have to hit the books again all weekend. If you've got a Monday quiz, you can study hard for it on Friday afternoon, and just review the material on Sunday night.

• Use all your afternoons well. Next to Fridays, late afternoons are usually the most wasted time for college students. What you do from 3:00 to 6:00 p.m. determines whether you'll be studying late that night or not. The more you do during the day, the more free your evening will be for other stuff. At the same time, don't think that you have to study *every* afternoon. If a friend suggests a bike ride or a tennis match on a gorgeous sunny day, go for it. Just don't do it *every* day.

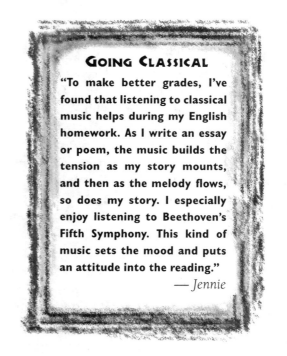

GOING CLASSICAL

"To make better grades, I've found that listening to classical music helps during my English homework. As I write an essay or poem, the music builds the tension as my story mounts, and then as the melody flows, so does my story. I especially enjoy listening to Beethoven's Fifth Symphony. This kind of music sets the mood and puts an attitude into the reading."

— *Jennie*

• Find a place to study. And it might not be your dorm room, especially at night. Dorms can be busy, noisy places at night. If you can concentrate under these circumstances, great. If not, you'll want to look for a quiet place—and the library is a good place to start.

• Know your work load and keep up with assignments. Avoid last-minute cramming for tests and exams. Don't put off term papers till the last couple of days. The things you "got away with" in high school aren't going to work in college. You can't fall behind and count on catching up. So keep up all along.

• Attend classes. Yeah, it sounds obvious. But in college, it's pretty easy to cut classes. Nobody's gonna send you to the principal's office. Professors rarely take roll, except on the first day. It's tempting to turn off the alarm clock and sleep through that 8:00 a.m. Spanish class. It's hard to pass up a sunny afternoon at the lake when your best friends are going, even though it conflicts with your chemistry lab. But it's even harder to catch up when you miss. Sure, you can get lecture notes from someone else in the class, but the prof just might explain something critical that day, something that will end up being on your final exam—and worth 40 percent of your grade, at that.

• Get a study buddy, or join a study group. Studying alone can be difficult, especially if you're putting in some 30 hours a week doing it. Studying with classmates can make it more interesting. They'll have ideas you won't have, and you'll have ideas they won't have. They'll understand things you didn't understand, and vice versa. Everybody benefits.

Q **Any suggestions on how to take better notes in class?**

A In college classes, you'll probably do a lot of listening while the professor talks. Obviously, you'll want to take good notes. Don't assume lectures are "secondary material." Don't make the mistake of thinking, *Well, I'll just be a good listener in class, but I'll really study the textbook hard, and that'll be enough.* Wrong. Sometimes what the prof says in class is just as important and counts for as many points on tests as what you've learned from the textbook.

On the first day of class, most profs distribute a *syllabus*, a preview of what's going to be covered in the class. The syllabus may include a test and quiz schedule, your reading assignments, topics covered each week. The syllabus might even say what percentage of your test scores is based on lectures and what percentage is based on textbook assignments. If the syllabus doesn't give this information, ask the prof after class about his or her expectations.

If you haven't done much note-taking, it'll take some getting used to. But by taking notes, you'll be more involved in the class, following along with every word, and less likely to drift away in a daydream.

You won't be able to write as fast as your professors talk, but that's OK. No professor expects you to take down every word, just the main points. If he or she writes something on the board, you should write it down, too. And if the prof says something you didn't understand, raise your hand and ask for clarification.

A few more tips for good note-taking:

• Do the assigned reading before class. That way you'll be more familiar with the material, and it won't seem so foreign when you hear it in class. Plus, you'll be prepared to ask more intelligent questions in class.

• Sit up front. You'll be less likely to daydream or be distracted—or read the morning paper while the prof is talking. Also, profs will get to know you more quickly.

• Sit up, period. Yes, it sounds like your third-grade teacher's advice. But it works. Slouching in a chair or desk makes you more likely to drift away. Plus, your notes get sloppy.

• Be careful who you sit next to. If you sit next to your best friend, you're more likely to whisper—and not necessarily about what you're learning in class. And think twice about sitting next to that incredibly good-looking student that you're just *dying* to get to know. Then you'll *really* daydream. Save the introductions for after class.

• You'll have to write fast when taking notes, but be as neat as possible. After all, to study them, you'll need to be able to read them!

STUDY TIP: SAVE TIME ON BIG READING ASSIGNMENTS BY READING EVERY OTHER WORD.

• Use a regular-sized spiral notebook, and use a different colored notebook for each course you take. That way, when you're rushing out the dorm room for English 101, you can just grab the green notebook instead of taking the time to figure out which one's the right one. Or, use a three-ring binder for each class. It's easier to re-arrange pages in a binder, if necessary.

• Use shorthand, or some variation of it. You probably haven't had a shorthand course, but you'll want to come up with your own ways to take shortcuts. Use abbreviations and symbols whenever possible. Eliminate verbs. For instance, if your anatomy professor says, "Thigh bone's connected to the knee bone, knee bone's connected to the shin bone, shin bone's connected to the ankle bone, ankle bone's connected to the foot bone," don't write it down word for word. Instead, write, "thigh connected to knee, kn to shin, sh to ankle, ank to ft." Cut words down even further by eliminating letters, especially vowels: "th-kn, kn-sh, sh-ank, ank-ft." Get it?

• Read your notes as soon as possible after class. When you're writing things down, they make sense, because the prof's explaining them as you write. But when you read them later, they might not make as much sense. Note these things, and ask the prof for needed clarifications. Also, abbreviations and shorthand might make sense as you're writing them, but they might not make any sense a month from now when you review for a test. When you re-read your notes shortly after class, spell out any words that have unusual abbreviations, while the material's still fresh in your mind.

• Don't try to "fix" your notes during class. Sometimes, you'll notice during class that your notes are disorganized. Don't try to correct this in class; you'll miss stuff while you're doing the fixing. Fix 'em later.

• Don't use a tape recorder to take notes. Too many things can go wrong—weak batteries; bad tape; malfunctioning microphone; the person next to you has a sneezing fit when the prof says something important. Besides, you'll just have to transcribe them later.

Q **What can I expect from my professors?**

A You can expect that they'll all look and act like the guy who played "The Professor" on *Gilligan's Island*. You know, the kind of guy who can make a nuclear reactor out of two coconuts, a palm leaf, and a little water from the infamous lagoon.

Uhh, we're kidding, of course. But the point is that many students head off to college with pre-conceived stereotypes of just what a professor is. No, they don't wander around desert islands in the South Pacific. No, they don't wear lab coats (unless you're in the lab) and talk in multi-syllabic, unintelligible ways.

Professors are just teachers, that's all. They just happen to teach at the college level. And they might go by the name *Dr.* So-and-so.

Many new students have fears about profs. But college students will tell you that those fears are largely unfounded. College profs do what they do because they are not only interested in your education, but your life. After all, profs are people, too.

Profs have an abundance of knowledge about the topics they teach. (Duh! Why else would they be there?) And they want to share this knowledge with you. They assume you're in their class because you want to learn this stuff, and they want to help you learn it. So they're going to do their best to teach it—whether it's through lectures, discussions, readings, experiments, field trips, or whatever.

You can expect profs to be masters of their material; that is, they know their subjects well. You can expect them to clearly tell you their expectations for the class—assignments, tests, due dates, etc. (But *don't* expect them to remind you when things are due; that's your responsibility.) You can expect them to have office hours, to be available to answer your questions.

But at a Christian college, you can expect more than just the "educational" side of profs. These instructors care about *you*, and they want to help you grow intellectually, spiritually, emotionally. They want to help prepare you for life after college. Because of their experience and knowledge, profs are a great resource.

Q Should I talk to my professor if I'm having trouble in a class?

A Yes. And you should talk to your prof even if you're not having trouble in class.

As we've already mentioned, profs care about you, and they want to help you succeed. Often, you can chat with them for at least a few minutes before or after class. But usually, college profs will let their students know of their office hours—specific times each week when they'll be available to answer questions, to further explain something, to help you with your classroom struggles. That's part of the professor's job, and you should take advantage of it. Feel free to ask your prof after class if you can come by his or her office to discuss something. Or call your prof and make an appointment. They'll be more than happy to make the time.

When you schedule an appointment with your prof, come prepared with a list of specific questions. But keep your questions *relevant*; ask questions about the class, about the textbook, about something you didn't quite understand, maybe about careers related to the subject. Don't schedule an appointment just to "shoot the breeze." Profs are people, yes, but profs are busy people, and other students need appointments, too. At the same time, if your conversation with your prof goes off on a tangent, that's OK, too.

Now, it's one thing to be having problems with your class. It's entirely another thing to be having problems with your professor. But it happens. Again, profs are people too, and sometimes people don't get along.

We know one student who said she couldn't stand one of her profs. She said the prof was very critical and always put students down. But dropping the class wasn't an option, because it was a required class. That student was advised to take a good look at her complaints. Were they fair? Had she had similar problems with other profs? Did other students have problems with that same prof? You might want to ask yourself the same questions if you're in a similar situation.

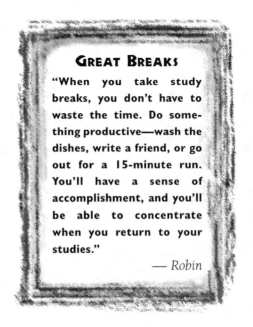

GREAT BREAKS

"When you take study breaks, you don't have to waste the time. Do something productive—wash the dishes, write a friend, or go out for a 15-minute run. You'll have a sense of accomplishment, and you'll be able to concentrate when you return to your studies."

— *Robin*

There are steps you can take if you find yourself in a situation like this. In the spirit of Matthew 18:15, it's a good idea to go right to your professor and share your concerns directly. If you're too nervous to go alone, ask a friend from the same class to come along for moral support—not to "gang up" on the prof. Tell your prof what you need from him or her to be more successful in the class, rather than putting the blame on his or her teaching style. That way, your prof won't be put on the defensive.

It might also help to study with a group from the class, or talk with an upperclassman who's had the same prof. Others may better understand or even appreciate the prof's style and be able to help you adjust to it.

If none of these suggestions help, it's appropriate to go to the chairperson of that prof's academic department. Tell the chairperson about your struggles, again making sure your comments are fair. Beyond that, your academic advisor may have some helpful suggestions.

Finally, at the end of the term, many schools give students an opportunity to offer written, anonymous evaluations of their professors. This will give you a chance to describe your experience and try to be helpful for future classes. If you're fair with your comments and specific with your examples, you may help improve the teaching of someone who truly desires to be more effective.

Q What about dropping and/or adding classes?

A   One of the many cool things about college is that, for a certain length of time each term, you can drop and/or add classes to your schedule. The "drop-add deadline" is usually a few weeks into the term, and until that deadline, you can make such changes without penalty. If you wait until after the deadline to drop a class, you may end up getting an "F" or "Incomplete" in the class. You might also lose the money you've paid for that class. Policies vary from college to college, so be sure to ask about the rules.

There are many advantages to the drop-add system. One *Campus Life* editor often used it to fine-tune his schedule every semester. He needed to average 15 hours (five classes) per semester to graduate, but he often signed up for 18 hours (six classes) or even 21 hours (seven classes), knowing he would end up dropping one or two of the classes. Taking six classes in a semester is difficult, and seven is downright brutal, especially if you're involved in extracurricular activities. But this guy signed up for that many classes, knowing he was headed for just a "trial run" in a couple of them. He'd attend all seven classes for a couple weeks, decide which five he liked best, and drop the other two. Often, there were classes he couldn't drop, because they were required for graduation or for his major. But sometimes, there were a few "elective" courses in the mix, and those were the ones he could drop.

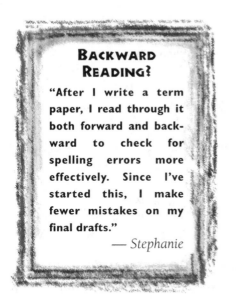

BACKWARD READING?

"After I write a term paper, I read through it both forward and backward to check for spelling errors more effectively. Since I've started this, I make fewer mistakes on my final drafts."

— *Stephanie*

What are some good reasons for dropping a class? One might be that the class is simply too difficult. Most college classes are hard, but some are much more difficult and time-consuming than others. If your schedule of required classes is incredibly difficult, you might want your electives to be a little easier. So, if you get into an elective class that, after two weeks, you're convinced is going to hinder your effectiveness in your required classes, you can consider dropping that elective—either dropping it outright, or replacing it by adding another. Caution: If you plan to add classes to replace your drops, do it as soon in the term as possible. It's hard to catch up in an added class if you've already missed the first few lectures.

At the same time, don't drop a class *just* because it's difficult. It's impossible to schedule a term of only easy classes. There just aren't many, if any, easy classes in college. You're going to have to take plenty of difficult ones, and you shouldn't abuse the drop-add system just to try to avoid them.

Also, don't drop a class just because you had a bad first impression of the prof. Maybe you don't like the clothes he wears, or her hairstyle, or something about their voice or manner. Something rubs you the wrong way. But that's life; someday, you might have a boss like that, but you're not going to be able to "drop" the job and "add" another. So, try to stick with the class and give the prof a chance.

Another reason to drop a class is schedule conflict. You might have a 9:00 a.m. class on one side of the campus, and a 10:00 a.m. class on the other, and it's just about impossible to get from one to the other on time. You might have to make a change.

If you sign up for a class that you're thinking *might* end up getting dropped, and you buy new textbooks, don't write in them. And save the receipt. If you do end up dropping the class, you can get a full refund.

Sometimes, you can drop *and* add the same class. Required courses and popular courses are often offered on different days and different times. If you're having trouble making it to your 1:00 p.m. Square Dancing 101 class, you might be able to drop it and add the 2:00 p.m. Square Dancing 101 class instead. *Promenade yer pardner!*

Sometimes, there might be a situation where you'd add a class without dropping another. Perhaps a class you wanted to take wasn't on the list when you signed up for classes, but when you arrived for the next term, there it was. (Maybe the professor decided not to take his Hawaiian sabbatical after all.) So you add it to your schedule.

Again, different colleges have different policies on drop-add. Ask the colleges you're considering about theirs, or talk to your academic advisor once you get on campus.

Q What's an academic advisor?

A When you start college, you'll probably be assigned an academic advisor, usually just a professor at the school. If you mentioned a preference for a major when you applied, your advisor might be from that department. If you said you're thinking about majoring in chemistry, your advisor will likely be a chemistry prof, but not necessarily.

An academic advisor is just what the title implies—someone to give you advice as you make your academic plans. Your academic advisor can give you general suggestions on scheduling classes, study tips, some career counseling, and basic "college survival" advice. Good stuff.

But you might not keep your academic advisor from your freshman year the whole time you're in college. By the time you're a sophomore, you might want to choose your own advisor, rather than the one the college chose for you as a freshman. As a sophomore, you'll probably be leaning toward a particular major, and you will have gotten to know certain professors. The advisor you were assigned to might be a math professor, but you might want to major in Ancient Egyptian Hieroglyphics. So, you might wanna switch advisors. Don't worry about "hurting the feelings" of the advisor you were assigned to as a freshman; students switch advisors all the time as they decide on a major and get to know other profs. On the other hand, if your assigned advisor is also a prof in your major field of study, and you've appreciated his or her advice during your freshman year, you can keep that same advisor.

But your advisor isn't your only source of academic advice. Ask other profs and older students for their suggestions, too.

Additionally, if you're struggling academically, or if you just want to improve your grades and study habits, look for a place on campus called a "study center" or "academic support center," or something like that. This place will offer all sorts of academic help and include a staff of professional advisors and trained student tutors. They can do everything from help you solve that pesky math homework problem, to teach you study and reading skills and time-management techniques. It's worth checking out, even if you're not having a hard time academically.

Q **What's a major? A minor? When do I have to decide on those, and can I change my mind later?**

A A major is a high-ranking military officer who . . .

Oops. Sorry, that's another book.

A major is a field of study that you decide to concentrate on and specialize in as a college student. Most colleges require you to major in something to graduate. You'll have to take a certain number of classes in your major field of study, some of them required, many of them electives (i.e., your choice).

And you'll probably do some "independent study" or "independent research," where you'll work with a prof to pursue a particular issue. For instance, if you decide to major in psychology, you might be particularly interested in child psychology. You might want to do your independent study on language development. You'd work with a prof who knows this field well, and you and the prof would essentially set up your own private class for the semester.

While most majors are in one field of study, many colleges also give you the option of pursuing a major in "interdisciplinary studies," where you take a variety of classes in a variety of academic fields. Sometimes the interdisciplinary major is a curriculum already set up by the college. But sometimes you can set it up yourself. Ask the colleges you're considering if they offer an interdisciplinary major.

FRESHMAN LISA DUBNER HADN'T CAUGHT ON TO THE FACT THAT
MOST COLLEGE CLASSES ARE HELD EVERY OTHER DAY.

Some students even decide to pursue a "double major," fulfilling the requirements in two major fields of study. For obvious reasons, a double major can be more demanding academically than a single major. Additionally, it means you probably won't have room for many—if any—electives during your junior and senior years.

You don't have to know what you want to major in when you arrive at college. The freshman year and at least some of the sophomore year are usually designed for you to get a "feel" for the variety of courses and fields of study available. At most colleges, you won't have to "declare" a major—which just means you tell the college what you want to major in—until at least your sophomore year. Until then, take classes that interest you in addition to your required courses. As you sit through these courses, think about what you like or don't like in each subject. That way, you'll be exploring your options and taking care of graduation requirements at the same time.

During this process, don't keep your thoughts totally to yourself. Talk to your academic advisor(s), and get their input. If you're considering a particular major and your advisor isn't in that department, schedule an appointment with a prof in that department to discuss the possibility of majoring in that field. Ask him or her what's involved in a major, and how that major might help you after graduating from college. Talk to someone at the college's career center to get their suggestions on how certain majors might affect your career choices and possibilities. Talk to your parents and close friends. Ask them what they picture you doing in the future; their thoughts might spark some ideas for you. And don't forget talking to God, who will guide you: "For I know the plans I have for you . . . plans to give you a hope and a future" (Jer. 29:11).

There are a few majors—usually in the sciences—which you might need to start in your freshman year in order to complete the necessary courses in four years. Your academic advisor can tell you what those majors are, and whether there are any freshman requirements. Sometimes, colleges hold special advising sessions for potential science majors during orientation week; attend one of these if you're thinking about a science major. If you're mildly interested in majoring in science, go ahead and sign up for the designated courses. If you change your mind and shift to another major later, that's OK. More than half of all college students end up changing their major anyway. But note: If you change from a non-science major, which you won't really concentrate on till your junior year, to a science major, you might find yourself fairly far behind in the necessary coursework. So, if you're going to major in a science, it's usually good to know this by the end of your freshman year.

If you do change majors, you can take the courses you've taken toward your old major and use them as electives. Or you can put them toward a minor.

A minor is someone who goes into caves with a shovel and pick-axe, looking for . . .

Oops. Sorry, again.

A minor is a topic you choose to study in some depth, but not as much depth as your major. You'll have to take about half as many courses for a minor as are required for a major. A minor doesn't replace a major, but supplements it. You have to major in something to graduate, but you don't have to minor in anything. A minor is just a way for you to further pursue a topic of particular interest.

Q   What about international study experiences?

A   Many colleges offer you an opportunity to study for a term, or even a whole year, in another country.

At Goshen College in Indiana, for example, most students spend 13 weeks in one of six foreign countries—learning the language and the customs of the people, living with a host family, attending lectures, going on field trips, and doing service work, often in rural areas. They work as aides in hospitals, teaching English in schools, running sports programs, doing construction. At the same time, they earn college credits for the experience.

Christian colleges are especially good at offering these "study abroad" opportunities. More than half of the 90 schools in the Coalition for Christian Colleges and Universities offer such programs, sending students all over the world.

The number of students participating in these programs varies from college to college. At Goshen, for instance, 85 percent of its 1,000-plus students take part. At Westmont in California, 15 percent take part. At Trinity Christian College in Illinois, it's 2 percent.

Ask the colleges you're considering for information about their study abroad programs.

Q   What if I can't hack it academically?

A   First of all, you need to decide what you mean by "hacking it academically." If you were a straight-A student in high school, you might be surprised when you get your first B, C, or even D in college. It can be quite a shock. You might say, "I don't get it! I'm studying more now than I ever did in high school. What's wrong?!?"

This is not to say that you *can't* make straight A's in college, because you can. It'll just take a lot more work than it did in high school. (The *Campus Life* editors have actually heard of people who did it, though none of us were lucky enough, or smart enough, to have been in their shoes. Shucks, we couldn't have even worn their socks!)

It's good to have high expectations in college. After all, grades *do* matter—not only to you, but to your parents, to graduate schools (if you decide to go), to the people who give you scholarships, and to your future employer.

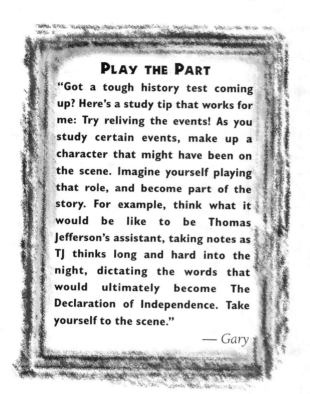

PLAY THE PART

"Got a tough history test coming up? Here's a study tip that works for me: Try reliving the events! As you study certain events, make up a character that might have been on the scene. Imagine yourself playing that role, and become part of the story. For example, think what it would be like to be Thomas Jefferson's assistant, taking notes as TJ thinks long and hard into the night, dictating the words that would ultimately become The Declaration of Independence. Take yourself to the scene."

— *Gary*

But if you make a B or C instead of an A, don't freak out. And keep in mind what the grades are for. If you're used to straight A's and you make a C on a quiz in one class the second week of college, don't sweat it. Just talk to the prof, ask what you can to do to improve, and then do what needs to be done. Besides, your final exam will likely be the biggest factor in determining your final grade in the course, and you'll long forget about the C on that quiz.

If you're struggling in a particular course, don't wait until the end of the term to deal with the situation. If your problem is that you're just not "getting it," talk to the professor right away. If you're trying as hard as you can, the prof will be happy to try to help you improve. Profs don't like to flunk students; they want you to learn, not fail. Your prof will be understanding and helpful. For more help, talk to your academic advisor, or get some assistance at the study center.

Your grades might slip for other reasons, too. Sometimes it's not a matter of you not understanding the material, but of personal challenges—like physical illness, emotional problems, depression and/or stress. Talk to your R.A. about these things. Talk to your parents. Talk to your pastor or the campus chaplain. And if your problems aren't "academic" in nature, you can still talk to your prof. He or she will be sensitive to your situation.

If you can't complete the requirements of the class for any of the above reasons, or because of something like a family emergency or extreme illness, your prof can give you a temporary "Incomplete" in the class, which appears on your transcript as an "I" until you finish the work. You have a certain amount of time, usually a semester, to complete the work.

You might decide there's no hope for you to catch up or make a good grade, or that you simply don't want to finish the class. In this case, you can withdraw by a certain date, and you'll get a "W" on your transcript. This is better than staying with the class and flunking it; a "W" looks better on your records than an "F."

If you're used to high grades and you get a C in a course, that's OK. A few C's aren't going to bring your cumulative GPA—your average GPA for *all* of your college years—down very far. Even a D won't sink you, especially if you're making mostly A's and B's otherwise.

When should you start getting concerned? If you start making all C's and D's—or worse. And if you flunk a course, that's a pretty big red flag; you need to determine what the problem is. Maybe you're pursuing a major that's not right for you. Maybe you're not studying as hard as you should. Talk to your professor and find out why you failed. But keep in mind that if you've applied yourself and tried your hardest, it's pretty difficult to outright flunk a class.

If you're not doing well academically, consider the courses you're not doing well in; if they're in your major area, you might want to consider changing majors. Or at least talking to your advisor. For example, what if, in your sophomore year, you make three A's, three B's, two C's and two D's? That's a 2.7 GPA for the year, which isn't great, but isn't awful, either. (It's actually a little above average, on a 4-point scale.) But what if the A's were in classes like "The Social Life of Cows" and "Treading Water," and the C's and D's all came in your major? Assuming you tried your hardest in those classes, this information *might* be enough for you to consider changing your major—or at least talking to your advisor and your parents about it. Maybe the lower grades mean it's a major you'll have trouble understanding. Maybe they mean you weren't as passionate about that topic as you originally thought. Whatever. Low grades in your major are a good reason to at least discuss your choice with someone.

If all of your grades are bad, ask yourself some questions:
- Am I trying as hard as I can?
- Is there anything else I can do to improve?
- Are there other things in my life distracting me from my studies?
- Have I lost the "fire" to do well academically?
- Do I even *care* about my grades?
- Do I really want a college degree after all?

Think about these questions alone, and then discuss them with others. Talk to your profs. Talk to your academic advisor. Talk to someone at the study center. Talk to your parents, your R.A., a pastor or counselor, some trusted friends.

Often, if you start making bad grades, a college will put you on "academic probation," which is essentially a warning that you need to improve your grades, or you might be asked to drop out. Bad grades could also endanger your financial aid. Ask the colleges you're considering about their rules and consequences concerning academic probation.

If you decide to leave the school, or the school asks you to leave for academic reasons, don't make a hasty decision about what you're going to do next. Go home, take some time, pray about it, and get advice from those you trust and love. If you didn't make it academically at your first choice of colleges, that doesn't mean you're not "cut out" for college. Any number of things could have contributed to your academic problems. You still might want to consider transferring to another college, perhaps one that's less demanding academically. Discuss your options with your college advisor, your parents, your pastor, and others whose opinions you trust.

Whatever happens academically, never lose sight that your grades are *not* a reflection of who you are as a person. God's love for you has nothing to do with your GPA. You cannot flunk out of his favor and mercy. Heaven is not just for valedictorians.

God doesn't care if you make an A or an F, or anything in between. There's no such thing as an "incomplete" in God's kingdom. His love for you is quite complete.

Q **Any suggestions on managing my time so I can get everything done?**

A Carry a day planner, and make schedules. Schedules will bring order to your life in college, and they'll keep you on track. Write down everything you need to do. If you don't write it down, you'll never remember what you need to do and when you need to do it.

We suggest keeping three types of schedules: a basic calendar to hang in your dorm room, highlighting the important events of the entire term (semester or quarter); a weekly schedule, kept in your day planner; and daily schedules, also in your day planner. (You can buy day planners at big stores like Wal-Mart, and at office supply stores.)

Here's a closer look at each:

A *calendar* is just, well, a regular calendar: A wall calendar or desk calendar, anything you can look at and see the whole term at a glance. At the beginning of each term, fill your calendar with important events, like due dates (for projects, term papers, and exams), special campus activities, holidays, sports events, whatever is a "can't-miss" for that term.

A *weekly schedule* will show you what a typical week looks like. When you know your class schedule, make a chart of the entire week. If your day planner doesn't have a weekly chart, make your own. Divide a sheet of paper into five vertical columns, with Monday through Friday at the top of each column. Down the left side, put the hours of the day: 6:00 a.m., 7:00 a.m., and so on. Now you've got the full week divided into one-hour blocks. Fill out your class schedule first. If you work, put in your work schedule. Block off time for meals, devotions, exercises, study times, laundry, shopping, recreation, and maybe even an occasional nap on especially hard days. Try to end each day by 11:00 p.m. or midnight, no matter what remains undone; you'll need the rest. Once you've made this "master" weekly schedule, make a bunch of copies to last you the whole term. Then, pull out a new copy at the beginning of each week, and fill in the details or any added activities for that particular week—committee meeting on Monday, psychology quiz on Tuesday, intramural basketball game Wednesday night, statistics project due Thursday, tennis with Bob on Friday, and so on.

A *daily schedule* spells out the specific demands of each day. Every night, write down the things you've got to do the next day, working from your weekly schedule and making any fine-tuning adjustments. If Bob calls Thursday night and says he can't make it to tennis on Friday, pencil something else into that time slot. Maybe it's an extra hour of studying—which means less studying over the weekend. Maybe it's calling someone else to try to find a tennis match. Maybe it's getting some exercise on your own, like going for a bike ride across campus. Or maybe it's just down time. If you're wiped out, you'll need it.

As you make your schedules, always keep in mind that their purpose is to *serve* you, not be your master. You won't want to stray too far from your schedule; your college life will be chaotic if you do. But don't be inflexible, either. Feel free to improvise and occasionally do something different.

EXCUSES, EXCUSES

"My Dog Ate It!"

by Steve and Alice Lawhead

In those tenuous moments when an excuse or an explanation is necessary—for that late paper, that missed appointment, that forgotten assignment—a masterful application of the fine art of obfuscation could save the day. Here are nine examples of what we mean:

- **Don't say: "I forgot."**

Instead, say: "Phrenialogically speaking, the aforementioned subject ineluctably eluded my short-term mnemonic functions, resulting in an unaccountable cognition void."

- **Don't say: "It'll be a little late."**

Instead, say: "Indefeasible difficulties necessitate a reassessment of allotted time parameters, vis-a-vis the restructuring of predesignated completion goals."

• **Don't say: "My dog ate it."**
Instead, say: "The ordinarily carnivorous domestic canine under my husbandry purloined unprecedented masticatory privileges with my unobserved project."

• **Don't say: "I lost it."**
Instead, say: "Indivertible circumstances misdirected the successful ensconcement of the errant property rendering possessorship inoperative."

• **Don't say: "I overslept."**
Instead, say: "Due to an avouched preponderancy for somnolent indulgence, I unilaterally misapprehended the foreordained commencement of this scholastic exercise."

• **Don't say: "It isn't finished."**
Instead, say: "The effectual consummation of the assignated object was inexplicably prolonged by irremediable forces unresponsive to my personal influence."

• **Don't say: "I broke it."**
Instead, say: "Owing to the delicate quiddity of the foredoomed article, my innoxious scrutiny stressed certain heretofore undisclosed flaws in manufacture, precipitating an inevitable fracture of the maldesigned subcomponents."

• **Don't say: "I didn't study."**
Instead, say: "The overwhelmingly addictive character of televised divertissements short-circuited my ambitionary regard for the apprehension and retention of the opusculatory material now under consideration."

• **Don't say: "I fell asleep in class."**
Instead, say: "Notwithstanding the scintillating repartee concomitant to this scholastic assemblage, intransigent preternatural biologic functions conspired to surmount my fragile resolve, plunging consciousness beneath my direct autonomy and thus insuring a rapid decline into somnolence."

From *The Total Guide to College Life,* by Alice and Steve Lawhead. Copyright 1997. Used by permission of Harold Shaw Publishers, Wheaton, IL 60189.

Your Spiritual Life

Q **What does my faith have to do with my education?**

A The best answer to that question comes from the presidents of Christian colleges. Here's what they say:

• "Your faith is very much a part of your education. It's like putting water and oil into a bowl and blending it together. Some things—like faith and education—might seem on the surface to be separate and unrelated. But with the right kind of support and environment—like you find at a Christian college—those things can become one without diluting either of them."

• "Your faith, beliefs, and values are *always* a part of your learning development. What's important is that those things are shaped by the Scriptures and energized by a vital personal relationship with Jesus Christ."

• "There's no point in attending a Christian college if you're not committed to combining faith and learning. It would be hard to avoid that integration when every faculty member is excited about pointing it out. Education apart from values is boring. At a college where you can really share your values, that's where it becomes exciting."

• "The opportunity to live away from your family, in the midst of a group of peers in an academic environment, will bring a maturity to your faith. Sometimes that is a very real challenge. Our commitment at a Christian college is to foster deeper commitment and understanding. We want you to embrace the faith for yourself. You will raise questions you may not have raised at home and in church. And you will raise them in a place where we believe in the reality of God and the truth of Scripture."

Q How do I grow in my faith at college?

A   Growing in your faith at college requires pretty much the same things it requires anywhere else. Typically, these things include:

• *Daily devotions.* You'll want to read your Bible and pray every day, if possible. You might even keep a "prayer journal" to record things you've prayed for and how you've seen those prayers answered. You might also note important Bible verses or spiritual lessons you've learned in this journal, too. It's important to actually schedule your devotion time. You may think you can just have a quiet time when you find a spare moment. But you'll be so busy during college that those spare moments will be hard to find. Deliberately set aside a block of time each day for devotions.

• *Fellowship.* You're probably involved in some kind of youth group in high school, and those meetings have helped you grow in your faith. The same thing will be true in college, so be sure to find some kind of a fellowship group. You might think, *I'll be at a Christian college, so I'll be hanging with Christians everywhere I go. Who needs a fellowship on top of that?* You do. Hanging with Christians in a chemistry class, in the dorm or in the cafeteria is not the same as real, live, Spirit-filled fellowship, where you're praising God and learning about him together. (We'll talk more about your fellowship options later in the chapter.)

• *Chapel and church.* These overlap the "fellowship" category a little bit, but the big thing here is the idea of "corporate worship"—getting together with a bunch of believers of all ages, singing hymns and praise songs, praying as a congregation, hearing and responding to the message. You'll have the opportunity to attend campus chapel services one or more times a week, and you'll head to a local church for the Sunday morning thing. (We'll talk more about chapel and church later in this chapter.)

• *Small groups.* While the "fellowship" and "church" categories apply to large groups, you'll also want to find some kind of small group for Bible study, prayer, accountability, and just good old friendship. Where do you find a small group? Often, you can find one through the fellowship you join; ask one of the leaders to get you plugged in. You might find one at the local church you attend; ask the college leader to give you information. Or you and your friends can start one in the dorm.

• *Discipleship.* You might want to find someone who can be your spiritual mentor, a person mature enough in their faith to help you mature in yours. This might be the campus chaplain, a prof, someone at church, an older student, your R.A. It might be a one-on-one relationship, or perhaps you and a friend or two might find someone to disciple you as a group. But discipleship is rarely done in a large group; Jesus pulled it off pretty well with a dozen guys, but you might want to look for something more personal.

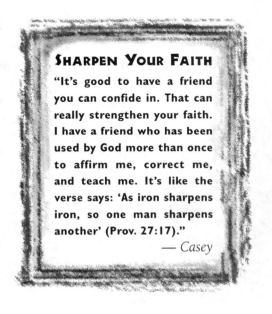

SHARPEN YOUR FAITH

"It's good to have a friend you can confide in. That can really strengthen your faith. I have a friend who has been used by God more than once to affirm me, correct me, and teach me. It's like the verse says: 'As iron sharpens iron, so one man sharpens another' (Prov. 27:17)."

— *Casey*

• *Service.* You'll want to find ways to serve others while you're in college. At a Christian college, you'll certainly find all sorts of service projects and missions opportunities. But don't just think about the "organized events" as opportunities for service. And don't just think that service needs to be extended to non-Christians. If you're a math whiz and your roommate is struggling with math, offer to be a tutor. That's service. If you were a state tennis champ and somebody down the hall wants to learn to play, give some free lessons. That's service. If your prof is carrying a giant box of supplies out to the car, offer to help. That's service. By keeping your eyes open, you'll find opportunities to serve every day.

• *Evangelism.* What? At a Christian college? Yes. Many Christian colleges admit non-Christians, so there might just be a nonbeliever on your hall. But even if your campus is exclusively Christian, there's still a community around you. Get involved in the community, and always look for a chance to tell someone about the heavenly hope you have.

Q What's chapel, and do I have to go?

A Chapel is essentially "college church." It's a church service held in your campus chapel, usually once a week, sometimes more, sometimes daily. Chapel is a "family experience" at the college, a regular time for all students to gather together to worship God. It's a pretty cool distinctive of the Christian college; you don't find anything like that on secular campuses . . . unless you count football games. That's the closest you'll get to finding something where students at a secular school gather in one place for one purpose.

One Christian college official told us, "Chapel is a vital part of student life. It's a key to spiritual vitality on any Christian campus. It's not only good for the individual; it also builds a sense of community."

Not all chapel services are the same. At one service, you might hear someone give a testimony. At another, a Bible message. At another, a worship band. You might see a video on world missions, or hear fellow students share a report on their service trip to Albania.

Often, you'll hear music and worship geared for and led by college students. Contemporary praise choruses are far more common than hymns, but many chapel services still include some of the great old classics.

Also, expect to hear outstanding speakers at chapel—like Chuck Colson, Tony Campolo, Josh McDowell, and Joni Eareckson Tada.

But many students say the chapels they most remember aren't the ones with the big names or the great sermons, but the ones that included messages from their fellow students.

Do you have to go to chapel? Many colleges require it. But whether it's required or not, you still have to make the choice whether to go or not. It's easy to "blow off" chapel, and, unfortunately, many students do, especially when it's not required. But don't blow it off. It's not only an important part of building "community," but a vital part of your spiritual growth.

Q What other kinds of fellowship are available?

A There should be a variety of opportunities for Christian clubs and fellowships on campus. Also, many Christian campuses include missions fellowships, if you're interested in learning more about missions and hanging out with other students who feel the same way. Ask the colleges you're considering about the fellowship groups that meet on campus.

And don't forget about fellowship opportunities in the local church.

But those are just the "organized" forms of fellowship. You can make your own fellowship, too. Get some dorm friends together on Sunday nights to sing songs and pray. Organize a hayride, and talk about what God is doing in your lives. Have a bonfire—get permission from the college first!—and roast marshmallows and sing. The opportunities are limitless.

Q Will my faith be challenged at college?

A Yes. In chapter 8, we discussed some of the temptations and peer pressure you'll likely face in college. But those aren't the only things that will challenge your faith.

In some ways, your faith might be challenged more at a Christian college than at a secular school. One Christian college president tells us, "Students at a Christian college sometimes think they can put their faith on hold for a few years. They don't work on developing their faith, because they believe no one is judging them, since everyone there is supposed to be a Christian. So it often takes more discipline on a Christian college campus to keep all of that in perspective and to continue growing in your faith."

Your faith will also be challenged though your academics. Another college president says, "A Christian college isn't about being in an isolated, sheltered, protected greenhouse kind of environment. Through your written assignments, readings, and lectures, you will find yourself examining many views that directly challenge your Christian worldview. But you'll face that challenge with an advantage at a Christian college, where you can examine those questions with the support, guidance, love, and care of faculty members who have examined those same issues and affirmed their Christian faith."

College is also a time when you really begin to take "ownership" of your faith. In other words, it won't just be something you grew up with, something "passed down" from your family or your church. Chances are, you'll even question your own beliefs. And this time of uncertainty can be scary. But out of these struggles, you'll develop a more solid faith that you can truly call your own.

"Be prepared to have your cherished opinions and ideas challenged," says one Christian college president. "You may find yourself questioning things you had just assumed to be true. You'll find that other people think differently on issues. That can be disconcerting."

Adds another college prez, "That's true. But keep in mind that a school wouldn't admit you unless it felt you could overcome the challenges you'll face."

Q Is church really important if I'm attending a Christian college?

A At a Christian college, you might sometimes feel like you're "up to your ears" in fellowship. You might even find yourself thinking, *I've already got chapel, dorm Bible study, prayer meetings, and a missions fellowship. Why plug into a local church, too?*

Well, here's how a few college students answered that question:
- "It's the perfect opportunity to worship with people of all ages."
- "I enjoy celebrating the Lord's Supper, and I've found a church that celebrates Communion every Sunday morning."
- "Our pastor preaches to everyone, not just students. I'm really growing through messages on marriage, teen-parent relationships, encouragement to widows and the elderly."
- "I began working in Pioneer Girls clubs on Wednesday nights, and discovered abilities and a love for children I never realized were there."

Here are a few more reasons for getting involved in a local church:
- *Corporate worship.* Obviously, you'll have the opportunity to worship God in chapel services, but generally, chapel is not as geared toward worship as the local church. And the key word here is "corporate," as in the "whole body" of Christ. A local church, with people of all ages and backgrounds, is a more complete cross-section of the universal body of Christ than a college chapel.
- *Sunday school classes.* In this setting, you'll have a chance not only to hear solid biblical teaching, but to discuss it as well. Discussion and occasional debate often make lessons more meaningful.

> ## BE ACCOUNTABLE
> "Get involved in a Bible study or accountability group. First Thessalonians 5:11 says we should 'encourage one another and build each other up.' Make this your motto as a group. Ask God for the strength to follow this advice."
> — Sara Ann

- *A "home away from home."* If you're a long way from your family and old friends, a church near your college campus can play the role of an "extended family." Some churches near colleges even arrange "adoption" programs, where a local family invites a college student for occasional meals and outings. It's a great feeling to go home with a family after church for a delicious meal and great conversation, and then chill out together in their den while watching a football game.

• *A place to serve.* A local church can serve you and meet your needs. But you can serve as well—by teaching a children's Sunday school class, singing in the choir, ushering, helping out on Clean-Up Day, and plenty of other ways. Ask the church how you might be able to serve.

Some Christian colleges have a church or churches very near the campus, so transportation won't be a problem. But if there isn't a church nearby, ask some older students for suggestions. Those who have cars might give you a ride. Some churches even offer shuttle services for college students.

Whatever you do, don't wait until Sunday morning to decide if you're going to church; it's too easy to roll over and go back to sleep. Make church a part of your regular schedule. Plan on going, and know how you're going to get there in advance. You'd hate to miss church just because you couldn't scrounge up a ride at the last minute.

If your college has a lot of churches nearby, that's good, but it can create a minor problem: You might be tempted to "shop around" for months and months without ever deciding which church you want to attend. Try to visit just a few churches at first, and decide on one church within a couple of months. The sooner you can become part of that church body, the better. If after a while you realize you're not comfortable at that church, you can change and start attending another one.

Q **Can I assume everyone on campus is a Christian?**

A Not really. In fact, it's pretty safe to assume there are non-Christians on campus.

Some Christian colleges have policies that say they won't admit non-Christians. One Christian college application includes this line: "To be considered for this admission, you must be a Christian for at least one year and a member of a Protestant evangelical church." Another application says, "The applicant should be a high-school graduate and born-again Christian for at least one year." But just because it's in the policy is no guarantee that every student on campus is a Christian.

Most Christian schools don't have such policies. But that doesn't mean most of the students are non-Christians. Usually, these colleges will admit a small number of non-believers every year, but the majority of students on campus will be Christians. After all, that's what the college is all about: educating students from a Christian perspective.

Don't be bothered by the possibility of having some non-Christians on campus. As a matter of fact, welcome it. Non-Christians will have some great questions about the Christian faith, questions you'll want to wrestle with as you make your faith "your own." Additionally, what better place for non-Christians to be than on a Christian campus? Where else would they have such a great opportunity to hear God's good news, and see it lived out in the lives of their fellow students? They may even make the life-changing decision to follow Christ.

Q **My friend went to a Christian college and came home with a lot of doubts. Is that normal?**

A Yes. We've already discussed some of things that will challenge your faith: peer pressure, temptations, classes, non-Christian students. Some of these challenges will get you asking questions about your faith.

And believe it or not, some professors might actually plant some of these questions. College profs want you to develop "critical thinking" skills—a means of looking at problems and solving them with reasoning, logic, and deep thought, not just pat answers. So profs might occasionally challenge what you believe in order to keep you on your toes. A prof might begin a class one day by saying, "Suppose for a moment that Christianity is *not* true. Suppose that Jesus was *not* resurrected . . . " And he or she might go on to give you some pretty good arguments to support these suppositions.

Or maybe a biology teacher will say, "You know, there's pretty good evidence that some species have evolved." And then he'll go on to list that evidence, apparently dissing Creation theory along the way.

> **BROAD SPECTRUM**
>
> "Going to church while I'm at college puts me in touch with people from so many different backgrounds, ages, and experiences. It's helped me to see that the body of Christ is much bigger and broader than just my college community. It's also a place where I'm discovering a lot about worship and about my Christian faith."
>
> — *Pete*

You might think, "WHAT?!? I thought I was at a Christian college, and now this guy's trying to gun down my faith?" Nope, he's trying to strengthen your faith, by getting you to question your assumptions and find answers. Sometimes the best way to solidify your faith is to probe it, to question it, to address the doubts about it.

A guy named Paul Little wrote a book called, *Know What You Believe*. It outlines all the basic beliefs of Christianity and has long been a great book to help new believers get grounded in their faith. The response to the book was overwhelming, and tons of people bought it. But then these new Christians were beginning to ask deeper questions about their faith: "OK, I believe these things, but I'm not sure *why* I believe them. Yes, I take them on faith. But can't I support my faith with some logical answers, too?" Paul Little heard the questions, and wrote another book, *Know Why You Believe*, to give people some answers. He saw the importance of defending your faith.

That's part of what they do at a Christian college. They figure you already know *what* you believe. They just want to help you know *why* you believe it.

Q If I'm struggling spiritually, will there be someone to help me?

A Yes. And you'll probably have several choices:

• *The campus chaplain.* This person is the pastor of the chapel, and when he's not leading chapel services, his main job is to oversee the spiritual growth of students. If you need help, don't hesitate to schedule an appointment.

• *The counseling center.* Found on many campuses, the counseling center was described in chapter 7 as a place you can go if you're struggling emotionally. But your emotions are often tied directly to your spiritual life. The counseling center will have people who can talk to you about both your emotional and spiritual struggles.

• *Your advisor.* Yes, your academic advisor might be a source for spiritual help. That's one thing that's cool about a Christian college: Your professors are usually going to be mature Christians who may be able to help with your non-academic struggles too. If not, they'll be able to point you toward someone who can.

• *Your R.A.* Your Resident Assistant probably won't have the training to handle a major crisis, but he or she can certainly help you work through typical day-to-day struggles. Your R.A. got the job partly because he or she is mature in the faith, so that might be a good place to start if you're struggling.

• *The local church.* Once you find a local church, take advantage of the resources there—the pastor or someone on the staff, your Sunday school teacher, a mature Christian.

• *Back home.* While the college will provide plenty of spiritual support, don't forget your resources back home. If you're more comfortable sharing your struggles with your parents than anyone else, talk to them. Or maybe it's your youth pastor, a teacher, or a mature friend. Don't forget the people who have helped you all along.

Q **Will I have the chance to put my faith into action through a service project or missions experience?**

A Most Christian colleges offer a variety of ways to put your faith into action. There are service clubs on most campuses set up for just this purpose. Some of the more popular clubs at Christian colleges include community service and outreach ministry groups, such as Habitat for Humanity. One school even has a club called Practical Christian Involvement; that says it all. Christian colleges will give you plenty of opportunities to serve. And again: Don't just look for the organized methods of serving. You'll have opportunities every day to reach out and put your love into action—to your roommate, your R.A., your profs, almost anyone on campus. Your service isn't just designated for people off-campus; it's for your college family, too.

Many colleges also provide opportunities for missions experiences, both domestic and international. You'll have opportunities in the surrounding community, and you'll have opportunities overseas. Most of the study-abroad programs, discussed in chapter 8, include service work and missions. That's part of the integration of faith and learning. You can go to another part of the world and study a culture, but the best way to learn about a culture is to immerse yourself in it. And the best way to immerse yourself in it is to serve the people who live there.

Often, you'll receive college credits for service projects, especially in the study-abroad programs. Ask the colleges you're considering what service and missions opportunities they offer, and whether they give credit for these programs.

God Bless Homer Crebbs!

by Ron Hafer

When you're at college, you'll to want to plug into a local church for several reasons.

One of those reasons is that a local church, with people of all ages and backgrounds, is a more complete cross-section of the universal body of Christ than a college chapel.

And that cross-section can come in handy if you're a long way from your family and old friends, because a church near your college campus can play the role of an extended family, sort of a second family away from home.

Plus, a local church can be a great food source! Here's what I mean:

When I was a junior in college, my roommate and I canceled our weekend meals at the cafeteria and went in search of creative, inexpensive food supplies. We found one local church that offered doughnuts for Sunday school, so we arrived early. After class, we went to the worship service and sat down to polish off the remaining doughnuts we had pocketed.

Suddenly, the biggest guy in the place whacked us on the back and introduced himself: "I'm Homer Crebbs, and I'll bet you guys are students at Biola!"

With doughnut crumbs falling off my chin, I shook Homer's hand. Before the service began, he bragged about his wife's cooking and invited us home for lunch. Little did he know how hungry we were! And little did we realize that Homer's invitation was part of the ministry of this little neighborhood church.

Almost every Sunday for that semester, we ate lunch with Homer and Dorothy Crebbs—and their gorgeous college-age daughter, Nancy. We relaxed on their living-room floor, played with their dog, and watched NFL games until we fell asleep.

Looking back, I realize that little church provided something (besides free food) we needed: the feeling of "family" and a diversity of ages.

When the apostle Paul wrote to Timothy, he underscored the value of the older teaching the younger. I am convinced this teaching happens more in the context of meals and relaxed times than during regularly-scheduled classes. Homer and Dorothy Crebbs taught us volumes about gracious hospitality.

I want you to know you can "have your cake and eat it too!" I encourage you to thoroughly enjoy your experience in college chapel — then head right on over to your local church and serve the Lord with all your might.

Who knows? You might even meet somebody like Homer Crebbs!

From *Campus Life* College Guide, March 1996. Used by permission.

Just for Homeschoolers

Editor's note: More and more homeschooled students are asking questions about what steps they need to take in the college search. Most of the advice in this book applies to homeschoolers as well as "conventional" students, but this section answers some of the most common questions homeschoolers ask.

Q **What do colleges think of homeschooling?**

A Many colleges view homeschooling as a legitimate form of education, and more colleges are adopting this view every year. This is especially true at Christian colleges, which are more likely to agree with the philosophical reasons for homeschooling. Many Christian colleges are even actively recruiting homeschooled students.

One Christian college's admissions department notes that "the experiences, learning opportunities, and instruction of homeschoolers are unique, beneficial, and effective. We open our doors to such students." Another "recognizes the hard work, dedication, and self-motivation behind your success in home education."

Colleges want a wide diversity of students on their campuses, and homeschoolers add to that diversity. One admissions official says he loves reading applications from homeschoolers, because he almost always finds something creative and interesting.

Some studies have shown that homeschooled students tend to do better academically in college, and colleges are always looking for students who excel academically.

Q **What do colleges look for in a homeschooled student?**

A Much the same thing they look for in any student. They want students who can think, speak, and write well. They want students who enjoy learning, who tend to be involved in activities, and who are good citizens. Christian colleges want students who are passionate about putting their faith into action—through the academic environment of the classroom, in the real-world environment of service opportunities, and in their everyday lives.

Colleges also want people who are unique, not only in their personality, but in the things they've done. Homeschoolers certainly have the opportunity to take part in some non-traditional learning experiences, and colleges will be especially interested in hearing about those.

Q **What steps should I take to prepare for college while I'm still in home school?**

A You can take many of the same steps as your friends in public and private schools: Excel in your curriculum, and make sure it's a challenging one. Take the ACT and/or SAT. Get involved in community and church activities, as well as activities organized by your local homeschool association, if there is one.

Develop good study habits, good reading and writing skills, good social skills. Learn to express yourself clearly. Cultivate a high level of curiosity.

What should you be reading? Here are a couple of suggested lists: *Reading Lists for College-Bound Students*, by Doug Estell, Michelle L. Satchwell, and Patricia S. Wright (Macmillan, 1993); or *Take & Read: Spiritual Reading: An Annotated List*, by Eugene H. Peterson (Wm. B. Eerdmans Publishing, 1996).

And learn to work with others. As a homeschooler, you spend a lot of time working on things alone. Make sure you do some projects—academic and otherwise—with other homeschooled students.

As a homeschooler, you can take advantage of your flexible schedule and pursue "alternative" educational opportunities. You may be able to work in a museum, a national park, or at the local TV station. You might take a class or two at an area college, and you might be able to get both high school *and* college credit for it.

Additionally, don't forget local public schools and/or private schools. You may be able to take AP or honors courses, a lab science course, or a foreign language—things that might not be available in a typical homeschool curriculum. Also, ask your local public school if you can be involved in its activities. For instance, you might be allowed to play in the band, sing in the choir, or be on the debate team. You might be allowed to compete in a varsity sport. The rules on such activities vary from state to state, and even school board to school board, so ask what's available to you.

Finally, consult with the local public-school guidance counselor if you have any questions about the college search-and-application process.

Q   Do colleges prefer homeschoolers to use a pre-packaged curriculum, or is it OK to design our own?

A   Either way is OK, as long as you meet the minimum standards required for college admission.

Many colleges require a minimum of 18 units from courses taken in grades 9–12. Colleges often have requirements that most of those units must be earned in the academic areas of English, math, science, social studies, and foreign languages. Some colleges require at least two years of one foreign language. Check with the colleges you're interested in to see what their requirements are.

There are some advantages to using a pre-packaged curriculum. Lesson preparation is often less time-consuming, and many of these curricula have "stood the test of time." Additionally, some pre-packaged curricula come with a more standard structure. For example, tests may be sent to a national center for grading, and there may even be a central office which issues grades, transcripts, and class rank. These things give colleges a helpful standard of measurement, telling them how you "stack up" against other students.

On the other hand, a self-designed curriculum can be more flexible and tailored just to your individual needs, talents, and interests. One admissions official says he enjoys reading applications from students and parents who have designed their programs "from scratch," as long as they're well-designed and creative.

Note: If you design your own curriculum, you'll have to do more work in record-keeping than if you used a pre-packaged curriculum. Keep detailed records not only of everything you do, but *why* you're doing it. For example, if you decide to visit every major-league ballpark in America instead of earning a unit in U.S. History, be prepared to explain why you did this and what made it a legitimate alternative to taking U.S. History.

Q **Do colleges require a transcript?**

A Most colleges will want to see some kind of transcript. They'll want to know what courses you've taken, and how you've done in those courses. Most often, that means they'll want to see grades, so keep a record of all your grades. Occasionally, homeschoolers choose not to use grades, opting instead to use the term *mastery* when completing a course. If you're going this route, be prepared to define what you mean by *mastery*.

Put yourself in the admissions officer's shoes. At many schools, the application process is competitive; more students apply than there are slots for incoming freshmen. Admissions officers must make difficult decisions on which applicants to admit, and which ones to turn away. Be prepared to state your case. You need to demonstrate why you're ready for the higher demands of collegiate academics.

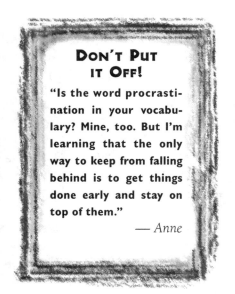

DON'T PUT IT OFF!

"Is the word procrastination in your vocabulary? Mine, too. But I'm learning that the only way to keep from falling behind is to get things done early and stay on top of them."

— *Anne*

So, make your transcript as "standard" as you possibly can. Keep detailed records for grades 9–12. Set a grading scale (95–100 is an A, 88–94 a B, and so on, or whatever scale you choose), and stick to it. Keep records of what courses you've taken, what grades you've earned, what textbooks you've used. Save a brief syllabus and samples of your work from every course.

For example, during your junior year, your transcript might be divided into two semesters, showing letter grades in English, U.S. History,

Trigonometry/Pre-Calculus, Chemistry, French III, and Music Composition. The more standard you can make your transcript, the easier it is for college admissions officials to make an evaluation.

Some colleges also will accept a detailed portfolio instead of a traditional transcript from a homeschooled student.

Some colleges may require an accredited diploma or GED (General Education Development) certificate for admission. (Note: A GED *may* be necessary, however, to obtain federal financial aid. See the question about financial aid later in this chapter.)

Finally, many colleges like to interview their homeschooled applicants to get a better "feel" for these students.

Again, check with the colleges you're considering to see what their requirements are.

Q   Most colleges want a teacher's recommendation. Should Mom write mine?

A   Colleges prefer recommendations from nonrelatives, but if Mom's your only teacher, yes, she should write yours.

Still, even if your mom does write a recommendation, it will help to have a nonrelative write one, too. You may be involved in group activities or cooperative programs with other area homeschoolers. In these cases, someone else—perhaps *another* homeschooler's parent—has probably taught you. That person would be a more objective source for a recommendation. If you've taken a college class, consider asking that professor for a recommendation. Or, you could ask a coach or a music instructor.

Note: Most colleges will also ask for a separate recommendation from your pastor or youth pastor. This recommendation does not replace the teacher recommendation.

Q   How important are my SAT or ACT scores?

A   They're especially important for homeschoolers. These tests are the most standardized, objective means by which an admissions officer can assess your academic progress—and your college readiness.

It's difficult for an admissions officer to know what grades or GPAs *really* mean. A "B-plus" in one place isn't necessarily a "B-plus" in another. Your criteria for making a certain grade in a certain course may be higher or lower than another homeschooler's.

This principle applies to more than just homeschoolers. Experts refer to a nationwide trend that they call "grade inflation." One high school, for instance, had *seven* valedictorians! The next three students were listed as salutatorians, and were given a class rank of No. 2. In other words, this school had 10 students in the top two of their class! Because of several more ties in class rank, the *entire class* graduated in the top half!

As a result of these kinds of situations, grades, GPAs, and class rank become suspect. Colleges might look at a homeschooler's grades with some suspicion; after all, most homeschoolers can claim they graduated number 1 in their class! So, what does a straight-A average really mean?

Because they're standardized and objective, the SAT and ACT have long been recognized by colleges as the great equalizers in this situation. So your SAT and/or ACT scores are quite important.

Q   What kinds of special adjustments will I have to make?

A   Academically, your main adjustment will probably be in the classroom—not necessarily the difficulty of the work, but the setting itself. As a homeschooler, you're probably accustomed to doing much of your work on your own in the quiet of your own home. In contrast, many college classes are set up as lectures; you sit, listen, and take detailed notes. Along with other assignments—like textbook readings, labs, term papers, and projects—these notes will be included in the material you're expected to learn.

As a homeschooler, you may not be used to working with other students on assignments. Since group projects are common in college, you'll need to adjust to this type of learning situation.

One way to prepare for the adjustment to the college classroom is to take a class or two at a local junior college while you're still in high school. This will help you get a feel for a typical college classroom environment.

Socially, your adjustment to college life depends a lot on what kinds of social interaction you've had as a homeschooler. If you've been doing projects and hanging out with students your age as a homeschooler, you'll keep doing that in college. If your homeschool situation has been more independent, where you've been more on your own, you'll have to get used to being a part of the crowd.

Whatever your social background, you'll run into both the positives and negatives of being surrounded by peers. On the positive side, you'll develop great friendships, you'll be encouraged, you'll find great fellowship, and you'll grow in your faith. On the negative side, you'll face peer pressure and temptations to do things that you know you shouldn't do.

For more on the academic, social, emotional, and spiritual adjustment to college life, see chapters 7–9.

Q **What about financial aid?**

A Financial aid comes in many forms, such as grants, loans and scholarships. For a detailed discussion on the subject, see chapter 5.

Homeschoolers apply for and receive financial-aid packages just like their peers in "standard" schools. Fill out the FAFSA (Free Application for Federal Student Aid) in January of your senior year, after your parents have done their tax forms. Ask the colleges you're interested in if they require additional financial-aid forms, and submit those as soon as possible. And look for private scholarships that you might be interested in and that might be just right for you. (All these steps are described in detail in chapter 5.)

To receive federal financial aid, in the form of grants, loans, or work-study, homeschoolers sometimes have more work to do than their "standard-school" friends. The federal government wants proof that you've graduated from high school before they'll give you money for college. But as many homeschoolers know, it's sometimes difficult to prove you're a high-school grad, especially if you live in a state where homeschooling isn't well-accepted and your diploma isn't recognized as legitimate.

Even in these cases, you can still be eligible for receiving federal aid by meeting one of the government's "Ability to Benefit" criteria. In most cases, this means taking the GED test, a substitute for a standard high-school diploma. There are a number of other tests you can take to meet the federal government's criteria for eligibility; a college admissions official can tell you what they are. Interestingly, at the time of this writing, neither the SAT nor ACT is on the government's list of criteria, so even a high score on one of those tests isn't enough to get you federal aid. If you have more questions about receiving federal aid, talk to a college financial-aid officer.

Some homeschoolers aren't interested in obtaining government financial aid for philosophical reasons. In this case, you can still fill out the FAFSA. Then, when you receive the college's financial-aid package, you can choose to decline the government money and accept only the college's portion of the offer. Of course, that means you and your family will have to pay that much more for college.

If you choose not to fill out the FAFSA because it's a government form, you should call the college(s) you're considering and ask their admissions and financial-aid officials for advice.

Special thanks to Dan Crabtree, Director of Admissions at Wheaton College, and to the Home School Legal Defense Association for their contributions to this section on homeschooling.

Afterword

by Ruth Senter

Ever wonder what your parents might be feeling as you're making college plans? It might not be as easy for them as it looks. Here's how one parent felt.

Dear Nick,

I drove by the college on my way home from the grocery store and saw they've put up the big blue-and-white striped tent. It reminded me that this is the week the freshmen come. It also reminded me of the week you went off to college.

In some ways, you'd been leaving for college since you entered high school. Your guidance counselor started talking to you right away about college fairs, ACTs, and SATs. I think you even attended a college fair in the fall of your freshman year, and you came home with a big pile of brochures that ended up collecting dust under your bed.

Then I remember, later, when your first college information packet arrived in the mail. You kept looking through the viewbook to find the pretty girls. I knew one college information packet would accomplish its purpose; it would convince you this college was right for you. You would be swapping home for college.

Not that I would have wanted it any different. I would not have missed, for anything, the fun of watching you plan for college—of seeing your excitement the day you finally made your decision. You came bounding down the stairs and called out, "Well. This is the day. I've made my choice. I'm going to _____." And you named your college with as much pleasure as if you'd just won a million bucks.

You and I and your dad had a party, right then and there. I think we celebrated with a whopping bowl apiece of your favorite Cookies 'n Cream ice cream. I saw the sparkle in your eye. For all practical purposes, you were already wearing your blue and orange college football uniform.

Dad and I celebrated. But we were also bracing ourselves for the day you would start lugging your stuff out the door and loading up the car. A parent can't really prepare for that day, but we tried.

For example, I remember promising myself I *would not cry* in front of you. I did not want to diminish the joy of your day. I tried to tell myself ahead of time, I would not remind you to be sure and take your Vitamin C if you felt a cold coming on. And I *would not,* repeat, I *would not* offer to do your laundry any time you decided to come home for the weekend.

For all my promises to myself that I would give you plenty of space—and all in all, I think I did pretty well, don't you?—I have to tell you this: It wasn't as easy as it looked.

I mean, moms and dads don't just suddenly stop being parents—we'd been parents since your sister was born 22 years earlier. For 18 years your dad and I were the ones who knew most about you—where you were, how you were feeling, what you'd eaten (or hadn't eaten) for breakfast, what you were wearing. One doesn't live that closely to someone for 18 years and then suddenly get used to the fact they're not living in your house anymore.

I knew your empty room was going to bother me. Maybe that's why I seemed to want you to hang around the house a little more your last week home. I knew I was going to miss your friends bursting through the back door and yelling, "Time to get up, Nick!" (Even if it was four o'clock in the afternoon.) Maybe that's why that last week, I stood talking to your friends longer than usual when they dropped by to go somewhere with you—while you stood by the door, jingling your car keys.

I knew I was going to miss sitting down with you every evening at dinner and hearing about your day. Maybe that's why I asked so many questions that last week and you had to say, "Mom. What *is* this? Fifty questions?" I knew I was going to worry a little about your eating right and staying healthy. Maybe that's why I slipped Vitamin C into one of your bags. (But I didn't say anything.) You just groaned when you saw them. But you didn't take them out.

For all the emotion of those last weeks before you left, I think we all knew everything would be OK. Your dad and I had prayed many times about your college decision. You had prayed. You had planned carefully. So, even though I felt the lump growing in my throat and my eyes getting moist when the time came for that final goodbye, we could drive out of that dormitory parking lot and not look back.

And somehow, I knew you would not be looking back either. You would be on to the next exciting adventure. And truly, Nick, a mother would not want it any other way.

I love you,

Mom

P.S. I did cry when we got home. So did your dad.

Countdown to College

As you start making your college plans, here's a schedule of what you need to do, and when you need to do it.

GRADE 9: FALL

- Meet with your guidance counselor. Talk about what you should be doing to help you make the most out of high school.
- Sign up for extracurricular activities. They'll help take your mind off all that classroom stress, give you something fun to do, and, besides, they look great on college applications.

GRADE 9: SPRING

- Talk to your guidance counselor about this past year. Discuss your strengths and weaknesses, and plan next year's schedule.
- Get some friends together and go to a college fair. But don't go with a "big agenda"; just go to look around. Afterward, go out for Cokes and talk about the experience.

GRADE 10: FALL

- Register for and take the PLAN (a preliminary version of the ACT); the PSAT (a preliminary version of the SAT). Or take the "real thing" (ACT or SAT), just for experience.
- Ask your guidance counselor about early admissions options and what you need to do to qualify.

GRADE 10: SPRING

- If you haven't done it already, talk to your guidance counselor about your college plans.
- Finalize your junior-year courses, keeping in mind college entrance requirements in foreign languages, math, English, science, etc.
- Consider taking some Advanced Placement courses that could earn you college credit.
- Attend a college fair to get some idea of what you might be looking for in a college.

11

GRADE 11: SUMMER

• Find a job to help earn money for college.

GRADE 11: FALL

• Study hard! College admissions officers want to see your grades stay strong throughout high school.

• Register for and take the PLAN and/or PSAT, even if you took it last year. Juniors with the highest scores in their state may be eligible for National Merit Scholarships.

• Start sorting all the mail you're getting from colleges. Keep a file of places that interest you the most.

• Consult the college and university listings at the back of this book, various other college directories at your guidance counselor's office, online sites, and college software to get more information on specific schools.

• If you haven't already been, check out a college fair.

GRADE 11: WINTER

• Decide where you'd like your ACT/SAT scores sent. Include any colleges you think you'd like to attend.

• Decide when you'll take the SAT and/or ACT. If you plan to take either in the spring, register now.

• Narrow your list of colleges to your Top 10.

GRADE 11: SPRING

• Take the SAT and/or ACT, and any Advanced Placement tests you might need.

• Once you get your SAT or ACT scores, meet with your guidance counselor to discuss which of your selected schools you've qualified for.

• Finalize your senior-year class schedule. Include courses that continue to prepare you for college.

• Visit the campuses of colleges you're most interested in.

12

GRADE 12: SUMMER

- Contact your Top 10 schools and request information. Even if you've already received their catalogs, you'll want to make sure you have the most current information.
- Continue to sort, file, and organize materials from various schools.
- Make a list of your extracurricular activities.
- Write down what you think will be your strengths and weaknesses as a college student. This will help when you answer essay questions on your college applications and interview with college admissions officials.
- Keep working hard and saving your money!

GRADE 12: FALL

- Keep your grades up. This is no time to coast.
- Narrow your list of "choice schools" down to your Top 5—or less.
- Ask selected adults (teacher, guidance counselor, pastor, boss) to fill out any required recommendation forms from the colleges.
- Write first drafts of your application essay. Ask your parents and a teacher to read it and give their suggestions.
- Take the SAT and/or ACT, if you haven't already. Or consider taking either test again if you weren't satisfied with your earlier scores.
- Find out test dates for any other exams required by the schools you're interested in, and sign up.
- Send in any early admission applications and transcripts, often due in November.
- Start work on the remaining applications.
- Continue visiting college campuses. Attend classes and stay in the dorms when possible.

GRADE 12: WINTER

- Finish the rest of your college applications, usually due between January 1 and March 1.
- Fill out the Free Application for Federal Student Aid (FAFSA) as soon after January 1 as possible. Complete all other needed financial-aid forms.

GRADE 12: SPRING

- Once you start receiving acceptance letters from colleges, decide which school you'll attend and notify all other applied-to schools by May 1.
- Meet all application and payment deadlines as required by the college admissions office.

Congratulations! You're now ready for college!

Colleges & Universities

All of the information in this list was submitted by college admissions departments.
The information was accurate at the time of printing.
To get the most current information, contact the colleges.

ABILENE CHRISTIAN UNIVERSITY

ACU Box 29000
Abilene, Texas 79699

Admissions department information:
Phone: (915) 674-2650 Fax: (915) 674-2130
E-mail: info@admissions.acu.edu
Web Site: http://www.acu.edu

Founded: 1906

Affiliation: Church of Christ

1996–1997 freshman admission statistics:
Number applied: 2,056 Number accepted: 993

Tests required: SAT or ACT

Total undergraduate enrollment: 1,829 men; 1,925 women

Faculty/student ratio: 1:18

Most popular majors: Biology, business, education, journalism,
religion studies

Setting: Urban

1997–98 expenses: Tuition: $8,730 Room & board: $3,810

Financial aid:
% of students receiving aid: 70% Average annual aid received: $8,700

ALASKA BIBLE COLLEGE

P.O. Box 289
Glennallen, Alaska 99588
Admissions department information:
 Phone: (907) 822-3201 Fax: (907) 822-5027
 E-mail: akbibcol@alaska.net
Founded: 1966
Affiliation: Interdenominational
1996–1997 freshman admission statistics:
 Number applied: 25 Number accepted: 20
Tests required: SAT or ACT
Total undergraduate enrollment: 20 men; 12 women
Faculty/student ratio: 1:4
Most popular majors: Pastoral studies, camping, Christian ed.,
 integrated studies, missions
Setting: Rural
1997–98 expenses: Tuition: $3,300 Room & board: $3,400
Financial aid:
 % of students receiving aid: 90% Average annual aid received: $700–$800

ALDERSON-BROADDUS COLLEGE

College Hill
Philippi, West Virginia 26416
Admissions department information:
 Phone: (304) 457-1700 Fax: (304) 457-6239
 E-mail: Admissions@AB.edu Web Site: http://www.Mountain.Net/AB
Founded: 1871
Affiliation: American Baptist
1996–1997 freshman admission statistics:
 Number applied: 693 Number accepted: 426
Tests required: SAT or ACT
Total undergraduate enrollment: 280 men; 412 women
Faculty/student ratio: 1:13
Most popular majors: Physician asst., nursing, education, music, liberal arts
Setting: Rural
1997–98 expenses: Tuition: $12,215 Room & board: $4,165
Financial aid:
 % of students receiving aid: 95% Average annual aid received: $4,200

AMERICAN BAPTIST COLLEGE
1800 Baptist World Center Dr.
Nashville, Tennessee 37207
Admissions department information:
Phone: (615) 228-7877   Fax: (615) 226-7855
Founded: 1924
Affiliation: Baptist
1996–1997 freshman admission statistics:
Number applied: 40   Number accepted: 29
Total undergraduate enrollment: 119 men; 35 women
Most popular majors: A.A., B.A. and B.T.
Setting: Urban
1997–98 expenses: Tuition: $1,265   Room & board: $514
Financial aid:
% of students receiving aid: 20%
Average annual aid received: $2,470

ANDERSON UNIVERSITY
1100 East 5th St.
Anderson, Indiana 46012
Admissions department information:
Phone: 1-800-428-6414   Fax: (765) 641-3851
E-mail: Info@Anderson.edu
Web Site: http://www.Anderson.edu
Founded: 1917
Affiliation: Church of God (Anderson, IN)
1996–97 freshman admission statistics:
Number applied: 1,836   Number accepted: 1,028
Tests required: SAT or ACT
Total undergraduate enrollment: 967 men; 1,284 women
Faculty/student ratio: 1:14
Most popular majors: Music, education, business, nursing, communications
Setting: Suburban
1997–98 expenses: Tuition: $12,500 Room & board: $4,150
Financial aid:
% of students receiving aid: 80%
Average annual aid received: $11,000

ARIZONA BIBLE COLLEGE

1718 W. Maryland
Phoenix, Arizona 85015
Admissions department information:
    Phone: 1-800-847-2138   Fax: (602) 242-1992
Affiliation: Nondenominational
1996–1997 freshman admission statistics:
    Number applied: 50   Number accepted: 42
Tests required: ACT
Total undergraduate enrollment: 75 men; 75 women
Faculty/student ratio: 1:8
Most popular majors: Pastoral, elementary ed, cross-cultural,
    youth ministry, music
Setting: Urban
1997–98 expenses: Tuition: $5,950   Room & board: $1,728
Financial aid:
    % of students receiving aid: 85%
    Average annual aid received: n/a

ARLINGTON BAPTIST COLLEGE

3001 W. Division
Arlington, Texas 76012
Admissions department information:
    Phone: (817) 461-8741   Fax: (817) 274-1138
Founded: 1939
Affiliation: Baptist
1996–1997 freshman admission statistics:
    Number applied: 95   Number accepted: 95
Total undergraduate enrollment: 115 men; 85 women
Faculty/student ratio: 1:17
Most popular majors: Pastoral ministry, education, general studies,
    youth ministry, missions
Setting: Urban
1997–98 expenses: Tuition: $2,650 Room & board: $1,700
Financial aid:
    % of students receiving aid: 52%
    Average annual aid received: $2,411

Asbury College

1 Macklem Dr.
Wilmore, Kentucky 40390
Admissions department information:
Phone: (606) 858-3511   Fax: (606) 858-3921
E-mail: admissions@asbury.edu   Web Site: http://www.asbury.edu
Founded: 1890
Affiliation: Interdenominational
1996–1997 freshman admission statistics:
Number applied: 762   Number accepted: 295
Tests required: SAT or ACT
Total undergraduate enrollment: 488 men; 679 women
Faculty/student ratio: 1:14
Most popular majors: Education, psychology, accounting/business
management, broadcast media, Christian ministries
Setting: Rural
1997–98 expenses: Tuition: $11,100   Room & board: $3,150
Financial aid:
% of students receiving aid: 82%   Average annual aid received: $7,000

Atlantic Union College

P.O. Box 1000, 338 Main St.
South Lancaster, Massachusetts 01561
Admissions department information:
Phone: (508) 368-2255   Fax: (508) 368-2015
E-mail: enroll@atlanticuc.edu   Web Site: http://www.atlanticuc.edu
Founded: 1882
Affiliation: Seventh-Day Adventist
1996–1997 freshman admission statistics:
Number applied: 428   Number accepted: 203
Tests required: SAT or ACT
Total undergraduate enrollment: 200 men; 463 women
Faculty/student ratio: 1:10
Most popular majors: Nursing, psychology, business, education, English
Setting: Rural
1997–98 expenses: Tuition: $11,330   Room & board: $3,900
Financial aid:
% of students receiving aid: 97%   Average annual aid received: $9,000

AZUSA PACIFIC UNIVERSITY

901 E. Alosta Ave.

Azusa, California 91702

Admissions department information:

Phone: 1-800-TALK-APU or (818) 812-3016   Fax: (818) 812-3096

E-mail: admissions@apu.edu

Web Site: http://www.apu.edu

Founded: 1899

Affiliation: Interdenominational

1996–1997 freshman admission statistics:

Number applied: 1,271   Number accepted: 1,111

Tests required: SAT or ACT

Total undergraduate enrollment: 950 men; 1,525 women

Faculty/student ratio: 1:15

Most popular majors: Nursing, music, business, liberal studies, psychology

Setting: Urban

1997–98 expenses: Tuition: $13,550   Room & board: $4,482

Financial aid:

% of students receiving aid: 82%   Average annual aid received: $12,000

BAPTIST BIBLE COLLEGE

628 E. Kearney

Springfield, Missouri 65803

Admissions department information:

Phone: (417) 268-6013   Fax: (417) 268-6694

E-mail: bbc@ncsi.net   Web Site: http://www.seebbc.edu

Founded: 1950

Affiliation: Baptist

1996–1997 freshman admission statistics:

Number applied: 434   Number accepted: 433

Tests required: ACT

Total undergraduate enrollment: 476 men; 389 women

Faculty/student ratio: 1:22

Most popular majors: Missions, pastors, youth, elementary ed, church music

Setting: Urban

1997–98 expenses: Tuition: $1,082–$1,233   Room & board: $1,607

Financial aid:

% of students receiving aid: 88%   Average annual aid received: $2,940

BAPTIST BIBLE COLLEGE

P.O. Box 800
Clarks Summit, Pennsylvania 18411
Admissions department information:
　Phone: 1-800-451-7664 or (717) 586-2400　Fax: (717) 586-1753
　E-mail: admissions@bbc.edu　Web Site: http://www.bbc.edu
Founded: 1932
Affiliation: General Association of Regular Baptist Churches
1996–1997 freshman admission statistics:
　Number applied: 314　Number accepted: 233
Tests required: SAT or ACT
Total undergraduate enrollment: 215 men; 325 women
Faculty/student ratio: 1:15
Most popular majors:
　Elementary ed., youth pastor, pastoral, counseling, missions
Setting: Suburban
1997–98 expenses: Tuition: $6,750　Room & board: $4,534
Financial aid:
　% of students receiving aid: 85%　Average annual aid received: n/a

BARCLAY COLLEGE

P.O. Box 288
Haviland, Kansas 67059
Admissions department information:
　Phone: 1-800-862-0226　Fax: (316) 862-5403
Founded: 1917
Affiliation: Interdenominational
1996–1997 freshman admission statistics:
　Number applied: 71　Number accepted: 70
Tests required: SAT or ACT
Total undergraduate enrollment: 52 men; 62 women
Faculty/student ratio: 1:11
Most popular majors: Pastoral ministries, youth ministries, business
　administration, teacher education for Christian schools, psychology
Setting: Rural
1997–98 expenses: Tuition: $4,400　Room & board: $2,900
Financial aid:
　% of students receiving aid: 95%　Average annual aid received: $5,604

BARTLESVILLE WESLEYAN COLLEGE

2201 Silver Lake Rd.

Bartlesville, Oklahoma 74006

Admissions department information:

Phone: 1-800-468-6292   Fax: (918) 335-6229

E-mail: Gotobwc@aol.com

Founded: 1909

Affiliation: Wesleyan Church

1996–1997 freshman admission statistics:

Number applied: 285   Number accepted: 140

Tests required: SAT or ACT

Faculty/student ratio: 1:14

Most popular majors: Education, business, pastoral ministries, MHR, nursing

Setting: Suburban

1997–98 expenses: Tuition: $7,800   Room & board: $3,700

Financial aid:

% of students receiving aid: 90%

Average annual aid received: $4,000

BAYLOR UNIVERSITY

P.O. Box 97056

Waco, Texas 76798

Admissions department information:

Phone: 1-800-BAYLOR-U or (817) 755-1811   Fax: (817) 755-3436

Web Site: http://www.baylor.edu

Founded: 1845

Affiliation: Baptist

1996–1997 freshman admission statistics:

Number applied: 6,791;   Number accepted: 2,476

Tests required: SAT or ACT

Total undergraduate enrollment: 4,565 men; 5,935 women

Faculty/student ratio: 1:18

Most popular majors: Pre-business, biology, psychology, interdisciplinary
studies (education), accounting

Setting: Urban

1997–98 expenses: Tuition: $8,640   Room & board: $4,483

Financial aid:

% of students receiving aid: 75%   Average annual aid received: n/a

BELHAVEN COLLEGE

1500 Peachtree St.

Jackson, Mississippi 39202

Admissions department information:

Phone: (601) 968-5940   Fax: (601) 968-9998

Founded: 1883

Affiliation: Presbyterian

1996–1997 freshman admission statistics:

Number applied: 498   Number accepted: 381

Tests required: SAT or ACT

Total undergraduate enrollment: 483 men; 725 women

Faculty/student ratio: 1:17

Most popular majors: Business administration, education, computer science, biology, psychology

Setting: Urban

1997–98 expenses: Tuition: $8,990   Room & board: $3,380

Financial aid:

% of students receiving aid: 92%   Average annual aid received: $6,820

BETHANY BIBLE COLLEGE

26 Western St.

Sussex, New Brunswick, Canada   E0E 1P0

Admissions department information:

Phone: 1-888-432-4422   Fax: (506) 432-4425

E-mail: jasteppe@nbnct.nb.ca

Web Site: http://www.bethany-ca.edu

Founded: 1945

Affiliation: Wesleyan

1996–1997 freshman admission statistics:

Number applied: 166   Number accepted: 114

Total undergraduate enrollment: 92 men; 85 women

Faculty/student ratio: 1:17

Most popular majors: Pastoral ministry, global ministry, music ministry, youth ministry, Christian school ed.

Setting: Rural

1997–98 expenses: Tuition: $4,900   Room & board: $4,100

Financial aid:

% of students receiving aid: 95%   Average annual aid received: $1,117

BETHANY COLLEGE

800 Bethany Dr.
Scotts Valley, California 95066
Admissions department information:
Phone: 1-800-843-9410   Fax: (408) 461-1533
Web Site: http://www.bethany.edu
Founded: 1919
Affiliation: Assemblies of God
1996–1997 freshman admission statistics:
Number applied: 359   Number accepted: 231
Tests required: SAT or ACT
Total undergraduate enrollment: 170 men; 209 women
Faculty/student ratio: 1:16
Most popular majors: Church leadership, teacher education, English,
business, psychology
Setting: Rural
1997–98 expenses: Tuition: $8,930   Room & board: $4,190
Financial aid:
% of students receiving aid: 92%   Average annual aid received: n/a

BETHANY COLLEGE

421 N. First St.
Lindsborg, Kansas 67042
Admissions department information:
Phone: 1-800-826-2281   Fax: (785) 227-2004
Founded: 1881
Affiliation: Lutheran
1996–1997 freshman admission statistics:
Number applied: 1,050   Number accepted: 223
Tests required: SAT or ACT
Total undergraduate enrollment: 364 men; 334 women
Faculty/student ratio: 1:13
Most popular majors: Education, business, pre-professional,
criminal justice, physical ed/recreation
Setting: Rural
1997–98 expenses: Tuition: $10,540   Room & board: $3,290
Financial aid:
% of students receiving aid: 91%   Average annual aid received: $6,400

BETHANY COLLEGE

Bethany, West Virginia 26032
Admissions department information:
Phone: 1-800-922-7611   Fax: (304) 829-7142
E-mail: admission@bethanywv.edu
Web Site: http://www.info.bethany.wvnet.edu
Founded: 1840
Affiliation: Disciples of Christ
1996–1997 freshman admission statistics:
Number applied: 870   Number accepted: 615
Tests required: SAT or ACT
Total undergraduate enrollment: 394 men; 354 women
Faculty/student ratio: 1:12
Most popular majors: Communication, economics, biology, political science, education
Setting: Rural
1997–98 expenses: Tuition: $17,022   Room & board: $5,700

BETHANY COLLEGE OF MISSIONS

6820 Auto Club Rd.
Minneapolis, Minnesota 55438
Admissions department information:
Phone: 1-800-328-3417   Fax: (612) 827-7535
E-mail: bcom@bethFel.org
Founded: 1945
Affiliation: Interdenominational
1996–1997 freshman admission statistics:
Number applied: 80   Number accepted: 66
Tests required: SAT or ACT
Total undergraduate enrollment: 62 men; 89 women
Faculty/student ratio: 1:15
Most popular major: Cross-cultural studies
Setting: Suburban
1997–98 expenses: Tuition: Paid   Room & board: Paid
Financial aid:
% of students receiving aid: 100%   Average annual aid received: $8,700

BETHANY LUTHERAN COLLEGE
734 Marsh St.
Mankato, Minnesota 56001
Admissions department information:
Phone: (507) 386-5331   Fax: (507) 386-5376
E-mail: admissions@blc.edu   Web Site: http://www.blc.edu
Founded: 1927
Affiliation: Lutheran/ELS
1996–1997 freshman admission statistics:
Number applied: 313   Number accepted: 260
Tests required: SAT or ACT
Total undergraduate enrollment: 48% men; 52% women
Faculty/student ratio: 1:13
Most popular majors: Education, business, music, health-related careers
Setting: Urban
1997–98 expenses: Tuition: $8,750   Room & board: $3,660
Financial aid:
% of students receiving aid: 93%   Average annual aid received: $9,300

BETHEL COLLEGE
1001 W. McKinley Ave.
Mishawaka, Indiana 46545
Admissions department information:
Phone: (219) 257-3339   Fax: (219) 257-3326
E-mail: admissions@bethel-in.edu   Web Site: http://www.bethel-in.edu
Founded: 1947
Affiliation: Missionary Church, Inc.
1996–1997 freshman admission statistics:
Number applied: 615 Number accepted: 376
Tests required: SAT or ACT
Total undergraduate enrollment: 541 men; 928 women
Faculty/student ratio: 1:18
Most popular majors: Education, nursing, business, American sign
language/English interpreting
Setting: Suburban
1997–98 expenses: Tuition: $11,100   Room & board: $3,500
Financial aid:
% of students receiving aid: 85%   Average annual aid received: n/a

BETHEL COLLEGE
300 E. 27th St.
North Newton, Kansas 67117
Admissions department information:
    Phone: 1-800-522-1887   Fax: (316) 284-5286
    E-mail: admissions@bethelks.edu   Web Site: http://www.bethelks.edu
Founded: 1887
Affiliation: Mennonite
1996–1997 freshman admission statistics:
    Number applied: 419   Number accepted: 374
Tests required: SAT or ACT
Total undergraduate enrollment: 248 men; 372 women
Faculty/student ratio: 1:11
Most popular majors: Nursing, education, social work, business, English
Setting: Suburban
1997–98 expenses: Tuition: $10,290   Room & board: $4,200
Financial aid:
    % of students receiving aid: 90%   Average annual aid received: $3,500

BETHEL COLLEGE
3900 Bethel Dr.
St. Paul, Minnesota 55112
Admissions department information:
    Phone: 1-800-255-8706 ext. 6242; Fax: (612) 635-1490
    E-mail: bcoll-admit@bethel.edu   Web Site: http://www.bethel.edu/
Founded: 1871
Affiliation: Baptist General Conference
1996–1997 freshman admission statistics:
    Number applied: 1,372   Number accepted: 1,107
Tests required: SAT & ACT
Total undergraduate enrollment: 788 men; 1,251 women
Faculty/student ratio: 1:16
Most popular majors: Education, business, biology, nursing, biblical &
    theological studies
Setting: Suburban
1997–98 expenses: Tuition: $13,840   Room & board: $4,950
Financial aid:
    % of students receiving aid: 90%   Average annual aid received: $10,000

BIOLA UNIVERSITY
13800 Biola Ave.
La Mirada, California 90639
Admissions department information:
  Phone: (562) 903-4752   Fax: (562) 903-4709
  E-mail: admissions@biola.edu   Web Site: http://www.biola.edu/
Founded: 1908
Affiliation: Interdenominational
1996–1997 freshman admission statistics:
  Number applied: 1,643   Number accepted: 1,255
Tests required: SAT or ACT
Total undergraduate enrollment: 811 men; 1,226 women
Faculty/student ratio: 1:17
Most popular majors: Communication, liberal studies, business, psychology,
  nursing
Setting: Suburban
1997–98 expenses: Tuition: $14,286   Room & board: $4,851
Financial aid:
  % of students receiving aid: 80%   Average annual aid received: $7,088

BLUE MOUNTAIN COLLEGE
201 W. Main St.
Blue Mountain, Mississippi 38610
Admissions department information:
  Phone: (601) 685-4161   Fax: (601) 685-4776
Founded: 1873
Affiliation: Southern Baptist
1996–1997 freshman admission statistics:
  Number applied: 85   Number accepted: 85
Tests required: SAT or ACT
Total undergraduate enrollment: 70 men; 347 women
Faculty/student ratio: 1:15
Most popular majors: Elementary ed., secondary ed., church-related
  vocations, biology/chemistry, social science
Setting: Rural
1997–98 expenses: Tuition: $4,640   Room & board: $2,350
Financial aid:
  % of students receiving aid: 90%   Average annual aid received: n/a

BLUFFTON COLLEGE
280 W. College Ave.
Bluffton, Ohio 45817
Admissions department information:
    Phone: 1-800-488-3257   Fax: (419) 358-3232
    E-mail: admissions@bluffton.edu   Web Site: http://www.bluffton.edu
Founded: 1899
Affiliation: Mennonite Church
1996–1997 freshman admission statistics:
    Number applied: 556   Number accepted: 497
Tests required: SAT or ACT
Total undergraduate enrollment: 495 men; 570 women
Faculty/student ratio: 1:15
Most popular majors: Business, education, criminal justice, fine arts, math
Setting: Rural
1997–98 expenses: Tuition: $11,835   Room & board: $4,872
Financial aid:
    % of students receiving aid: 100%   Average annual aid received: $8,961

BOB JONES UNIVERSITY
1700 Wade Hampton Blvd.
Greenville, South Carolina 29614
Admissions department information:
    Phone: 1-800-252-6363   Fax: 1-800-232-9258
    E-mail: admissions@bju.edu   Web Site: http://www.bju.edu
Founded: 1927
Affiliation: Protestant
1996–1997 freshman admission statistics:
    Number applied: 2,185   Number accepted: 1,759
Tests required: ACT
Total undergraduate enrollment: 1,545 men; 1,813 women
Faculty/student ratio: 1:11
Most popular majors: Elementary ed., accounting, guidance & counseling,
    Bible
Setting: Urban
1997–98 expenses: Tuition: $5,220   Room & board: $4,020
Financial aid:
    % of students receiving aid: 50%   Average annual aid received: n/a

BOISE BIBLE COLLEGE

8695 Marigold
Boise, Idaho 83714

Admissions department information:
Phone: 1-800-893-7755   Fax: (208) 376-7743
E-mail: boibible@micron.net

Founded: 1945

Affiliation: Nondenominational

1996–1997 freshman admission statistics:
Number applied: 94   Number accepted: 78

Tests required: SAT or ACT

Total undergraduate enrollment: 88 men; 59 women

Faculty/student ratio: 1:12

Most popular majors: Bible, ministry, Christian ed., music

Setting: Suburban

1997–98 expenses: Tuition: $2,170/semester   Room & board: $1,712/sem.

Financial aid:
% of students receiving aid: 90%   Average annual aid received: $3,500

BREWTON-PARKER COLLEGE

Highway 280
Mt. Vernon, Georgia 30445

Admissions department information:
Phone: (912) 583-3268   Fax: (912) 583-4498
Web Site: http://www.bpc.edu

Founded: 1904

Affiliation: Baptist

1996–1997 freshman admission statistics:
Number applied: 378   Number accepted: 378

Tests Required: None

Faculty/student ratio: 1:16

Most popular majors: Education, business, health sciences, psychology,
sociology

Setting: Rural

1997–98 expenses: Tuition: $5,265   Room & board: $2,565

Financial aid:
% of students receiving aid: 93%   Average annual aid received: n/a

BRIERCREST BIBLE COLLEGE

510 College Dr.
Caronport, Saskatchewan, Canada S0H 050
Admissions department information:
Phone: 1-800-667-5199 Fax: 1-800-667-2329
E-mail: enrollment@briercrest.ca Web Site: http://www.briercrest.ca
Founded: 1935
Affiliation: Nondenominational
1996–1997 freshman admission statistics:
Number applied: 602 Number accepted: 503
Tests required: None
Total undergraduate enrollment: 53% men; 47% women
Faculty/student ratio: 1:20
Most popular majors: Youth ministry, sports ministry, theology, worship
ministry, inter-cultural studies
Setting: Rural
1997–98 expenses: Tuition: $4,576/Canadian Room & board: $3,180/Can.
Financial aid:
% of students receiving aid: n/a Average annual aid received: n/a

BRYAN COLLEGE

P.O. Box 7000
Dayton, Tennessee 37321
Admissions department information:
Phone: (423) 775-7204 Fax: (423) 775-7199
E-mail: admiss@bryannet.bryan.edu Web Site: http://www.bryan.edu
Founded: 1930
Affiliation: Nondenominational
1996–1997 freshman admission statistics:
Number applied: 457 Number accepted: 291
Tests required: ACT
Total undergraduate enrollment: 216 men; 264 women
Faculty/student ratio: 1:14
Most popular majors: Education, business admin., psychology, biology,
communication arts
Setting: Rural
1997–98 expenses: Tuition: $9,700 Room & board: $3,950
Financial aid:
% of students receiving aid: 94% Average annual aid received: $9,950

CALIFORNIA BAPTIST COLLEGE

8432 Magnolia Ave.
Riverside, California 92504
Admissions department information:
Phone: (909) 343-4212   Fax: (909) 351-1808
E-mail: admissions@calbaptist.edu
Web Site: http://www.calbaptist.edu
Founded: 1950
Affiliation: Southern Baptist
1996–1997 freshman admission statistics:
Number applied: 538   Number accepted: 387
Tests required: SAT or ACT
Faculty/student ratio: 1:15
Most popular majors: Education (elementary/secondary), psychology,
business admin., biblical studies, kinesiology
Setting: Urban
1997–98 expenses: Tuition: $8,190   Room & board: $4,594
Financial aid:
% of students receiving aid: 85%   Average annual aid received: $3,500

CALVARY BIBLE COLLEGE & THEOLOGICAL SEMINARY

15800 Calvary Rd.
Kansas City, Missouri 64147
Admissions department information:
Phone: 1-800-326-3960   Fax: (816) 331-4474
E-mail: alum205@aol.com
Web Site: http://www.Calvary.edu
Founded: 1932
Affiliation: Interdenominational
1996–1997 freshman admission statistics:
Number applied: 450   Number accepted: 300
Tests required: SAT or ACT
Faculty/student ratio: 1:10
Most popular majors: Elementary ed., SC ed., counseling, pastoral studies,
aviation
Setting: Suburban
1997–98 expenses: Tuition: $150/credit hr.   Room & board: $875/semester
Financial aid:
% of students receiving aid: 80%   Average annual aid received: n/a

CALVIN COLLEGE
3201 Burton St. S.E.
Grand Rapids, Michigan 49546
Admissions department information:
Phone: (616) 957-6106   Fax: (616) 957-8551
E-mail: admissions@calvin.edu   Web Site: http://www.calvin.edu
Founded: 1876
Affiliation: Christian Reformed
1996–1997 freshman admission statistics:
Number applied: 1,847   Number accepted: 1,789
Tests required: SAT or ACT
Total undergraduate enrollment: 1,771 men; 2,222 women
Faculty/student ratio: 1:16
Most popular majors: Business, education, biology, English, psychology
Setting: Suburban
1997–98 expenses: Tuition: $12,225   Room & board: $4,340
Financial aid:
% of students receiving aid: 90%   Average annual aid received: $7,460

CAMPBELL UNIVERSITY
P.O. Box 546
Buies Creek, North Carolina 27506
Admissions department information:
Phone: 1-800-334-4111   Fax: (910) 893-1280
E-mail: Satterfi@mailcenter.campbell.edu
Web Site: http://www.campbell.edu
Founded: 1887
Affiliation: Baptist
1996–1997 freshman admission statistics:
Number applied: 1,818   Number accepted: 1,098
Tests required: SAT or ACT
Total undergraduate enrollment: 912 men; 1,261 women
Faculty/student ratio: 1:18
Most popular majors: Mass communications, business, education, pre-law, biology
Setting: Rural
1997–98 expenses: Tuition: n/a   Room & board: n/a
Financial aid:
% of students receiving aid: 84%   Average annual aid received: $6,000

CAMPBELLSVILLE UNIVERSITY
1 University Dr.
Campbellsville, Kentucky 42718
Admissions department information:
Phone: (502) 789-5220   Fax: (502) 789-5050
E-mail: admissions@campbellsvil.edu
Web Site: http://www.campbellsvil.edu
Founded: 1906
Affiliation: Southern Baptist
1996–1997 freshman admission statistics:
Number applied: 1,262   Number accepted: 830
Tests required: SAT or ACT
Total undergraduate enrollment: 653 men; 812 women
Faculty/student ratio: 1:16
Most popular majors: Education, business administration
Setting: Rural
1997–98 expenses: Tuition: $7,200   Room & board: $3,610
Financial aid:
% of students receiving aid: 91%   Average annual aid received: n/a

CANADIAN BIBLE COLLEGE
4400 4th Ave.
Regina, Saskatchewan, Canada S4T 0H8
Admissions department information:
Phone: (306) 545-1515 Fax: (306) 545-0210
E-mail: admissions@CBCCTS.SK.CA
Web Site: http://www.CBCCTS.SK.CA
Founded: 1941
Affiliation: Christian & Missionary Alliance
1996–1997 freshman admission statistics:
Number applied: 278   Number accepted: 201
Total undergraduate enrollment: 220 men; 173 women
Faculty/student ratio: 1:18.7
Most popular majors: Access program, BT, BRE, youth ministry,
BA in religion, BRE/missions
Setting: Suburban
1997–98 expenses: Tuition: $4,400/Canadian   Room & board: $3,556/Can.
Financial aid:
% of students receiving aid: 22%   Average annual aid received: $1,181

CAPITAL UNIVERSITY

2199 E. Main St.
Columbus, Ohio 43209
Admissions department information:
Phone: (614) 236-6101   Fax: (614) 236-6820
E-mail: admissions@capital.edu
Web Site: http://www.capital.edu
Founded: 1830
Affiliation: Lutheran/ELCA
1996–1997 freshman admission statistics:
Number applied: 1,932   Number accepted: 1,604
Tests required: SAT or ACT
Total undergraduate enrollment: 689 men; 1,141 women
Faculty/student ratio: 1:13
Most popular majors: Nursing, education, music, business, political science
Setting: Suburban
1997–98 expenses: Tuition: $14,760   Room & board: $4,200
Financial aid:
% of students receiving aid: 90%   Average annual aid received: $11,000

CARSON-NEWMAN COLLEGE

1646 Russell Ave., P.O. Box 72025
Jefferson City, Tennessee 37760
Admissions department information:
Phone: (423) 471-3223   Fax: (423) 471-3502
E-mail: SGray@cncadm.cn.edu   Web Site: http://www.cn.edu
Founded: 1851
Affiliation: Baptist
1996–1997 freshman admission statistics:
Number applied: 1,176   Number accepted: 970
Tests required: SAT or ACT
Total undergraduate enrollment: 872 men; 1,188 women
Faculty/student ratio: 1:13
Most popular majors: Education, biology, communication arts, psychology
Setting: Rural
1997–98 expenses: Tuition: $9,540   Room & board: $3,670
Financial aid:
% of students receiving aid: 90%   Average annual aid received: $8,000

CEDARVILLE COLLEGE

P.O. Box 601
Cedarville, Ohio 45314-0601
Admissions department information:
  Phone: (937) 766-7700   Fax: (937) 766-7575
  E-mail: admissions@cedarville.edu   Web Site: http://www.cedarville.edu
Founded: 1887
Affiliation: Baptist
1996–1997 freshman admission statistics:
  Number applied: 1,872   Number accepted: 1,511
Tests required: SAT or ACT
Total undergraduate enrollment: 1,147 men; 1,362 women
Faculty/student ratio: 1:19
Most popular majors: Education, business, science, engineering, nursing
Setting: Rural
1997–98 expenses: Tuition: $9,168   Room & board: $4,716
Financial aid:
  % of students receiving aid: 87.4%   Average annual aid received: $6,636

CENTRAL BAPTIST COLLEGE

1501 College Ave.
Conway, Arkansas 72032
Admissions department information:
  Phone: 1-800-205-6872   Fax: (501) 329-2941
  E-mail: gmcallister@admin.cbc.edu
Founded: 1952
Affiliation: Baptist Missionary Association of Arkansas
1996–1997 freshman admission statistics:
  Number applied: 137   Number accepted: 119
Tests required: ACT
Total undergraduate enrollment: 152 men; 131 women
Faculty/student ratio: 1:16
Most popular majors: AA general ed., BA Bible, BS Bible, AA education,
  AA science
Setting: Suburban
1997–98 expenses: Tuition: $4,176   Room & board: $3,032
Financial aid:
  % of students receiving aid: 98%   Average annual aid received: n/a

CENTRAL BIBLE COLLEGE
3000 N. Grant
Springfield, Missouri 65803
Admissions department information:
Phone: (417) 833-2551   Fax: (417) 833-5141
Founded: 1922
Affiliation: Assemblies of God
1996–1997 freshman admission statistics:
Number applied: 291   Number accepted: 289
Tests required: ACT
Total undergraduate enrollment: 556 men; 420 women
Faculty/student ratio: 1:17
Most popular majors: Biblical studies, pastoral ministry, missions, youth ministry, sacred music
Setting: Suburban
1997–98 expenses: Tuition: $148/semester hr. Room & board: $1,600/sem.
Financial aid:
% of students receiving aid: 63%   Average annual aid received: n/a

CENTRAL CHRISTIAN COLLEGE OF THE BIBLE
911 Urbandale Dr. E.
Moberly, Missouri 65270
Admissions department information:
Phone: (816) 263-3900   Fax: (816) 263-3936
E-mail: iwant2be@cccb.edu   Web Site: http://www.cccb.edu
Founded: 1957
Affiliation: Nondenominational
1996–1997 freshman admission statistics:
Number applied: 106   Number accepted: 74
Tests required: SAT or ACT
Total undergraduate enrollment: 68 men; 61 women
Faculty/student ratio: 1:13
Most popular majors: Preaching, youth ministry, Christian music, Christian ed., counseling
Setting: Urban
1997–98 expenses: Tuition: $115/credit hr.
Room & board: $1,280 double/semester — $1,600 single/semester
Financial aid:
% of students receiving aid: 98%   Average annual aid received: $4,113

CHARLESTON SOUTHERN UNIVERSITY

P.O. Box 118087

Charleston, South Carolina 29423-8087

Admissions department information:

Phone: 1-800-947-7474 or (803) 863-7050   Fax: (803) 863-7070

E-mail: enroll@csuniv.edu   Web Site: http://www.csuniv.edu

Founded: 1964

Affiliation: Southern Baptist

1996–1997 freshman admission statistics:

Number applied: 1,088   Number accepted: 973

Tests required: SAT or ACT

Faculty/student ratio: 1:17

Most popular majors: Business, education, nursing, religion/youth ministry, psychology

Setting: Suburban

1997–98 expenses: Tuition: $9,248   Room & board: $3,562

Financial aid: % of students receiving aid: 90%

Average annual aid received: $8,499/residents — $7,525/nonresidents

CHOWAN COLLEGE

P.O. Box 1848

Murfreesboro, North Carolina 27855

Admissions department information:

Phone: 1-800-488-4101   Fax: (919) 398-1190

E-mail: admissions@micah.chowan.edu   Web Site: http://www.chowan.edu

Founded: 1848

Affiliation: Baptist

1996–1997 freshman admission statistics:

Number applied: 1,018   Number accepted: 907

Tests required: SAT or ACT

Total undergraduate enrollment: 396 men; 340 women

Faculty/student ratio: 1:12

Most popular majors: Business administration, printing production and imaging technology, graphic design, education, biology

Setting: Rural

1997–98 expenses: Tuition: $10,760   Room & board: $4,170

Financial aid:

% of students receiving aid: 100%   Average annual aid received: $8,100

Christian Heritage College

2100 Greenfield Dr.
El Cajon, California 92019
Admissions department information:
Phone: 1-800-676-2CHC   Fax: (619) 440-0209
E-mail: chcinfo@1sat.com
Web Site: http://www.christianheritage.edu
Founded: 1970
Affiliation: Nondenominational
1996–1997 freshman admission statistics:
Number applied: 225   Number accepted: 186
Tests required: SAT
Total undergraduate enrollment: 229 men; 331 women
Faculty/student ratio: 1:15
Most popular majors: Business administration, education, counseling,
psychology, Bible
Setting: Suburban
1997–98 expenses: Tuition: $9,670   Room & board: $4,326
Financial aid: % of students receiving aid: 95%
Average annual aid received: $3,000 w/o loans, federal or state aid

Cincinnati Bible College and Seminary

2700 Glenway Ave.
Cincinnati, Ohio 45204
Admissions department information:
Phone: (513) 244-8141   Fax: (513) 244-8140
E-mail: admissions@cincybible.edu
Web Site: http://www.cincybible.edu
Founded: 1924
Affiliation: Christian Churches / Churches of Christ
Tests required: SAT or ACT
Faculty/student ratio: 1:19
Most popular majors: Preaching ministry, youth min., urban & international
affairs, Christian education, primary/secondary ed.
Setting: Urban
1997–98 expenses: Tuition: $5,775   Room & board: $3,650
Financial aid:
% of students receiving aid: 80%   Average annual aid received: $4,000

CIRCLEVILLE BIBLE COLLEGE

P.O. Box 458
Circleville, Ohio 43113
Admissions department information:
  Phone: (614) 477-7701   Fax: (614) 477-7755
Founded: 1948
Affiliation: Churches of Christ in Christian Union
Tests required: ACT
Faculty/student ratio: 1:10
Most popular majors: Christian ministry, psychology, elementary ed.,
  chemical dependency counseling
Setting: Rural
1997–98 expenses:
  Tuition: $5,696   Room & board: $4,011
Financial aid:
  % of students receiving aid: 95%
  Average annual aid received: $7,500

CLEAR CREEK BAPTIST BIBLE COLLEGE

300 Clear Creek Rd.
Pineville, Kentucky 40977
Admissions department information:
  Phone: (606) 337-3196   Fax: (606) 337-2372
  E-mail: clearcreek@tcnet.net
  Web Site: http://www.ccbbc.edu
Founded: 1926
Affiliation: Southern Baptist
1996–1997 freshman admission statistics:
  Number applied: 65   Number accepted: 52
Total undergraduate enrollment: 125 men; 27 women
Faculty/student ratio: 1:12
Most popular majors: Bible
Setting: Rural
1997–98 expenses:
  Tuition: $2,420   Room & board: $2,480
Financial aid:
  % of students receiving aid: 91%
  Average annual aid received: $1,800

COLLEGE OF THE OZARKS

Point Lookout, Missouri 65726

Admissions department information:

Phone: (417) 334-6411 ext. 4219   Fax: (417) 335-2618

E-mail: admiss4@cofo.edu

Web Site: http://www.cofo.edu

Founded: 1906

Affiliation: Presbyterian (USA)

1996–1997 freshman admission statistics:

Number applied: 2,824   Number accepted: 388

Tests required: SAT or ACT

Total undergraduate enrollment: 716 men; 809 women

Faculty/student ratio: 1:14

Most popular majors: Business, biology, education, criminal justice, psychology

Setting: Rural

1997–98 expenses: Tuition: -0-   Room & board: $2,200

Financial aid:

% of students receiving aid: 100%   Average annual aid received: $13,260

COLORADO CHRISTIAN UNIVERSITY

180 S. Garrison St.

Lakewood, Colorado 80226

Admissions department information:

Phone: 1-800-44-FAITH or (303) 202-0100 ext. 120

Fax: (303) 238-2191

E-mail: admissions@ccu.edu

Web Site: http://www@ccu.edu

Founded: 1914

Affiliation: Nondenominational

Tests required: SAT or ACT

Faculty/student ratio: 1:18

Most popular majors: Education, business, psychology, youth ministry, biology

Setting: Suburban

1997–98 expenses: Tuition: $9,360   Room & board: $4,560

Financial aid:

Average annual aid received: $7,961

COLUMBIA BIBLE COLLEGE

2940 Clearbrook Rd.
Abbotsford, British Columbia, Canada V2T 7Z8
Admissions department information:
Phone: 1-800-283-0881 or (604) 853-3567 ext. 308
Fax: (604) 853-3063
Founded: 1936
Affiliation: Mennonite
1996–1997 freshman admission statistics:
Number applied: 200   Number accepted: 185
Total undergraduate enrollment: 185 men; 135 women
Faculty/student ratio: 1:20
Most popular majors: Youth work, missions, Biblical studies,
early childhood ed., caregiving
Setting: Urban
1997–98 expenses:
Tuition: $4,420/Canadian   Room & board: $3,880/Canadian

CONCORDIA COLLEGE

800 N. Columbia
Seward, Nebraska 68434
Admissions department information:
Phone: 1-800-535-5494   Fax: (402) 643-4073
E-mail: admiss@seward.ccsn.edu
Web Site: http://www.ccsn.edu/
Founded: 1894
Affiliation: Lutheran Church - Missouri Synod
1996–1997 freshman admission statistics:
Number applied: 654   Number accepted: 551
Tests required: SAT or ACT
Total undergraduate enrollment: 406 men; 507 women
Faculty/student ratio: 1:15
Most popular majors: Education, business, psychology, biology-life sciences,
visual & performing arts
Setting: Rural
1997–98 expenses: Tuition: $10,650   Room & board: $3,640
Financial aid:
% of students receiving aid: 98%   Average annual aid received: n/a

CONCORDIA COLLEGE

171 White Plains Rd.
Bronxville, New York 10708
Admissions department information:
Phone: (914) 337-9300 ext. 255   Fax: (914) 395-4500
E-mail: admission@concordia-ny.edu
Web Site: http://www.concordia-ny.edu
Founded: 1881
Affiliation: Lutheran Church - Missouri Synod
1996–1997 freshman admission statistics:
Number applied: 503   Number accepted: 407
Tests required: SAT or ACT
Total undergraduate enrollment: 227 men; 250 women
Faculty/student ratio: 1:10
Most popular majors: Education, business, biology, social work
Setting: Suburban
1997–98 expenses: Tuition: $11,990   Room & board: $5,550
Financial aid:
% of students receiving aid: 85%   Average annual aid received: $5,300

CONCORDIA UNIVERSITY

1530 Concordia West
Irvine, California 92612
Admissions department information:
Phone: (714) 854-8002 ext. 106   Fax: (714) 854-6854
E-mail: admission@cui.edu   Web Site: http://www.cui.edu
Founded: 1972
Affiliation: Lutheran Church - Missouri Synod
1996–1997 freshman admission statistics:
Number applied: 637   Number accepted: 527
Tests required: SAT or ACT
Total undergraduate enrollment: 216 men; 387 women
Faculty/student ratio: 1:18
Most popular majors: Business, religion studies, education,
biology, psychology
Setting: Suburban
1997–98 expenses: Tuition: $12,880   Room & board: $5,180
Financial aid:
% of students receiving aid: 70%   Average annual aid received: $6,000

CONCORDIA UNIVERSITY - WISCONSIN

12800 N. Lake Shore Dr.

Mequon, Wisconsin 53097

Admissions department information:

Phone: (414) 243-5700   Fax: (414) 243-4544

E-mail: kgasck@bach.cuw.edu   Web Site: http://www.cuw.edu

Founded: 1881

Affiliation: Lutheran Church - Missouri Synod

1996–1997 freshman admission statistics:

Number applied: 1,085   Number accepted: 793

Tests required: SAT or ACT

Total undergraduate enrollment: 52% men; 48% women

Faculty/student ratio: 1:17

Most popular majors: Education, liberal arts, physical therapy, occupational therapy, business

Setting: Suburban

1997–98 expenses: Tuition/Room & board: $15,200

Financial aid:

% of students receiving aid: 85%   Average annual aid received: $7,100

CORNERSTONE COLLEGE

1001 E Beltline N.E.

Grand Rapids, Michigan 49505

Admissions department information:

Phone: 1-800-787-9778   Fax: (616) 222-1400

E-mail: admissions@cornerstone.edu

Web Site: http://www.cornerstone.edu

Founded: 1941

Affiliation: Regular Baptist

1996–1997 freshman admission statistics:

Number applied: 754   Number accepted: 662

Tests required: SAT or ACT

Total undergraduate enrollment: 452 men; 566 women

Faculty/student ratio: 1:19

Most popular majors: Business, teacher ed., youth ministry, music, psychology

Setting: Suburban

1997–98 expenses: Tuition: $9,450   Room & board: $4,418

Financial aid:

% of students receiving aid: 90%   Average annual aid received: $7,300

COVENANT COLLEGE

Scenic Highway
Lookout Mountain, Georgia 30750
Admissions department information:
Phone: (706) 820-2398   Fax: (706) 820-0893
E-mail: admissions@covenant.edu   Web site: http://www.covenant.edu
Founded: 1955
Affiliation: Presbyterian Church in America
1996–1997 freshman admission statistics:
Number applied: 378   Number accepted: 372
Tests required: SAT or ACT
Total undergraduate enrollment: 304 men; 361 women
Faculty/student ratio: 1:14
Most popular majors: Education, sciences, social sciences, business, humanities
Setting: Suburban
1997–98 expenses: Tuition: $12,550   Room & Board: $3,960
Financial aid:
% of students receiving aid: 90%   Average annual aid received: $10,342

CRICHTON COLLEGE

6655 Winchester Rd.
Memphis, Tennessee 38115
Admissions department information:
Phone: (901) 367-3888   Fax: (901) 367-3883
Founded: 1944
Affiliation: Nondenominational
1996–1997 freshman admission statistics:
Number applied: 236   Number accepted: 171
Tests required: SAT or ACT
Total undergraduate enrollment: 44 men; 109 women
Faculty/student ratio: 1:15
Most popular majors: Teacher ed., business, organizational management,
psychology, biblical studies
Setting: Suburban
1997–98 expenses:
Tuition: $6,360   Room & board: $1,750 (room only)
Financial aid:
% of students receiving aid: 80%   Average annual aid received: $650

THE CRISWELL COLLEGE

4010 Gaston Ave.
Dallas, Texas 75246
Admissions department information:
Phone: (214) 821-5433   Fax: (214) 818-1310
E-mail: egrimm@criswell.edu
Web Site: http://www.criswell.edu
Founded: 1970
Affiliation: Southern Baptist
1996–1997 freshman admission statistics: n/a
Tests required: SAT or ACT
Total undergraduate enrollment: 251 men; 76 women
Faculty/student ratio: 1:15
Most popular majors: Counseling, pastoral
Setting: Urban
1997–98 expenses: Tuition: $3,090   Room & board: n/a
Financial aid:
% of students receiving aid: 62%   Average annual aid received: $616

CROWN COLLEGE

6425 Co. Rd. 30
St. Bonifacius, Minnesota 55375
Admissions department information:
Phone: (612) 446-4142 Fax: (612) 446-4149
E-mail: Info@gw.crown.edu
Web Site: http://www.crown.edu
Founded: 1916
Affiliation: Christian & Missionary Alliance
1996–1997 freshman admission statistics:
Number applied: 448   Number accepted: 430
Tests required: SAT or ACT
Total undergraduate enrollment: 158 men; 270 women
Faculty/student ratio: 1:14
Most popular majors: Business, teacher ed., youth ministry, music
Setting: Suburban
1997–98 expenses: Tuition: $8,640   Room & board: $4,020
Financial aid:
% of students receiving aid: 92%   Average annual aid received: $8,800

CUMBERLAND COLLEGE
6178 College Station Dr.
Williamsburg, Kentucky 40769
Admissions department information:
Phone: 1-800-343-1609   Fax: (606) 539-4303
E-mail: adruss@cc.cumber.edu
Web Site: http://www.cumber.edu
Founded: 1889
Affiliation: Kentucky Baptist Convention
1996–1997 freshman admission statistics:
Number applied: 1,111   Number accepted: 709
Tests required: SAT or ACT
Total undergraduate enrollment: 727 men; 887 women
Faculty/student ratio: 1:15
Most popular majors: Education, biology, business, psychology, chemistry
Setting: Rural
1997–98 expenses: Tuition: $8,430   Room & board: $3,776
Financial aid:
% of students receiving aid: 86%   Average annual aid received: $8,397

DALLAS BAPTIST UNIVERSITY
3000 Mountain Creek Pkwy.
Dallas, Texas 75211
Admissions department information:
Phone: (214) 333-5360   Fax: (214) 333-5447
E-mail: admiss@dbu.edu   Web Site: http://www.dbu.edu
Founded: 1965
Affiliation: Southern Baptist
1996–1997 freshman admission statistics:
Number applied: 388   Number accepted: 342
Tests required: SAT or ACT
Total undergraduate enrollment: 1,102 men; 1,559 women
Faculty/student ratio: 1:18
Most popular majors: Business, education, music, psychology, biblical studies
Setting: Suburban
1997–98 expenses: Tuition: $248 semester/hr   Room & board: $1,770/sem.
Financial aid:
% of students receiving aid: 70%   Average annual aid received: n/a

DALLAS CHRISTIAN COLLEGE
2700 Christian Parkway
Dallas, Texas 75234-7299
Admissions department information:
Phone: (972) 241-3371 Fax: (972) 241-8021
Web site: http://www.papi.net/dcc
Founded: 1950
Affiliation: Independent Christian Church
1996–1997 freshman admission statistics:
Number applied: 85 Number accepted: 75
Tests required: ACT
Total undergraduate enrollment: 140 men; 100 women
Faculty/student ratio: 1:8
Most popular majors: BA Bible, BS Bible, ministry & leadership, management, ethics
Setting: Urban
1997–98 expenses: Tuition: $1,560/semester Room & board: $1,320
Financial aid:
% of students receiving aid: 95% Average annual aid received: $1,900

DAVID LIPSCOMB UNIVERSITY
3901 Granny White Pike
Nashville, Tennessee 37204
Admissions department information:
Phone: (615) 269-1776 Fax: (615) 269-1804
E-mail: admissions@dlu.edu Web Site: http://www.dlu.edu
Founded: 1891
Affiliation: Church of Christ
1996–1997 freshman admission statistics:
Number applied: 1,318 Number accepted: 1,176
Tests required: SAT or ACT
Total undergraduate enrollment: 1,082 men; 1,375 women
Faculty/student ratio: 1:18
Most popular majors: Business, education, history & political science, biology, psychology
Setting: Urban
1997–98 expenses: Tuition: $8,430 Room & board: $3,910
Financial aid:
% of students receiving aid: 75% Average annual aid received: $6,558

DORDT COLLEGE

498 4th Ave. N.E.
Sioux Center, Iowa 51250
Admissions department information:
Phone: (712) 722-6081   Fax: (712) 722-1967
E-mail: admission@dordt.edu
Web Site: http://www.dordt.edu
Founded: 1955
Affiliation: Christian Reformed
1996–1997 freshman admission statistics:
Number applied: 726   Number accepted: 683
Tests required: SAT or ACT
Total undergraduate enrollment: 642 men; 627 women
Faculty/student ratio: 1:15
Most popular majors: Education, engineering, agriculture, social work, sciences
Setting: Rural
1997–98 expenses: Tuition: $11,300   Room & board: $3,030
Financial aid:
% of students receiving aid: 95%   Average annual aid received: $10,000

EAST COAST BIBLE COLLEGE

6900 Wilkinson Blvd.
Charlotte, North Carolina 28214
Admissions department information:
Phone: (704) 394-2307   Fax: (704) 393-3689
Founded: 1976
Affiliation: Church of God, Cleveland, Tennessee
1996–1997 freshman admission statistics:
Number applied: 50   Number accepted: 50
Tests required: SAT or ACT
Total undergraduate enrollment: 94 men; 85 women
Faculty/student ratio: 1:17
Most popular majors: Biblical studies, Christian ed., elementary ed.,
Christian education, church music
Setting: Urban
1997–98 expenses: Tuition: $5,500   Room & board: $2,700
Financial aid:
% of students receiving aid: 74%   Average annual aid received: $5,329

East Texas Baptist University

1209 N. Grove
Marshall, Texas 75670
Admissions department information:
  Phone: 1-800-804-3828   Fax: (903) 938-1705
  E-mail: mbender@etbu.edu   Web Site: http://www.etbu.edu
Founded: 1912
Affiliation: Southern Baptist
1996–1997 freshman admission statistics:
  Number applied: 766   Number accepted: 561
Tests required: SAT or ACT
Total undergraduate enrollment: 519 men; 787 women
Faculty/student ratio: 1:16
Most popular majors: Education, business, religion, nursing, psychology
Setting: Rural
1997–98 expenses: Tuition: $6,800   Room & board: $3,500
Financial aid: % of students receiving aid: 85%
  Average annual aid received: $3,700 (without loans) – $6,500 (with loans)

Eastern College

1300 Eagle Rd.
St. Davids, Pennsylvania 19087
Admissions department information:
  Phone: (610) 341-5967   Fax: (610) 341-1723
  E-mail: ugadm@eastern.edu   Web Site: http://www.eastern.edu
Founded: 1952
Affiliation: American Baptist
1996–1997 freshman admission statistics:
  Number applied: 850   Number accepted: 595
Tests required: SAT or ACT
Total undergraduate enrollment: 1,100
Faculty/student ratio: 1:13
Most popular majors: Youth ministry, business, sciences, education,
  social work, psychology
Setting: Suburban
1997–98 expenses: Tuition: $12,200   Room & board: $5,130
Financial aid:
  % of students receiving aid: 95%   Average annual aid received: n/a

EASTERN MENNONITE UNIVERSITY

1200 Park Rd.
Harrisonburg, Virginia 22801-2462
Admissions department information:
    Phone: 1-800-368-2665   Fax: (540) 432-4444
    E-mail: admiss@emu.edu
    Web Site: http://www.emu.edu
Founded: 1917
Affiliation: Mennonite
1996–1997 freshman admission statistics:
    Number applied: 525   Number accepted: 482
Tests required: SAT or ACT
Total undergraduate enrollment: 396 men; 626 women
Faculty/student ratio: 1:13
Most popular majors: Education, business, nursing, biology, social work
Setting: Suburban
1997–98 expenses: Tuition: $12,000   Room & board: $4,500
Financial aid:
    % of students receiving aid: 92%   Average annual aid received: $12,000

EASTERN NAZARENE COLLEGE

23 E. Elm Ave.
Quincy, Massachusetts 02170
Admissions department information:
    Phone: 1-800-88-ENC-88   Fax: (617) 745-3490
    E-mail: admissions@enc.edu
    Web Site: http://www.enc.edu
Founded: 1918
Affiliation: International Church of the Nazarene
1996–1997 freshman admission statistics:
    Number applied: 629   Number accepted: 493
Tests required: SAT or ACT
Total undergraduate enrollment: 302 men; 407 women
Faculty/student ratio: 1:12
Most popular majors: Business administration, communication arts,
    education, psychology, social work
Setting: Suburban
1997–98 expenses: Tuition: $11,442   Room & board: $3,975

Eastern Pentecostal Bible College

780 Argyle St.

Peterborough, Ontario, Canada K9H 5T2

Admissions department information:

Phone: 1-800-295-6368   Fax: (705) 748-3931

E-mail: jmann@epbc.edu

Web Site: http://www.epbc.edu

Founded: 1939

Affiliation: Pentecostal

1996–1997 freshman admission statistics:

Number applied: 183   Number accepted: 147

Tests required: SAT or ACT

Total undergraduate enrollment: 200 men; 140 women

Faculty/student ratio: 1:21

Most popular majors: Pastoral, education, youth, missions, vocational

Setting: Urban

1997–98 expenses: Tuition: $4,320   Room & board: $3,999

Financial aid:

% of students receiving aid: 70%   Average annual aid received: $9,350

Emmanuel Bible College

100 Fergus Ave.

Kitchener, Ontario, Canada N2A 2H2

Admissions department information

Phone: (519) 894-8900   Fax: (519) 894-5331

E-mail: Admission@EBcollege.ON.CA

Web Site: http://www.EBCollege.ON.CA

Founded: 1940

Affiliation: Evangelical Missionary Church of Canada

1996–1997 freshman admission statistics:

Number applied: 120   Number accepted: 91

Total undergraduate enrollment: 142 men; 132 women

Faculty/student ratio: 1:21

Most popular majors: Counseling, pastoral studies, theology, missions

Setting: Urban

1997–98 expenses: Tuition: $2,016/semester   Room & board: $1,900/sem.

Financial aid:

% of students receiving aid: 34.7%   Average annual aid received: n/a

EMMANUEL COLLEGE

P.O. Box 129
Franklin Springs, Georgia 30639
Admissions department information:
    Phone: 1-800-860-8800 or (706) 245-7226   Fax: (706) 245-4424
    E-mail: admissions@emmanuel-college.edu
    Web Site: http://www.emmanuel-college.edu
Founded: 1919
Affiliation: Pentecostal Holiness
1996–1997 freshman admission statistics:
    Number applied: 1,121   Number accepted: 767
Tests required: SAT or ACT
Total undergraduate enrollment: 270 men; 369 women
Faculty/student ratio: 1:17
Most popular majors: Psychology, early childhood ed., middle grades ed.,
    business, Christian ministry
Setting: Rural
1997–98 expenses: Tuition: $6,060   Room & board: $3,420
Financial aid:
    % of students receiving aid: 92%   Average annual aid received: n/a

EMMAUS BIBLE COLLEGE

2570 Asbury Rd.
Dubuque, Iowa 52001
Admissions department information:
    Phone: (319) 588-8000   Fax: (319) 588-1216
    Web Site: http://www.xicom.com/edu/emmaus
Founded: 1941
Affiliation: Nondenominational
Tests required: SAT or ACT
Total undergraduate enrollment: 116 men; 120 women
Faculty/student ratio: 1:16
Most popular majors: Bible, elementary ed.
Setting: Rural
1997–98 expenses: Tuition: $2,270   Room & board: $4,730
Financial aid:
    % of students receiving aid: 87%   Average annual aid received: $3,200

ERSKINE COLLEGE
2 Washington
Due West, South Carolina 29639
Admissions department information:
Phone: (864) 379-8838   Fax: (864) 379-8533
E-mail: kfry@erskine.edu
Web Site: http://www.erskine.edu
Founded: 1839
Affiliation: Associate Reformed Presbyterian
1996–1997 freshman admission statistics:
Number applied: 539   Number accepted: 462
Tests required: SAT
Total undergraduate enrollment: 212 men; 311 women
Faculty/student ratio: 1:13
Most popular majors: Physics, biology, chemistry, education, history
Setting: Rural
1997–98 expenses: Tuition: $17,500   Room & board: $6,130
Financial aid:
% of students receiving aid: 90%   Average annual aid received: $6,000

EUGENE BIBLE COLLEGE
2155 Bailey Hill Rd.
Eugene, Oregon 97405
Admissions department information:
Phone: 1-800-322-2638   Fax: (541) 343-5801
E-mail: admissions@ebc.edu
Web Site: http://www.ebc.edu
Founded: 1925
1996–1997 freshman admission statistics:
Number applied: 196   Number accepted: 133
Tests required: SAT or ACT
Total undergraduate enrollment: 132 men; 116 women
Faculty/student ratio: 1:15
Most popular majors: Youth Ministry, Christian Counseling
Setting: Urban
1997–98 expenses: Tuition: $4,745   Room & board: $3,181
Financial aid:
% of students receiving aid: 75%   Average annual aid received: $2,700

EVANGEL COLLEGE
1111 N. Glenstone
Springfield, Missouri 65802
Admissions department information:
Phone: (417) 865-2811   Fax: (417) 865-9599
E-mail: admissions@mail4.evangel.edu
Web Site: http://www.evangel.edu/
Founded: 1955
Affiliation: Assemblies of God
1996–1997 freshman admission statistics:
Number applied: 722   Number accepted: 654
Tests required: SAT or ACT
Total undergraduate enrollment: 666 men; 908 women
Faculty/student ratio: 1:17
Most popular majors: Education, business, psychology, biology, communications
Setting: Urban
1997–98 expenses: Tuition: $7,700   Room & board: $3,440
Financial aid:
% of students receiving aid: 90%   Average annual aid received: n/a

FAITH BAPTIST BIBLE COLLEGE & THEOLOGICAL SEMINARY
1900 N.W. 4th St.
Ankeny, Iowa 50021
Admissions department information:
Phone: 1-888-FAITH-4U   Fax: (515) 964-1638
E-mail: FBBCenroll@aol.com   Web Site: http://www.Faith.edu
Founded: 1921
Affiliation: General Association of Regular Baptist
1996–1997 freshman admission statistics:
Number applied: 113   Number accepted: 99
Tests required: SAT or ACT
Total undergraduate enrollment: 118 men; 138 women
Faculty/student ratio: 1:16
Most popular majors: Pastoral, youth pastor, elementary ed., Bible, missions
Setting: Urban
1997–98 expenses: Tuition: $6,094   Room & board: $3,276
Financial aid:
% of students receiving aid: 95%   Average annual aid received: n/a

Faulkner University

5345 Atlanta Hwy.
Montgomery, Alabama 36109
Admissions department information:
  Phone: 1-800-879-9816   Fax: (334) 260-6137
  E-mail: Kmock@Faulkner.edu
  Web Site: http://www.Faulkner.edu
Founded: 1942
Affiliation: Church of Christ
1996–1997 freshman admission statistics:
  Number applied: 550   Number accepted: 450
Tests required: SAT or ACT
Faculty/student ratio: 1:18
Most popular majors: Bible, business, criminal justice, education, computer
  sciences
Setting: Urban
1997–98 expenses: Tuition: $215 per semester/hr.   Room & board: $3,700
Financial aid:
  % of students receiving aid: 95%
  Average annual aid received: $4,000

Florida Baptist Theological College

P.O. Box 1306
Graceville, Florida 32440
Admissions department information:
  Phone: (904) 263-3261 ext.460   Fax: (904) 263-7506
Founded: 1943
Affiliation: Southern Baptist
1996–1997 freshman admission statistics:
  Number applied: 208   Number accepted: 191
Tests required: SAT or ACT
Total undergraduate enrollment: 328 men; 107 women
Most popular majors: Theology, Christian ed., elementary ed., church music
Setting: Rural
1997–98 expenses: Tuition: $2,880   Room: $1,800
Financial aid:
  % of students receiving aid: 84%
  Average annual aid received: $3,078

FLORIDA CHRISTIAN COLLEGE

1011 Bill Beck Blvd.
Kissimmee, Florida 34744
Admissions department information:
Phone: 1-888-468-6322   Fax: (407) 847-3925
Founded: 1975
Affiliation: Christian Church/Churches of Christ
1996–1997 freshman admission statistics:
Number applied: 115   Number accepted: 85
Tests required: SAT or ACT
Total undergraduate enrollment: 90 men; 95 women
Faculty/student ratio: 1:15
Most popular majors: Preaching, youth ministry, elementary ed., music, missions
Setting: Suburban
1997–98 expenses: Tuition: $140/credit hr.   Room & board: $2,300
Financial aid:
% of students receiving aid: 80%   Average annual aid received: $4,000

FLORIDA COLLEGE

119 N. Glen Arven Ave.
Temple Terrace, Florida 33617
Admissions department information:
Phone: 1-800-326-7655   Fax: (813) 899-6772
E-mail: admissions@flcoll.edu
Web Site: http://www.flcoll.edu
Founded: 1946
Affiliation: Church of Christ
1996–1997 freshman admission statistics:
Number applied: 312   Number accepted: 278
Tests required: ACT
Total undergraduate enrollment: 181 men; 198 women
Faculty/student ratio: 1:12
Most popular majors: Religious studies, education, business, pre-engineering
Setting: Suburban
1997–98 expenses: Tuition: $6,270   Room & board: $3,690
Financial aid:
% of students receiving aid: 80%   Average annual aid received: $2,000

FREE WILL BAPTIST BIBLE COLLEGE

3606 West End Ave.

Nashville, Tennessee 37205

Admissions department information:

Phone: (615) 383-1340   Fax: (615) 269-6028

Founded: 1942

Affiliation: National Association of Free Will Baptists

1996–1997 freshman admission statistics:

Number applied: 90   Number accepted: 75

Tests required: ACT

Total undergraduate enrollment: 183 men; 157 women

Faculty/student ratio: 1:18

Most popular majors: Elementary ed., pastoral ministry, business management, missions track, youth ministry

Setting: Suburban

1997–98 expenses: Tuition: $159/semester hr.   Room & board: $3,498

Financial aid:

% of students receiving aid: 95%   Average annual aid received: $3,614

FREED-HARDEMAN UNIVERSITY

158 E. Main St.

Henderson, Tennessee 38340

Admissions department information:

Phone: 1-800-FHU-FHU1   Fax: (901) 989-6775

E-mail: admissions@fhu.edu

Web Site: http://www.fhu.edu

Founded: 1869

Affiliation: Church of Christ

1996–1997 freshman admission statistics:

Number applied: 767   Number accepted: 544

Tests required: ACT

Total undergraduate enrollment: 549 men; 674 women

Faculty/student ratio: 1:18

Most popular majors: Business, education, Bible, biology, communication

Setting: Rural

1997–98 expenses: Tuition: $6,504   Room & board: n/a

Financial aid:

% of students receiving aid: 85%   Average annual aid received: n/a

FRESNO PACIFIC UNIVERSITY
1717 S Chestnut Ave.
Fresno, California 93702
Admissions department information:
Phone: 1-800-660-6089
Fax: (209) 453-2039
E-mail: ugadmis@fresno.edu
Web Site: http://www.fresno.edu
Founded: 1944
Affiliation: Mennonite Brethren
1996–1997 freshman admission statistics:
Number applied: 343   Number accepted: 266
Tests required: SAT or ACT
Total undergraduate enrollment: 307 men; 501 women
Faculty/student ratio: 1:15
Most popular majors: Liberal studies, business, psychology, English
Setting: Suburban
1997–98 expenses: Tuition: $11,936   Room & board: $4,100
Financial aid:
% of students receiving aid: 90%   Average annual aid received: $7,182

FRUITLAND BAPTIST BIBLE INSTITUTE
Rt. 2, Box 116
Hendersonville, North Carolina 28792
Admissions department information:
Phone: (704) 685-8886   Fax: (704) 685-8888
Founded: 1946
Affiliation: Southern Baptist
1996–1997 freshman admission statistics:
Number applied: 85   Number accepted: 80
Total undergraduate enrollment: 199 men; 2 women
Faculty/student ratio: 1:8
Most popular majors: Religion/church ministries
Setting: Rural
1997–98 expenses: Tuition: $155-190/per qtr.   Room & board: $435/per qtr.
Financial aid:
% of students receiving aid: 20%
Average annual aid received: $500

GARDNER-WEBB UNIVERSITY
Box 817
Boiling Springs, North Carolina 28017
Admissions department information:
Phone: (704) 434-4498   Fax: (704) 434-448
E-mail: admissions@gardner-webb.edu
Web Site: http://www.gardner-webb.edu
Founded: 1905
Affiliation: Southern Baptist
1996–1997 freshman admission statistics:
Number applied: 1,445   Number accepted: 1,212
Tests required: SAT or ACT
Total undergraduate enrollment: 862 men; 1,439 women
Faculty/student ratio: 1:17
Most popular majors: Business, education, ministry, nursing, psychology
Setting: Rural
1997–98 expenses: Tuition, room & board: $14,250
Financial aid:
% of students receiving aid: 90%   Average annual aid received: $8,000

GENEVA COLLEGE
3200 College Ave.
Beaver Falls, Pennsylvania 15010
Admissions department information:
Phone: (412) 847-6500   Fax: (412) 847-6776
E-mail: admissions@geneva.edu Web Site: http://www.geneva.edu
Founded: 1848
Affiliation: Reformed Presbyterian
1996–1997 freshman admission statistics:
Number applied: 815   Number accepted: 682
Tests required: SAT or ACT
Total undergraduate enrollment: 776 men; 852 women
Faculty/student ratio: 1:20
Most popular majors: Biology, business, education, psychology
Setting: Suburban
1997–98 expenses: Tuition: $11,250   Room & board: $4,750
Financial aid:
% of students receiving aid: 95%   Average annual aid received: n/a

GEORGE FOX UNIVERSITY

414 N. Meridian St.

Newberg, Oregon 97132

Admissions department information:

Phone: 1-800-765-4369   Fax: (503) 538-7234

E-mail: jrickey@georgefox.edu   Web Site: http://www.georgefox.edu

Founded: 1891

Affiliation: Evangelical Friends

1996–1997 freshman admission statistics:

Number applied: 943   Number accepted: 824

Tests required: SAT or ACT

Total undergraduate enrollment: 614 men; 926 women

Faculty/student ratio: 1:16

Most popular majors: Teacher ed., business & economics, biology, sociology, psychology

Setting: Rural

1997–98 expenses: Tuition: $15,250   Room & board: $4,920

Financial aid:

% of students receiving aid: 91%   Average annual aid received: $12,300

GEORGETOWN COLLEGE

400 E. College St.

Georgetown, Kentucky 40324

Admissions department information:

Phone: (502) 863-8009   Fax: (502) 868-8891

E-mail: admissions@gtc.georgetown.ky.us

Web Site: http://www.gtc.georgetown.ky.us

Founded: 1829

Affiliation: Baptist

1996–1997 freshman admission statistics:

Number applied: 745   Number accepted: 668

Tests required: SAT or ACT

Faculty/student ratio: 1:13

Most popular majors: Education, biology, communication arts, English, psychology

Setting: Suburban

1997–98 expenses: Tuition: $9,990   Room & board: $4,180

Financial aid:

% of students receiving aid: 90%   Average annual aid received: $11,000

GOD'S BIBLE SCHOOL & COLLEGE
1810 Young St.
Cincinnati, Ohio 45210
Admissions department information:
    Phone: (513) 721-7944   Fax: (513) 721-3971
    E-mail: GBS4U@juno.com
Founded: 1900
Affiliation: Interdenominational
1996–1997 freshman admission statistics:
    Number applied: 92   Number accepted: 87
Tests required: SAT or ACT
Total undergraduate enrollment: 83 men; 90 women
Faculty/student ratio: 1:11
Most popular majors: Ministerial studies, music,
    elementary Christian ed., missions
Setting: Urban
1997–98 expenses: Tuition: $3,560   Room & board: $3,050
Financial aid:
    % of students receiving aid: 86%   Average annual aid received: $1,500

GORDON COLLEGE
255 Grapevine Rd.
South Hamilton, Massachusetts 01984
Admissions department information:
    Phone: 1-800-343-1379   Fax: (508) 524-3704
    E-mail: admissions@hope.gordonc.edu   Web Site: http://www.gordonc.edu
Founded: 1889
Affiliation: Nondenominational
1996–1997 freshman admission statistics:
    Number applied: 957   Number accepted: 807
Tests required: SAT or ACT
Total undergraduate enrollment: 454 men; 770 women
Faculty/student ratio: 1:14
Most popular majors: English, psychology, biology, social work, biblical studies
Setting: Suburban
1997–98 expenses: Tuition: $14,520   Room & board: $4,840
Financial aid:
    % of students receiving aid: 86%   Average annual aid received: $13,213

GOSHEN COLLEGE
1700 S. Main
Goshen, Indiana 46526
Admissions department information:
Phone: (219) 535-7535   Fax: (219) 535-7609
E-mail: admissions@goshen.edu   Web Site: http://www.goshen.edu
Founded: 1894
Affiliation: Mennonite
1996–1997 freshman admission statistics:
Number applied: 451   Number accepted: 393
Tests required: SAT or ACT
Total undergraduate enrollment: 435 men; 579 women
Faculty/student ratio: 1:13
Most popular majors: Biology, nursing, education, art, psychology
Setting: Rural
1997–98 expenses: Tuition: $11,450   Room & board: $4,000
Financial aid:
% of students receiving aid: 95%   Average annual aid received: n/a

GRACE COLLEGE
200 Seminary Drive
Winona Lake, Indiana 46590
Admissions department information:
Phone: (219) 372-5131   Fax: (219) 372-5114
E-mail: rhenry@grace.edu   Web Site: http://www.grace.edu
Founded: 1948
Affiliation: Fellowship of Grace Brethren Churches
1996–1997 freshman admission statistics:
Number applied: 525   Number accepted: 380
Tests required: SAT or ACT
Total undergraduate enrollment: 265 men; 380 women
Faculty/student ratio: 1:16
Most popular majors: Elementary ed., psychology, business,
biology, youth ministries
Setting: Rural
1997–98 expenses: Tuition: $9,820   Room & board: $4,280
Financial aid:
% of students receiving aid: 90%   Average annual aid received: $4,500

Grace Bible College

1011 Aldon S.W., P.O. Box 910
Grand Rapids, Michigan 49509
Admissions department information
Phone: 1-800-968-1887   Fax: (616) 538-0599
Founded: 1945
Affiliation: Grace Gospel Fellowship
1996–1997 freshman admission statistics:
Number applied: 140   Number accepted 88
Tests required: ACT
Total undergraduate enrollment: 66 men; 80 women
Faculty/student ratio: 1:10
Most popular majors: Christian music industry, business, human services, education, pastoral/youth ministry
Setting: Suburban
1997–98 expenses: Tuition: $6,200   Room & board: $3,700
Financial aid:
% of students receiving aid: 94%   Average annual aid received: $4,750

Grace University

1311 S. 9th Street
Omaha, Nebraska 68108
Admissions department information:
Phone: 1-800-383-1422   Fax: (402) 341-9587
E-mail: admissions@GraceU.edu   Web Site: http://www.graceu.edu
Founded: 1943
Affiliation: Nondenominational
1996–1997 freshman admission statistics:
Number applied: n/a   Number accepted: 336
Tests required: ACT
Total undergraduate enrollment: 214 men; 200 women
Faculty/student ratio: 1:14
Most popular majors: Bible humanities, management and organizational leadership
Setting: Urban
1997–98 expenses: Tuition: $229/credit hr.   Room & board: $3,230
Financial aid:
% of students receiving aid: 85%   Average annual aid received: $4,040

GRAND CANYON UNIVERSITY
3300 W. Camelback Rd., P.O. Box 1097
Phoenix, Arizona 85061-1097
Admissions department information:
Phone: (602) 589-2855   Fax: (602) 589-2580
E-mail: admiss@grand-canyon.edu   Web Site: http://www.grand-canyon.edu
Founded: 1949
Affiliation: Southern Baptist
1996–1997 freshman admission statistics:
Number applied: 622   Number accepted: 563
Tests required: SAT or ACT
Total undergraduate enrollment: 632 men; 1,009 women
Faculty/student ratio: 1:21
Most popular majors: Biology (general), human biology, elementary ed., psychology
Setting: Urban
1997–98 expenses: Tuition: $8,600   Room & board: $3,400
Financial aid:
% of students receiving aid: 84%   Average annual aid received: $8,521

GREAT LAKES CHRISTIAN COLLEGE
6211 W. Willow Hwy.
Lansing, Michigan 48917
Admissions department information:
Phone: 1-800-937-4522   Fax: (517) 321-5902
E-mail: admissions@glcc.edu   Web Site: http://www.glcc.edu
Founded: 1949
Affiliation: Christian Churches/Churches of Christ
1996–1997 freshman admission statistics:
Number applied: 71   Number accepted: 68
Tests required: SAT or ACT
Total undergraduate enrollment: 86 men; 59 women
Faculty/student ratio: 1:12
Most popular majors: Christian counseling, Christian ministry, music, humanities, education
Setting: Suburban
1997–98 expenses: Tuition: $4,054   Room & board: $3,450
Financial aid:
% of students receiving aid: 87%   Average annual aid received: $6,461

GREENVILLE COLLEGE

315 E. College Ave.
Greenville, Illinois 62246
Admissions department information:
Phone: 1-800-345-4440   Fax: (618) 664-9841
E-mail: admissions@greenville.edu
Web Site: http://www.greenville.edu
Founded: 1892
Affiliation: Free Methodist
Tests required: SAT or ACT
Total undergraduate enrollment: 401 men; 452 women
Faculty/student ratio: 1:14
Most popular majors: Contemporary Christian music, education
Setting: Rural
1997–98 expenses: Tuition: $12,576   Room & board: $4,750
Financial aid:
% of students receiving aid: 92%   Average annual aid received: $11,740

GROVE CITY COLLEGE

100 Campus Dr.
Grove City, Pennsylvania 16127-2104
Admissions department information:
Phone: (412) 458-2100   Fax: (412) 458-3395
E-mail: admissions information@gcc.edu
Web Site: http://www.gcc.edu
Founded: 1876
Affiliation: Presbyterian
1996–1997 freshman admission statistics:
Number applied: 2,301   Number accepted: 1,115
Tests required: SAT or ACT
Total undergraduate enrollment: 1,156 men; 1,118 women
Faculty/student ratio: 1:21
Most popular majors: Business, education, biology, engineering, accounting
Setting: Rural
1997–98 expenses: Tuition: $6,567   Room & board: $3,816
Financial aid:
% of students receiving aid: 55%   Average annual aid received: n/a

HANNIBAL-LAGRANGE COLLEGE

2800 Palmyra Rd.
Hannibal, Missouri 63401
Admissions department information:
    Phone: (573) 221-3113   Fax: (573) 221-6594
    E-mail: admission@hlg.edu   Web Site: http://www.hlg.edu
Founded: 1858
Affiliation: Southern Baptist
1996–1997 freshman admission statistics:
    Number applied: 248   Number accepted: 230
Tests required: ACT
Total undergraduate enrollment: 327 men; 555 women
Faculty/student ratio: 1:14
Most popular majors: Education, business, nursing, human services
Setting: Rural
1997–98 expenses: Tuition: $7,330   Room & board: $2,920
Financial aid:
    % of students receiving aid: 98%   Average annual aid received: n/a

HARDIN-SIMMONS UNIVERSITY

2200 Hickory
Abilene, Texas 79698
Admissions department information
    Phone: 1-800-568-2692   Fax: (915) 670-1263
    E-mail: enroll.services@hsutx.edu   Web Site: http://www.hsutx.edu
Founded: 1891
Affiliation: Baptist
1996–1997 freshman admission statistics:
    Number applied: 740   Number accepted: 653
Tests required: SAT or ACT
Total undergraduate enrollment: 944 men; 987 women
Faculty/student ratio: 1:16
Most popular majors: Education, biology, psychology, business,
    religious studies
Setting: Urban
1997–98 expenses: Tuition: $7,500   Room & board: $3,240
Financial aid:
    % of students receiving aid: 80%   Average annual aid received: $6,456

HARDING UNIVERSITY
Box 2255
Searcy, Arkansas 72149
Admissions department information:
Phone: (501) 279-4407   Fax: (501) 275-4865
E-mail: admissions@harding.edu
Web Site: http://www.harding.edu
Founded: 1924
Affiliation: Church of Christ
1996–1997 freshman admission statistics:
Number applied: 1,713   Number accepted: 1,104
Tests required: SAT or ACT
Total undergraduate enrollment: 1,607 men; 1,933 women
Faculty/student ratio: 1:18
Most popular majors: Education, business, Bible, health, communications
Setting: Rural
1997–98 expenses:
Tuition: $7,230   Room & board: $4,088
Financial aid:
% of students receiving aid: 80%
Average annual aid received: $6,800

HERITAGE BAPTIST COLLEGE
175 Holiday Inn Dr.
Cambridge, Ontario, Canada N3C 3T2
Admissions department information:
Phone: 1-800-465-1961   Fax: (519) 651-2870
Affiliation: Independent/Baptist
1996–1997 freshman admission statistics:
Number applied: 121   Number accepted: 121
Total undergraduate enrollment: 120 men; 92 women
Faculty/student ratio: 1:17
Setting: Urban
1997–98 expenses:
Tuition: $2,312/Canadian   Room & board: $1,335/Canadian
Financial aid:
% of students receiving aid: 35.8%
Average annual aid received: n/a

HESSTON COLLEGE

P.O. Box 3000, 325 S. College Dr.
Hesston, Kansas 67062
Admissions department information:
    Phone: 1-800-99-LARKS   Fax: (316) 327-8300
    E-mail: admissions@hesston.edu
    Web Site: http://www.hesston.edu
Founded: 1909
Affiliation: Mennonite
1996–1997 freshman admission statistics:
    Number applied: 371   Number accepted: n/a
Tests required: SAT or ACT
Total undergraduate enrollment: 186 men; 252 women
Faculty/student ratio: 1:14
Most popular majors: Liberal arts, nursing, business, aviation, pastoral ministries
Setting: Rural
1997–98 expenses: Tuition: $10,400   Room & board: $4,050
Financial aid:
    % of students receiving aid: 95%
    Average annual aid received: $9,500

HOBE SOUND BIBLE COLLEGE

P.O. Box 1065
Hobe Sound, Florida 33475
Admissions department information:
    Phone: 1-800-881-5534   Fax: (561) 545-1422
    E-mail: HSBCUWIN@aol.com
Founded: 1960
Affiliation: Wesleyan
1996–1997 freshman admission statistics:
    Number applied: 24   Number accepted: 23
Tests required: ACT
Total undergraduate enrollment: 64 men; 59 women
Most popular majors: Ministerial, missions, education
Setting: Rural
1997–98 expenses: Tuition: $3,940   Room & board: $2,610
Financial aid:
    % of students receiving aid: 95%   Average annual aid received: n/a

HOPE COLLEGE

P.O. Box 9000
Holland, Michigan 49422-9000
Admissions department information:
   Phone: (616) 395-7850   Fax: (616) 395-7130
   E-mail: admissions@hope.edu   Web Site: http://www.hope.edu
Founded: 1866
Affiliation: Reformed Church in America
1996–1997 freshman admission statistics:
   Number applied: 1,771   Number accepted:1,608
Tests required: SAT or ACT
Total undergraduate enrollment: 1,189 men; 1,660 women
Faculty/student ratio: 1:13
Most popular majors: Business, biology, English, psychology, education
Setting: Suburban
1997–98 expenses: Tuition: $14,788   Room & board: $4,696
Financial aid:
   % of students receiving aid: 58% Average annual aid received: $11,642

HOUGHTON COLLEGE

1 Willard Ave.
Houghton, New York 14744
Admissions department information:
   Phone: 1-800-777-2556   Fax: (716) 567-9522
   E-mail: admissions@houghton.edu   Web Site: http://www.houghton.edu
Founded: 1883
Affiliation: The Wesleyan Church
1996–1997 freshman admission statistics:
   Number applied: 1,031   Number accepted: 796
Tests required: SAT or ACT
Total undergraduate enrollment: 424 men; 782 women
Faculty/student ratio: 1:15
Most popular majors: Education, biology, music, psychology, English
Setting: Rural
1997–98 expenses: Tuition: $12,344   Room & board: $4,238
Financial aid:
   % of students receiving aid: 94%   Average annual aid received: $6,500
   (excluding loans)

HOUSTON BAPTIST UNIVERSITY

7502 Fondrin Rd.
Houston, Texas 77074

Admissions department information:
Phone: (281) 649-3211   Fax: (281) 649-3217
E-mail: unadmin@hbu.edu
Web Site: http://www.hbu.edu

Founded: 1963

Affiliation: Baptist

Tests required: SAT or ACT

Total undergraduate enrollment: 592 men; 1,078 women

Faculty/student ratio: 1:17

Most popular majors: Biology, nursing, business administration,
music, education

Setting: Urban

1997–98 expenses: Tuition: $7,500   Room & board: $2,970

Financial aid:
% of students receiving aid: 65%   Average annual aid received: n/a

HOWARD PAYNE UNIVERSITY

1000 Fisk Ave.
Brownwood, Texas 76801

Admissions department information:
Phone: (915) 649-8020   Fax: (915) 649-8901
E-mail: admissions@hputx.edu   Web Site: http://www.hputx.edu

Founded: 1889

Affiliation: Baptist

1996–1997 freshman admission statistics:
Number applied: 548   Number accepted: 494

Tests required: SAT or ACT

Total undergraduate enrollment: 748 men; 720 women

Faculty/student ratio: 1:18

Most popular majors: Business, education, exercise & sports science,
religious studies, communication

Setting: Rural

1997–98 expenses: Tuition: $7,620   Room & board: $3,630

Financial aid:
% of students receiving aid: 86%   Average annual aid received: $5,878

HUNTINGTON COLLEGE

2303 College Ave.

Huntington, Indiana 46750

Admissions department information:

Phone: 1-800-642-6423　Fax: (219) 358-3699

E-mail: admissions@huntcol.edu

Web Site: http://www.huntcol.edu

Founded: 1897

Affiliation: United Brethren Church

1996–1997 freshman admission statistics:

Number applied: 510　Number accepted: 465

Tests required: SAT or ACT

Total undergraduate enrollment: 300 men; 345 women

Faculty/student ratio: 1:14

Most popular majors: Elementary ed., youth ministry, business administration, psychology, graphic arts

Setting: Rural

1997–98 expenses: Tuition: $11,700　Room & board: $4,570

Financial aid:

% of students receiving aid: 90%　Average annual aid received: $8,500

INDIANA WESLEYAN UNIVERSITY

4201 S. Washington

Marion, Indiana 46953

Admissions department information:

Phone: (765) 677-2710　Fax: (765) 677-2333

E-mail: admissions@indwes.edu

Web Site: http://www.indwes.edu

Founded: 1920

Affiliation: Wesleyan

1996–1997 freshman admission statistics:

Number applied: 1,278　Number accepted: 1,003

Tests required: SAT or ACT

Faculty/student ratio: 1:17

Most popular majors: Nursing, education, Christian ministry

1997–98 expenses: Tuition: $10,720　Room & board: $4,158

Financial aid:

% of students receiving aid: 96%　Average annual aid received: $10,000

INTERNATIONAL BIBLE COLLEGE

3625 Helton Dr.
P.O. Box IBC
Florence, Alabama 35630
Admissions department information:
Phone: (205) 766-6610
Fax: (205) 760-0981
E-mail: J.D.CollinsIBC@juno.com
Founded: 1971
Affiliation: Church of Christ
Most popular major: Bible
Setting: Suburban
1997–98 expenses:
Tuition: $149/semester hr.

JOHN BROWN UNIVERSITY

2000 W. University
Siloam Springs, Arkansas 72761
Admissions department information:
Phone: 1-800-634-6969
Fax: (501) 524-4196
E-mail: jbuinfo@acc.jbu.edu
Web Site: http://www.jbu.edu
Founded: 1919
Affiliation: Nondenominational
1996–1997 freshman admission statistics:
Number applied: 720   Number accepted: 490
Tests required: SAT or ACT
Total undergraduate enrollment: 573 men; 722 women
Faculty/student ratio: 1:16
Most popular majors: Engineering, business, teacher education,
communication, psychology
Setting: Rural
1997–98 expenses: Tuition: $9,120   Room & board: $4,390
Financial aid:
% of students receiving aid: 80%
Average annual aid received: $6,400

John Wesley College

2314 N. Centennial St.

High Point, North Carolina 27265

Admissions department information:

Phone: (910) 889-2262   Fax: (910) 889-2261

Founded: 1932

Affiliation: Interdenominational

1996–1997 freshman admission statistics:

Number applied: 16   Number accepted: 16

Total undergraduate enrollment: 82 men; 79 women

Faculty/student ratio: 1:11

Most popular majors: Pastoral ministry, Christian ministry, Bible theology, psychology/Christian counseling, elementary education

Setting: Suburban

1997–98 expenses: Tuition: $2,235/semester   Room & board: $800/semester

Financial aid:

% of students receiving aid: 50%   Average annual aid received: $2,500

Judson College

1151 N. State St.

Elgin, Illinois 60123

Admissions department information:

Phone: 1-800-TRY-JDSN   Fax: (847) 695-0216

E-mail: admission@mail.judson-il.edu

Web Site: http://www.judson-il.edu

Founded: 1963

Affiliation: American Baptist

1996–1997 freshman admission statistics:

Number applied: 751   Number accepted: 552

Tests required: SAT or ACT

Total undergraduate enrollment: 296 men; 415 women

Faculty/student ratio: 1:16

Most popular majors: Elementary ed., art (architecture & graphic design), business, youth ministry, psychology

Setting: Suburban

1997–98 expenses: Tuition: $10,900   Room & board: $4,780

Financial aid:

% of students receiving aid: 94%   Average annual aid received: $7,300

KING COLLEGE

1350 King College Rd.
Bristol, Tennessee 37620
Admissions department information:
  Phone: 1-800-362-0014   Fax: (423) 652-4727
  E-mail: admissions@king.bristol.tn.us
  Web Site: http://www.king.bristol.tn.us
Founded: 1867
Affiliation: Presbyterian
1996–1997 freshman admission statistics:
  Number applied: 442   Number accepted: 375
Tests required: SAT or ACT
Total undergraduate enrollment: 224 men; 313 women
Faculty/student ratio: 1:13
Most popular majors: Business, English, political science, history, education
Setting: Urban
1997–98 expenses: Tuition: $9,830   Room & board: $3,444
Financial aid:
  % of students receiving aid: 95%   Average annual aid received: $9,379

THE KING'S UNIVERSITY COLLEGE

9125 50 St.
Edmonton, Alberta, Canada T6B 2H3
Admissions department information:
  Phone: (403) 465-3500   Fax: (403) 465-3534
  E-mail: registrar@kingsu.ab.ca
  Web Site: http://www.kingsu.ab.ca
Founded: 1979
Affiliation: Transdenominational
1996–1997 freshman admission statistics:
  Number applied: 383   Number accepted: 300
Total undergraduate enrollment: 235 men; 285 women
Faculty/student ratio: 1:15
Most popular majors: Psychology, biology, education
Setting: Urban
1997–98 expenses: Tuition: $4,590   Room & board: $4,150
Financial aid:
  % of students receiving aid: 100%   Average annual aid received: $300

KENTUCKY CHRISTIAN COLLEGE

100 Academic Pkwy.
Grayson, Kentucky 41143
Admissions department information:
Phone: 1-800-KCC-3181   Fax: (606) 474-3155
E-mail: ad80382@KCC.edu   Web Site: http://www.kcc.edu
Founded: 1919
Affiliation: Christian Church/Churches of Christ
1996–1997 freshman admission statistics:
Number applied: 298   Number accepted: 257
Tests required: SAT or ACT
Total undergraduate enrollment: 210 men; 267 women
Faculty/student ratio: 1:16
Most popular majors: Teacher ed., ministry, music, business administration, social work
Setting: Rural
1997–98 expenses: Tuition: $5,984   Room & board: $3,764
Financial aid:
% of students receiving aid: 94%   Average annual aid received: $5,377

KENTUCKY MOUNTAIN BIBLE COLLEGE

P.O. Box 10
Vancleve, Kentucky 41385
Admissions department information:
Phone: (606) 666-5000
E-mail: kmbc@kmbc.edu   Web Site: http://www.kmbc.edu
Founded: 1931
Affiliation: Interdenominational
1996–1997 freshman admission statistics:
Number applied: 20   Number accepted: 15
Tests required: SAT or ACT
Total undergraduate enrollment: 28 men; 34 women
Faculty/student ratio: 1:4
Most popular majors: Ministerial, missions, Christian ed., communications, music
Setting: Rural
1997–98 expenses: Tuition: $3,650   Room & board: $2,900
Financial aid:
% of students receiving aid: 50%   Average annual aid received: $1,250

LANCASTER BIBLE COLLEGE

901 Eden Rd.
Lancaster, Pennsylvania 17601
Admissions department information:
Phone: (717) 560-8271
Fax: (717) 560-8213
Founded: 1933
Affiliation: Nondenominational
1996–1997 freshman admission statistics:
Number applied: 363   Number accepted: 268
Total undergraduate enrollment: 332 men; 396 women
Faculty/student ratio: 1:15
Most popular majors: Teacher ed., Christian ed., pastoral studies, biblical counseling, missions
Setting: Suburban
1997–98 expenses: Tuition: $8,250   Room & board: $3,850
Financial aid:
% of students receiving aid: 85%   Average annual aid received: $7,503

LEE UNIVERSITY

P.O. Box 3450
Cleveland, Tennessee 37320-3450
Admissions department information:
Phone: (423) 614-8500   Fax: (423) 614-8533
E-mail: admissions@LeeCollege.edu
Web Site: http://www.LeeCollege.edu
Founded: 1918
Affiliation: Church of God
1996–1997 freshman admission statistics:
Number applied: 875   Number accepted: 638
Tests required: SAT or ACT
Total undergraduate enrollment: 1,237 men; 1,420 women
Most popular majors: Pre-med (biology), education, communications, psychology, business administration
Setting: Suburban
1997–98 expenses: Tuition: $5,496   Room & board: $3,680
Financial aid:
% of students receiving aid: 85%   Average annual aid received: n/a

LeTourneau University

2100 S. Mobberly Ave.

Longview, Texas 75607

Admissions department information:

Phone: (903) 233-3400

Fax: (903) 233-3411

E-mail: admissions@james.letu.edu

Web Site: http://www.letu.edu

Founded: 1951

Affiliation: Interdenominational

Tests required: SAT or ACT

Total undergraduate enrollment: 612 men; 206 women

Faculty/student ratio: 1:15

Setting: Suburban

1997–98 expenses:

Tuition: $10,594   Room & board: $4,770

Liberty University

1971 University Blvd.

Lynchburg, Virginia 24502

Admissions department information

Phone: 1-800-543-5317

Fax: 1-800-628-7977

E-mail: webmaster@liberty.edu

Web Site: http://www.liberty.edu

Founded: 1971

Affiliation: Baptist

1996–1997 freshman admission statistics:

Number applied: 3,800   Number accepted: 3,649

Tests required: SAT or ACT

Most popular majors: Education, business, nursing, psychology, youth ministry

Setting: Urban

1997–98 expenses:

Tuition: $7,950   Room & board: $4,800

Financial aid:

% of students receiving aid: 80%

Average annual aid received: $4,500

LIFE BIBLE COLLEGE
1100 Covina Blvd.
San Dimas, California 91773
Admissions department information:
 Phone: (909) 599-5433   Fax: (909) 599-6690
 E-mail: info@lifebible.edu
 Web Site: http://www.lifebible.edu
Founded: 1923
Affiliation: Foursquare
1996–1997 freshman admission statistics:
 Number applied: 164   Number accepted: 147
Tests required: SAT or ACT
Total undergraduate enrollment: 211 men; 200 women
Faculty/student ratio: 1:16
Most popular major: Bible
Setting: Suburban
1997–98 expenses: Tuition: $4,680   Room & board: $3,000
Financial aid:
 % of students receiving aid: 60%   Average annual aid received: $1,200

LINCOLN CHRISTIAN COLLEGE
100 Campus View Dr.
Lincoln, Illinois 62656
Admissions department information:
 Phone: (217) 732-3168   Fax: (217) 732-5914
Founded: 1944
Affiliation: Christian Church
1996–1997 freshman admission statistics:
 Number applied: 218   Number accepted: 188
Tests required: ACT
Total undergraduate enrollment: 266 men; 314 women
Faculty/student ratio: 1:15
Most popular majors: Preaching, teacher ed., Christian ed., early childhood, business
Setting: Suburban
1997–98 expenses: Tuition: $157/credit hr.   Room & board: $1,776
Financial aid:
 % of students receiving aid: 83%   Average annual aid received: $6,296

LINCOLN CHRISTIAN COLLEGE - EAST COAST

P.O. Box 624

Bel Air, Maryland 21014

Admissions department information:

Phone: (410) 836-2000   Fax: (410) 734-4271

E-mail: Admit@Lincolneast.edu

Web Site: http://www.Lincolneast.edu

Founded: 1946

Affiliation: Christian/Church of Christ

Tests required: SAT or ACT

Total undergraduate enrollment: 16 men; 14 women

Faculty/student ratio: 1:5

Most popular majors: Bible, general ministry

Setting: Suburban

1997–98 expenses:

Tuition: $135/credit hr.   Room & board: $1,000/semester (rm. only)

Financial aid:

% of students receiving aid: 95%   Average annual aid received: n/a

LOUISIANA COLLEGE

1140 College Dr.

Pineville, Louisiana 71359

Admissions department information:

Phone: 1-800-487-1906   Fax: (318) 487-7550

E-mail: Admission@lacollege.edu

Founded: 1906

Affiliation: Baptist

1996–1997 freshman admission statistics:

Number applied: 520   Number accepted: 404

Tests required: SAT or ACT

Total undergraduate enrollment: 342 men; 494 women

Faculty/student ratio: 1:16

Most popular majors: Biology, pre-med, nursing

Setting: Suburban

1997–98 expenses: Tuition: $196/credit hr.   Room & board: $3,058/yr.

Financial aid:

% of students receiving aid: 87%   Average annual aid received: $1,300

MALONE COLLEGE
515 25th St. N.W.
Canton, Ohio 44709
Admissions department information
Phone: (330) 471-8145   Fax: (330) 471-8149
E-mail: admissions@malone.malone.edu   Web Site: http://www.malone.edu
Founded: 1892
Affiliation: Evangelical Friends Church (Eastern Region)
1996–1997 freshman admission statistics:
Number applied: 859   Number accepted: 755
Tests required: ACT preferred, SAT accepted
Total undergraduate enrollment: 714 men; 1,188 women
Faculty/student ratio: 1:14
Most popular majors: Elementary ed., nursing, Christian ministry, business administration, social work
Setting: Suburban
1997–98 expenses: Tuition: $11,130   Room & board: $4,600
Financial aid:
% of students receiving aid: 92%   Average annual aid received: $8,880

MANHATTAN CHRISTIAN COLLEGE
1415 Anderson
Manhattan, Kansas 66502
Admissions department information:
Phone: (913) 539-3571   Fax: (913) 539-0832
Web Site: http://www.meeks.edu
Founded: 1927
Affiliation: Independent Christian Church
1996–1997 freshman admission statistics:
Number applied: 173   Number accepted: 147
Tests required: SAT or ACT
Total undergraduate enrollment: 141 men; 140 women
Faculty/student ratio: 1:11
Most popular majors: Pastoral ministry, education ministry, church music ministry, Christian service ministry, missions ministry
Setting: Suburban
1997–98 expenses: Tuition: $5,620   Room & board: $2,920
Financial aid:
% of students receiving aid: 72%   Average annual aid received: n/a

THE MASTER'S COLLEGE

21726 Placerita Canyon Rd.
Santa Clarita, California 91321-1200
Admissions department information:
  Phone: 1-800-568-6248   Fax: (805) 288-1037
  E-mail: enrollment@masters.edu   Web Site: http://www.masters.edu
Founded: 1927
Affiliation: Nondenominational
1996–1997 freshman admission statistics:
  Number applied: 524   Number accepted: 410
Tests required: SAT or ACT
Total undergraduate enrollment: 371 men; 422 women
Faculty/student ratio: 1:18
Most popular majors: Biblical studies, education, business,
  music, communications
Setting: Suburban
1997–98 expenses: Tuition: $11,980   Room & board: $4,786
Financial aid:
  % of students receiving aid: 85%   Average annual aid received: $9,000

MERCER UNIVERSITY

1400 Coleman Ave.
Macon, Georgia 31207
Admissions department information
  Phone: 1-800-637-2378 ext. 2650   Fax: (912) 752-2828
  E-mail: admissions@mercer.edu   Web Site: http://www.mercer.edu/admissions/
Founded: 1833
Affiliation: Georgia Baptist Convention
1996–1997 freshman admission statistics:
  Number applied: 2,503   Number accepted: 2,170
Tests required: SAT or ACT
Total undergraduate enrollment: 1,182 men; 1,475 women
Faculty/student ratio: 1:13
Most popular majors: Management, marketing, education,
  English, communications
Setting: Urban
1997–98 expenses: Tuition: $14,656   Room & board: $4,882
Financial aid:
  % of students receiving aid: 85%   Average annual aid received: $14,130

Messiah College

College Ave.
Grantham, Pennsylvania 17027
Admissions department information:
Phone: (717) 691-6000   Fax: (717) 796-5374
E-mail: admiss@messiah.edu   Web Site: http://www.messiah.edu
Founded: 1909
Affiliation: Brethren in Christ Church
1996–1997 freshman admission statistics:
Number applied: 1,904   Number accepted: 1,618
Tests required: SAT or ACT
Total undergraduate enrollment: 988 men; 1,529 women
Faculty/student ratio: 1:15
Most popular majors: Elementary ed., biology, nursing, psychology, business administration
Setting: Rural
1997–98 expenses: Tuition: $12,900   Room & board: $5,500
Financial aid:
% of students receiving aid: 92%   Average annual aid received: $10,064

Michigan Christian College

800 West Avon Rd.
Rochester Hills, Michigan 48307
Admissions department information:
Phone: 1-800-521-6010   Fax: (248) 218-2015
E-mail: admissions@michristian.edu   Web Site: http://www.michristian.edu
Founded: 1959
Affiliation: Church of Christ
1996–1997 freshman admission statistics:
Number applied: 222   Number accepted: 122
Tests required: ACT
Total undergraduate enrollment: 176 men; 187 women
Faculty/student ratio: 1:17
Most popular majors: Business management, human services, Christian ministry
Setting: Suburban
1997–98 expenses: Tuition: $6,524   Room & board: $3,700
Financial aid:
% of students receiving aid: 92%   Average annual aid received: $7,521

MID-AMERICA BIBLE COLLEGE

3500 S.W. 119th St.
Oklahoma City, Oklahoma 73170
Admissions department information:
Phone: (405) 691-3800   Fax: (405) 692-3165
E-mail: mbcok@cris.com
Founded: 1953
Affiliation: Church of God, Anderson, IN
1996–1997 freshman admission statistics:
Number applied: 300   Number accepted: 150
Tests required: SAT or ACT
Total undergraduate enrollment: 288 men; 224 women
Most popular majors: Pastoral ministry, specialized ministry, elementary/
secondary ed., business administration, behavioral science
Setting: Suburban
1997–98 expenses: Tuition: $4,032   Room & board: $3,098
Financial aid:
% of students receiving aid: 91%   Average annual aid received: $2,500

MIDAMERICA NAZARENE UNIVERSITY

2030 E. College Way
Olathe, Kansas 66062
Admissions department information:
Phone: (913) 791-3380   Fax: (913) 791-3481
E-mail: admissions@mnu.edu
Founded: 1966
Affiliation: Nazarene
1996–1997 freshman admission statistics:
Number applied: 447   Number accepted: 447
Tests required: SAT or ACT
Total undergraduate enrollment: 255 men; 347 women
Faculty/student ratio: 1:18
Most popular majors: Behavioral science & P.E., science and math,
business administration, education, humanities
Setting: Suburban
1997–98 expenses: Tuition: $272/credit hr. Room & board: $2,101/semester
Financial aid:
% of students receiving aid: 85%   Average annual aid received: $6,700

MILLIGAN COLLEGE

P.O. Box 210
Milligan College, Tennessee 37602
Admissions department information:
Phone: (423) 461-8730   Fax: (423) 461-8982
E-mail: admissions@milligan.edu
Web Site: http://www.milligan.edu
Founded: 1866
Affiliation: Christian Churches/Churches of Christ
1996–1997 freshman admission statistics:
Number applied: 599   Number accepted: 485
Tests required: SAT or ACT
Faculty/student ratio: 1:12
Most popular majors: Nursing, education, business, communications, biology
Setting: Suburban
1997–98 expenses: Tuition: $9,880   Room & board: $3,670
Financial aid:
% of students receiving aid: 90%   Average annual aid received: $3,500

MINNESOTA BIBLE COLLEGE

920 Mayowood Rd. S.W.
Rochester, Minnesota 55902
Admissions department information:
Phone: (507) 288-4563   Fax: (507) 288-9046
Web Site: http://www.mnbc.edu
Founded: 1913
Affiliation: Christian Church/Churches of Christ
1996–1997 freshman admission statistics:
Number applied: 63   Number accepted: 41
Tests required: SAT or ACT
Total undergraduate enrollment: 60 men; 56 women
Faculty/student ratio: 1:12
Most popular majors: Biblical studies & theology, pastoral leadership,
Christian ed., youth & families ministries, general studies
Setting: Urban
1997–98 expenses: Tuition: $5,270   Room & board: $2,900
Financial aid:
% of students receiving aid: 90%   Average annual aid received: $5,928

MISSISSIPPI COLLEGE

Box 4203
Clinton, Mississippi 39058
Admissions department information:
Phone: (601) 925-3240 Fax: (601) 925-3804
E-mail: admissions@mc.edu
Web Site: http://www.mc.edu
Founded: 1826
Affiliation: Southern Baptist
1996–1997 freshman admission statistics:
Number applied: 593 Number accepted: 511
Tests required: SAT or ACT
Total undergraduate enrollment: 1,357 men; 1,788 women
Faculty/student ratio: 1:16
Most popular majors: Biology/chemistry (pre-med), education, business, music, Christian studies
Setting: Suburban
1997–98 expenses: Tuition: $7,200 Room & board: $3,570
Financial aid:
% of students receiving aid: 89% Average annual aid received: $8,155

MISSOURI BAPTIST COLLEGE

One College Park Dr.
St. Louis, Missouri 63141
Admissions department information:
Phone: (314) 434-1115 Fax: (314) 434-7596
E-mail: admissions@mobap.edu Web Site: http://www.mobap.edu
Founded: 1964
Affiliation: Southern Baptist
1996–1997 freshman admission statistics:
Number applied: 262 Number accepted: 197
Tests required: SAT or ACT
Total undergraduate enrollment: 921 men; 1,502 women
Faculty/student ratio: 1:20
Most popular majors: Business, education, sports medicine, religion/religious ed., communications
Setting: Suburban
1997–98 expenses: Tuition: $8,170 Room & board: $4,030
Financial aid:
% of students receiving aid: 90% Average annual aid received: $6,907

MONTREAT COLLEGE

P.O. Box 1267
Montreat, North Carolina 28757
Admissions department information:
Phone: 1-800-669-6869   Fax: (704) 669-0120
E-mail: admissions@montreat.edu
Affiliation: Presbyterian
1996–1997 freshman admission statistics:
Number applied: 414   Number accepted: 292
Tests required: SAT or ACT
Total undergraduate enrollment: 71 men; 60 women
Faculty/student ratio: 1:7
Most popular majors: Business, outdoor ed., environmental science, music, human services
Setting: Rural
1997–98 expenses:
Tuition: $10,038   Room & board: $3,944
Financial aid:
% of students receiving aid: 87%   Average annual aid received: $9,000

MOODY BIBLE INSTITUTE

820 N. LaSalle Blvd.
Chicago, Illinois 60610
Admissions department information:
Phone: 1-800-967-4MBI or (312) 329-4400   Fax: (312) 329-8987
E-mail: admissions@mood.edu
Web Site: http://www.moody.edu
Founded: 1886
Affiliation: Nondenominational
1996–1997 freshman admission statistics:
Number applied: 860   Number accepted: 657
Tests required: ACT
Total undergraduate enrollment: 810 men; 592 women
Faculty/student ratio: 1:18
Most popular majors: Missions, educational ministries, Bible/theology
Setting: Urban
1997–98 expenses:
Tuition: Paid   Room & board: $4,300

MOUNT VERNON NAZARENE COLLEGE
800 Martinsburg Rd.
Mount Vernon, Ohio 43050
Admissions department information:
Phone: 1-800-782-2435   Fax: (614) 393-0511
E-mail: admissions@mvnc.edu   Web Site: http://www.mvnc.edu
Founded: 1968
Affiliation: Church of the Nazarene
1996–1997 freshman admission statistics:
Number applied: 833   Number accepted: 756
Tests required: ACT
Total undergraduate enrollment: 686 men; 999 women
Faculty/student ratio: 1:18
Most popular majors: Elementary education, business administration,
religion/Christian education, psychology, biology
Setting: Rural
1997–98 expenses: Tuition: $9,430   Room & board: $3,843
Financial aid:
% of students receiving aid: 91%   Average annual aid received: $8,031

MULTNOMAH BIBLE COLLEGE
8435 N.E. Glisan St.
Portland, Oregon 97220
Admissions department information:
Phone: 1-800-275-4672   Fax: (503) 254-1268
E-mail: admiss@multnomah.edu   Web Site: http://www.multnomah.edu
Founded: 1936
Affiliation: Interdenominational
1996–1997 freshman admission statistics:
Number applied: 420   Number accepted: 324
Tests required: SAT or ACT
Total undergraduate enrollment: 300 men; 234 women
Faculty/student ratio: 1:20
Most popular majors: Biblical studies, youth ministry, educational ministry,
intercultural ministry, pastoral ministry
Setting: Urban
1997–98 expenses: Tuition: $7,590   Room & board: $3,500
Financial aid:
% of students receiving aid: 75%   Average annual aid received: $5,000

NEBRASKA CHRISTIAN COLLEGE

1800 Syracuse Ave.
Norfolk, Nebraska 68701
Admissions department information:
    Phone: (402) 379-5000
    Fax: (402) 379-5100
Founded: 1946
Affiliation: Christian Churches/Churches of Christ
1996–1997 freshman admission statistics:
    Number applied: 146   Number accepted: 117
Tests required: SAT or ACT
Total undergraduate enrollment: 71 men; 76 women
Faculty/student ratio: 1:14
Most popular majors: Pastoral ministry, general studies, youth ministry,
    Christian ed., missions
Setting: Rural
1997–98 expenses: Tuition: $4,160   Room & board: $2,690
Financial aid:
    % of students receiving aid: 95%   Average annual aid received: $4,700

NORTH AMERICAN BAPTIST COLLEGE

11525 23 Avenue
Edmonton, Alberta, Canada T6J 4T3
Admissions department information:
    Phone: 1-800-567-4988 or (403) 437-1960
    Fax: (403)436-9416
Founded: 1939
Affiliation: North American Baptist Conference
1996–1997 freshman admission statistics:
    Number applied: 155 Number accepted: 124
Total undergraduate enrollment: 120 men; 100 women
Faculty/student ratio: 1:17
Most popular majors: Bible, general arts, education, music
Setting: Urban
1997–98 Expenses:
    Tuition: $3,950/Canadian   Room & board: $2,500/Canadian
Financial aid:
    % of students receiving aid: 21%   Average annual aid received: $450

NORTH GREENVILLE COLLEGE

P.O. Box 1892
Tigerville, North Carolina 29688
Admissions department information:
Phone: (864) 977-7001
Fax: (864) 977-7177
Founded: 1898
Affiliation: Baptist
1996–1997 freshman admission statistics:
Number applied: 810   Number accepted: 505
Tests required: SAT or ACT
Total undergraduate enrollment: 560 men; 380 women
Faculty/student ratio: 1:15
Most popular majors: Religion, business, education, mass communications, music
Setting: Rural
1997–98 expenses: Tuition: $6,900   Room & board: $4,080
Financial aid:
% of students receiving aid: 95%   Average annual aid received: $7,200

NORTH PARK UNIVERSITY

3225 W. Foster Ave.
Chicago, Illinois 60625
Admissions department information:
Phone: 1-800-888-6728 or (773) 244-5500
Fax: (773) 244-4953
E-mail: afao@northpark.edu
Web Site: http://www.northpark.edu
Founded: 1891
Affiliation: Evangelical Covenant Church
1996–1997 freshman admission statistics:
Number applied: 735   Number accepted: 571
Tests required: SAT or ACT
Faculty/student ratio: 1:16
Setting: Urban
1997–98 expenses: Tuition: $14,690   Room & board: $4,800
Financial aid
% of students receiving aid: 95%   Average annual aid received: n/a

Northwest Baptist College

22606 76A Avenue, Box 790
Langley, British Columbia, Canada V3A 8B8
Admissions department information:
Phone: (604) 888-3310   Fax: (604) 888-3354
E-mail: admissions@nbtc.bc.ca
Web Site: http://www.nbtc.bc.ca
Founded: 1934
Affiliation: Fellowship of Evangelical Baptist Churches
1996–1997 freshman admission statistics:
Number applied: 125   Number accepted: 102
Total undergraduate enrollment: 111 men; 100 women
Most popular majors: B.R.E., early childhood ed., A.R.E.
Setting: Rural
1997–98 expenses:: Tuition: $119-277/semester hr.   Room & board: n/a
Financial aid:
% of students receiving aid: 22%   Average annual aid received: $466

Northwest Christian College

828 E. 11th Ave.
Eugene, Oregon 97401
Admissions department information:
Phone: (541) 684-7201   Fax: (541) 343-9159
E-mail: admissions@eve.nwcc.edu
Web site: http://www.nwcc.edu
Founded: 1895
Affiliation: Christian Churches/Churches of Christ
1996–1997 freshman admission statistics:
Number applied: 191   Number accepted: 153
Tests Required: SAT or ACT
Total undergraduate enrollment: 163 men; 216 women
Faculty/student ratio: 1:14
Most popular majors: Business administration, psychology, elementary ed.,
Christian ministry, communications
Setting: Urban
1997–98 Expenses: Tuition: $10,665   Room & Board: $4,750
Financial aid:
% of students receiving aid: 88%   Average annual aid received: $11,500

Northwest College

5520 108th Ave. N.E., P.O. Box 579
Kirkland, Washington 98083-0579
Admissions department information:
    Phone: (425) 889-5231   Fax: (425) 827-0148
    E-mail: admissions@ncag.edu
    Web Site: http://www.say64k.com/nwcollege
Founded: 1934
Affiliation: Assemblies of God
1996–1997 freshman admission statistics:
    Number applied: 212   Number accepted: 207
Tests required: SAT or ACT
Total undergraduate enrollment: 360 men; 442 women
Faculty/student ratio: 1:17
Most popular majors: Education, behavioral science, business,
    church ministry, music
Setting: Suburban
1997–98 expenses: Tuition: $8,940   Room & board: $4,310
Financial aid:
    % of students receiving aid: 92%   Average annual aid received: $7,859

Northwest Nazarene College

623 Holly St.
Nampa, Idaho 83686
Admissions department information:
    Phone: (208) 467-8469   Fax: (208) 467-8645
    E-mail: admissions@nnc.edu
    Web Site: http://www.nnc.edu
Founded: 1913
Affiliation: Church of the Nazarene
Tests required: ACT
Faculty/student ratio: 1:13
Most popular majors: Education, business, social work,
    religious studies, biology
Setting: Suburban
1997–98 expenses: Tuition: $11,823   Room & board: $3,417
Financial aid:
    % of students receiving aid: 95%   Average annual aid received: $9,257

NORTHWESTERN COLLEGE

101 College Lane
Orange City, Iowa 51041
Admissions department information:
   Phone: (712) 737-7130   Fax: (712) 737-7164
   E-mail: markb@nwciowa.edu   Web Site: http://www.nwciowa.edu
Founded: 1882
Affiliation: Reformed Church in America
1996–1997 freshman admission statistics:
   Number applied: 988   Number accepted: 922
Tests required: SAT or ACT
Total undergraduate enrollment: 500 men; 660 women
Faculty/student ratio: 1:16
Most popular majors: Elementary ed., business admin., biology
Setting: Rural
1997–98 expenses: Tuition: $11,300   Room & board: $3,300
Financial aid:
   % of students receiving aid: 95%   Average annual aid received: $8,500

NORTHWESTERN COLLEGE

3003 Snelling Ave. N.
St. Paul, Minnesota 55113-1598
Admissions department information:
   Phone: 1-800-827-6827   Fax: (612) 631-5680
   E-mail: admissions@nwc.edu
   Web Site: http://www.nwc.edu
Founded: 1902
Affiliation: Nondenominational
1996–1997 freshman admission statistics:
   Number applied: 1,160   Number accepted: 872
Tests required: SAT or ACT
Total undergraduate enrollment: 553 men; 809 women
Faculty/student ratio: 1:16
Most popular majors: Education, business, psychology, Bible, communication
Setting: Suburban
1997–98 expenses: Tuition: $13,125   Room & board: $4,380
Financial aid:
   % of students receiving aid: 85%   Average annual aid received: $11,335

NYACK COLLEGE

1 S. Boulevard
Nyack, New York 10960-3698
Admissions department information:
  Phone: 1-800-33-NYACK   Fax: (914) 358-3047
  E-mail: enroll@nyack.edu   Web Site: http://www.nyackcollege.edu
Founded: 1882
Affiliation: Christian & Missionary Alliance
1996–1997 freshman admission statistics:
  Number applied: 784   Number accepted: 569
Tests required: SAT or ACT
Total undergraduate enrollment: 320 men; 408 women
Faculty/student ratio: 1:15
Most popular majors: Elementary ed., business administration, psychology,
  music ed., youth ministries
Setting: Suburban
1997–98 expenses: Tuition: $10,400   Room & board: $4,860
Financial aid:
  % of students receiving aid: 74%   Average annual aid received: $8,500

OAK HILLS BIBLE COLLEGE

1600 Oak Hills Road, S.W.
Bemidji, Minnesota 56601
Admissions department information:
  Phone: (218) 751-8670   Fax: (218) 751-8825
  E-mail: ohadmit@northernnet.com
  Web Site: http://www.digitmaster.com/hp/ohf/ohbc/
Founded: 1946
Affiliation: Interdenominational
1996–1997 freshman admission statistics:
  Number applied: 98   Number accepted: 52
Tests required: ACT
Total undergraduate enrollment: 62 men; 79 women
Faculty/student ratio: 1:10
Most popular majors: Applied psychology, pastoral, youth ministry, missions
Setting: Rural
1997–98 expenses: Tuition: $7,170   Room & board: $2,475
Financial aid:
  % of students receiving aid: 97.3%   Average annual aid received: $3,248

OKLAHOMA BAPTIST UNIVERSITY

500 West University
Shawnee, Oklahoma 74801
Admissions department information:
    Phone: (405) 878-2033 Fax: (405) 878-2046
    E-mail: admissions@mail.okbu.edu Web Site: http://www.okbu.edu
Founded: 1910
Affiliation: Southern Baptist
1996–1997 freshman admission statistics:
    Number applied: 950   Number accepted: 850
Tests required: SAT or ACT
Total undergraduate enrollment: 2,375
Faculty/student ratio: 1:14
Most popular majors: Pre-med, applied ministry, education, vocal music
Setting: Suburban
1997–98 expenses: Tuition: $7,090   Room & board: $3,180
Financial aid:
    % of students receiving aid: 85% Average annual aid received: $1,500

OLIVET NAZARENE UNIVERSITY

P.O. Box 592
Kankakee, Illinois 60901-0592
Admissions department information:
    hone: 1-800-648-1463 or (815) 939-5203 Fax: (815) 939-5203
    E-mail: admissions@olivet.edu Web Site: http://www.olivet.edu
Founded: 1907
Affiliation: Church of the Nazarene
1996–1997 freshman admission statistics:
    Number applied: 1,239 Number accepted: 1,094
Tests required: ACT
Total undergraduate enrollment: 743 men; 1,070 women
Faculty/student ratio: 1:18
Most popular majors: Nursing, elementary ed., business administration,
    biology, psychology
Setting: Suburban
1997–98 expenses: Tuition: $10,696   Room & board: $4,560
Financial aid:
    % of students receiving aid: 87% Average annual aid received: $9,318

ONTARIO BIBLE COLLEGE

25 Ballyconner Ct.

North York, Ontario, Canada M2M 4B3

Admissions department information:

Phone: (416) 226-6380 Fax: (416) 226-4210

E-mail: admissions@obcots.on.ca

Web Site: http://www.obcots.on.ca

Founded: 1894

Affiliation: Interdenominational

1996–1997 freshman admission statistics:

Number applied: 245 Number accepted: 170

Total undergraduate enrollment: 37% men; 63% women

Faculty/student ratio: 1:24

Most popular majors: Youth, pastoral, humanities, intercultural, Christian ed.

Setting: Suburban

1997–98 expenses:

Tuition: $5,280/Canadian Room & board: $3,400-$4,200/Canadian

Financial aid:

% of students receiving aid: 40% Average annual aid received: n/a

ORAL ROBERTS UNIVERSITY

7777 S. Lewis Ave.

Tulsa, Oklahoma 74171

Admissions department information:

Phone: (918) 495-6518 Fax: (918) 495-6222

E-mail: admissions@oru.edu

Web Site: http://www.oru.edu

Founded: 1963

1996–1997 freshman admission statistics:

Number applied: 1,326 Number accepted: 806

Tests required: SAT or ACT

Total undergraduate enrollment: 1,079 men; 1,488 women

Faculty/student ratio: 1:16

Most popular majors: Business, accounting, theology, nursing, biology

Setting: Suburban

1997–98 expenses: Tuition: $9,674 Room & board: $2,362

Financial aid:

% of students receiving aid: 68% Average annual aid received: $6,500

OUACHITA BAPTIST UNIVERSITY
410 Ouachita St.
Arkadelphia, Arkansas 71998
Admissions department information:
Phone: (501) 245-5110   Fax: (501) 245-5500
E-mail: admissions@sigma.obu.edu   Web Site: http://www.obu.edu
Founded: 1886
Affiliation: Southern Baptist
1996–1997 freshman admission statistics:
Number applied: 1,031   Number accepted: 925
Tests required: SAT or ACT
Total undergraduate enrollment: 720 men; 880 women
Faculty/student ratio: 1:11
Most popular majors: Business, education, religion, biology, mass communication
Setting: Rural
1997–98 expenses: Tuition: $7,970   Room & board: $3,040
Financial aid:
% of students receiving aid: 90%   Average annual aid received: $3,000

OZARK CHRISTIAN COLLEGE
1111 N. Main St.
Joplin, Missouri 64801
Admissions department information:
Phone: 1-800-299-4622   Fax: (417) 624-0090
E-mail: ozarkcc@aol.com   Web Site: http://www.occ.edu
Founded: 1942
Affiliation: Christian Churches/Churches of Christ
1996–1997 freshman admission statistics:
Number applied: 258   Number accepted: 258
Tests required: SAT or ACT
Total undergraduate enrollment: 356 men; 305 women
Faculty/student ratio: 1:20
Most popular majors: Youth ministry, preaching ministry, education, missions, music ministry
Setting: Urban
1997–98 expenses: Tuition: $3,520   Room & board: $3,100
Financial aid:
% of students receiving aid: 92%   Average annual aid received: $1,100

PACIFIC CHRISTIAN COLLEGE

2500 E. Nutwood Ave.
Fullerton, California 92831
Admissions department information:
  Phone: (714) 879-3901   Fax: (714) 526-0231
Founded: 1928
Affiliation: Christian Churches/Churches of Christ
Tests required: SAT or ACT
Faculty/student ratio: 1:14
Most popular majors: Youth ministry, psychology, physical therapy,
  biblical studies, general studies
Setting: Suburban
1997–98 expenses:
  Tuition: $8,950   Room & board: $3,619
Financial aid:
  % of students receiving aid: 82%   Average annual aid received: n/a

PALM BEACH ATLANTIC COLLEGE

901 S. Flagler Dr., P.O. Box 24708
West Palm Beach, Florida 33416-4708
Admissions department information:
  Phone: (561) 803-2100   Fax: (561) 803-2115
  E-mail: admit@pbac.edu
  Web Site: http://www.pbac.edu
Founded: 1968
Affiliation: Interdenominational
1996–1997 freshman admission statistics:
  Number applied: 999   Number accepted: 801
Tests required: SAT or ACT
Total undergraduate enrollment: 529 men; 762 women
Faculty/student ratio: 1:17
Most popular majors: Management of human resources, business,
  education, psychology, biology
Setting: Urban
1997–98 expenses:
  Tuition: $9,900   Room & board: $4,300
Financial aid
  % of students receiving aid: 90%   Average annual aid received: $11,500

PATTEN COLLEGE

2433 Coolidge Ave.
Oakland, California 94601
Admissions department information:
Phone: (510) 533-8300   Fax: (510) 534-4344
Founded: 1944
Affiliation: Interdenominational
1996–1997 freshman admission statistics:
Number applied: 160   Number accepted: 145
Tests required: SAT or ACT
Total undergraduate enrollment: 342 men; 262 women
Faculty/student ratio: 1:12
Setting: Urban
1997–98 expenses:
Tuition: $7,008   Room & board: $2,350
Financial aid:
% of students receiving aid: 85%   Average annual aid received: $7,200

PEPPERDINE UNIVERSITY

24255 Pacific Coast Hwy.
Malibu, California 90263-4392
Admissions department information:
Phone: (310) 456-4392   Fax: (310)456-4861
E-mail: admission-plong@pepperdine.edu
Web Site: http://www.pepperdine.edu
Founded: 1937
Affiliation: Church of Christ
1996–1997 freshman admission statistics:
Number applied: 3,499   Number accepted: 2,785
Tests required: SAT or ACT
Total undergraduate enrollment: 45% men; 55% women
Faculty/student ratio: 1:13
Most popular majors: Business, telecommunications, sports medicine,
psychology, biology
Setting: Suburban
1997–98 expenses: Tuition: $21,100   Room & board: $6,980
Financial aid:
% of students receiving aid: 75%   Average annual aid received: $18,352

PHILADELPHIA COLLEGE OF BIBLE

200 Manor Ave.
Langhorne, Pennsylvania 19047
Admissions department information:
Phone: (215) 752-5800   Fax: (215) 702-4248
E-mail: admissions@pcb.edu
Founded: 1958
Affiliation: Nondenominational
1996–1997 freshman admission statistics:
Number applied: 907   Number accepted: 560
Tests required: SAT or ACT
Total undergraduate enrollment: 393 men; 409 women
Faculty/student ratio: 1:16
Most popular majors: Bible, social work, education, music, business
Setting: Suburban
1997–98 expenses: Tuition: $8,850   Room & board: $4,820
Financial aid:
% of students receiving aid: 81%   Average annual aid received: $7,462

PIEDMONT BIBLE COLLEGE

716 Franklin St.
Winston-Salem, North Carolina 27101-5197
Admissions department information:
Phone: 1-800-937-5097   Fax: (910) 725-5522
E-mail: Admissions@pbc.edu   Web Site: http://www.ibnet.org/pbc.htm
Founded: 1945
Affiliation: Baptist
1996–1997 freshman admission statistics:
Number applied: 77   Number accepted: 69
Tests required: SAT or ACT
Total undergraduate enrollment: 148 men; 101 women
Faculty/student ratio: 1:14
Most popular majors: Biblical studies, aviation, elementary ed.,
  missions, music
Setting: Urban
1997–98 expenses: Tuition: $4,790   Room & board: $3,090
Financial aid:
% of students receiving aid: 70%   Average annual aid received: $1,071

Point Loma Nazarene College

3900 Lomaland Dr.
San Diego, California 92106
Admissions department information:
Phone: (619) 849-2273   Fax: (619) 849-2601
E-mail: discover@ptloma.edu   Web Site: http://www.ptloma.edu
Founded: 1902
Affiliation: Church of the Nazarene
1996–1997 freshman admission statistics:
Number applied: 1,088   Number accepted: 992
Tests required: SAT or ACT
Total undergraduate enrollment: 845 men; 1,297 women
Faculty/student ratio: 1:15
Most popular majors: Liberal studies, business administration, nursing,
psychology, biology-chemistry
Setting: Urban
1997–98 expenses: Tuition: $12,224   Room & board: $4,970
Financial aid:
% of students receiving aid: 85%   Average annual aid received: $10,320

Practical Bible College

400 Riverside Dr., P.O. Box 601
Bible School Park, New York 13737
Admissions department information:
Phone: 1-800-331-4137   Fax: (607) 729-2962
E-mail: PBC@lakenet.org   Web Site: http://www.lakenet.org/~pbc
Founded: 1900
Affiliation: Independent
1996–1997 freshman admission statistics:
Number applied: 110   Number accepted: 85
Tests required: ACT
Total undergraduate enrollment: 140 men; 100 women
Faculty/student ratio: 1:15
Most popular majors: Christian counseling ministries, youth ministries,
pastoral ministries, church ministries, 1-yr. Bible certificate program
Setting: Suburban
1997–98 expenses: Tuition: $2,300/semester   Room & board: $1,650/sem.
Financial aid:
% of students receiving aid: 85%   Average annual aid received: $2,500

Providence College & Theological Seminary

Otterburne, Manitoba
Canada R0A 1G0

Admissions department information:
Phone: (204) 433-7488   Fax: (204) 433-7158
E-mail: dthiele@providence.mb.ca
Web Site: http://www.Providence.mb.ca

Founded: 1925

Affiliation: Interdenominational

1996–1997 freshman admission statistics:
Number applied: 185   Number accepted: 175

Total undergraduate enrollment: 162 men; 188 women

Faculty/student ratio: 1:13

Most popular majors: Social sciences, pre-education, youth leadership,
biblical studies, music

Setting: Rural

1997–98 expenses: Tuition: $3,790/Canadian   Room & board: $3,040/Can.

Financial aid:
% of students receiving aid: 30%
Average annual aid received: $5,600 (student loans only)

Puget Sound Christian College

410 4th Ave N.
Edmonds, Washington 98020

Admissions department information
Phone: (425) 775-8686   Fax: (425) 775-8688

Founded: 1950

1996–1997 freshman admission statistics:
Number applied: 90   Number accepted: 56

Tests required: SAT or ACT

Total undergraduate enrollment: 101 men; 78 women

Faculty/student ratio: 1:15

Most popular majors: Preaching ministry, world missions, Christian ed./
youth ministry, music ministry, Christian ed./social science

Setting: Suburban

1997–98 expenses: Tuition: $5,550   Room & board: $3,870

Financial aid:
% of students receiving aid: 75%   Average annual aid received: $3,300

REDEEMER COLLEGE

777 Highway 53 East

Ancaster, Ontario, Canada L9J 1K4

Admissions department information:

Phone: (905) 648-2131 ext. 280   Fax: (905) 648-2134

Founded: 1982

Affiliation: Nondenominational

1996–1997 freshman admission statistics:

Number applied: 272   Number accepted: 206

Total undergraduate enrollment: 166 men; 253 women

Faculty/student ratio: 1:14

Most popular majors: English, psychology, education, history, business

Setting: Suburban

1997–98 expenses:

Tuition: $7,950   Room & board: $4,180

Financial aid:

% of students receiving aid: n/a   Average annual aid received: n/a

REFORMED BIBLE COLLEGE

3333 E. Beltline N.E.

Grand Rapids, Michigan 49505

Admissions department information

Phone: (616) 222-3000   Fax: (616) 222-3045

E-mail: rbc-go@ix.netcom.com

Founded: 1939

Affiliation: Interdenominational

1996–1997 freshman admission statistics:

Number applied: 100   Number accepted: 97

Tests required: SAT or ACT

Total undergraduate enrollment: 95 men; 85 women

Faculty/student ratio: 1:15

Most popular majors: Pre-seminary, missions, youth ministry, social work, urban ministry

Setting: Suburban

1997–98 expenses:

Tuition: $6,750   Room & board: $3,550

Financial aid:

% of students receiving aid: 80%   Average annual aid received: $2,732

Roanoke Bible College

714 First St.
Elizabeth City, North Carolina 27909
Admissions department information:
  Phone: (919) 338-5191 ext. 222   Fax: (919) 338-0801
  E-mail: roanoke@interpath.com
  Web Site: http://www.geocities.com/Athens/Acropolis/1003
Founded: 1948
Affiliation: Church of Christ/Christian Church
1996–1997 freshman admission statistics:
  Number applied: 129   Number accepted: 87
Tests required: SAT or ACT
Total undergraduate enrollment: 80 men; 81 women
Faculty/student ratio: 1:12
Most popular majors: Bible/theology, Bible/counseling, Bible/youth ministry
Setting: Urban
1997–98 expenses: Tuition: $140/credit hr.   Room & board: $1,600/sem.
Financial aid:
  % of students receiving aid: 96%   Average annual aid received: $1,112

Roberts Wesleyan College

2301 Westside Dr.
Rochester, New York 14624
Admissions department information:
  Phone: (716) 594-6400   Fax: (716) 594-6371
  E-mail: admissions@roberts.edu
  Web Site: http://www.nysernet.org/Roberts
Founded: 1866
1996–1997 freshman admission statistics:
  Number applied: 476   Number accepted: 425
Tests required: SAT or ACT
Total undergraduate enrollment: 362 men; 655 women
Faculty/student ratio: 1:14
Most popular majors: Elementary ed., nursing, music, social work, business
Setting: Suburban
1997–98 expenses: Tuition: $11,930   Room & board: $4,260
Financial aid:
  % of students receiving aid: 94%   Average annual aid received: n/a

ROCKY MOUNTAIN COLLEGE

4039 Brentwood Rd. N.W.

Calgary, Alberta, Canada T2L 1L1

Admissions department information

Phone: (403) 284-5100   Fax: (403) 220-9567

E-mail: rockymc@tewsplanet.net

Affiliation: Evangelical Missionary Church

1996–1997 freshman admission statistics:

Number applied: 151   Number accepted: 113

Total undergraduate enrollment: 99 men; 122 women

Faculty/student ratio: 1:18

Most popular majors: Youth, counseling, pastoral, post-professional, music

Setting: Urban

1997–98 expenses:

Tuition: $3,900/Canadian   Room & board: $1,450/Canadian

Financial aid:

% of students receiving aid: n/a   Average annual aid received: n/a

SAMFORD UNIVERSITY

800 Lakeshore Dr.

Birmingham, Alabama 35229

Admissions department information:

Phone: 1-800-888-7208 Fax: (205) 870-2171

Founded: 1841

Affiliation: Southern Baptist

1996–1997 freshman admission statistics:

Number applied: 1,779;   Number accepted: 1,571

Tests required: SAT or ACT

Total undergraduate enrollment: 1,132 men; 1,786 women

Faculty/student ratio: 1:17

Most popular majors: Business, health professions, biological sciences, home economics, education

Setting: Suburban

1997–98 expenses:

Tuition: $9,432   Room & board: $4,308

Financial aid:

% of students receiving aid: 75%   Average annual aid received: $6,453

San Jose Christian College

790 S. 12th St.
San Jose, California 95112
Admissions department information:
Phone: (408) 293-9058   Fax: (408) 293-7352
E-mail: SJCC1939@aol.com   Web Site: http://www.SJChristianCol.edu
Founded: 1939
Affiliation: Nondenominational
1996–1997 freshman admission statistics:
Number applied: 132   Number accepted: 79
Tests required: SAT or ACT
Total undergraduate enrollment: 185 men; 165 women
Faculty/student ratio: 1:12
Most popular majors: Bible & theology, youth ministry, counseling, Christian ed.
Setting: Urban
1997–98 expenses: Tuition: $6,672   Room & board: $3,689
Financial aid:
% of students receiving aid: 80%   Average annual aid received: $2,000

Seattle Pacific University

3307 Third Ave. W.
Seattle, Washington 98119
Admissions department information:
Phone: 1-800-366-3349   Fax: (206) 281-2669
E-mail: admissions@spu.edu   Web Site: http://www.spu.edu
Founded: 1891
Affiliation: Free Methodist
1996–1997 freshman admission statistics:
Number applied: 1,364   Number accepted: 1,244
Tests required: SAT or ACT
Total undergraduate enrollment: 901 men; 1,605 women
Faculty/student ratio: 1:15
Most popular majors: Teacher certification, nursing,
business administration, psychology, electrical engineering
Setting: Urban
1997–98 expenses: Tuition: $14,130   Room & board: $5,418
Financial aid:
% of students receiving aid: 76%   Average annual aid received: $12,635

SHORTER COLLEGE
315 Shorter Ave.
Rome, Georgia 30165
Admissions department information
Phone: 1-800-868-6980   Fax: (706) 233-7224
E-mail: admissions@shorter.edu   Web Site: http://www.shorter.edu
Founded: 1873
Affiliation: Georgia Baptist
1996–1997 freshman admission statistics:
Number applied: 553   Number accepted: 458
Tests required: SAT or ACT
Total undergraduate enrollment: 285 men; 517 women
Faculty/student ratio: 1:13
Most popular majors: Education, business, fine arts, sciences, social sciences
Setting: Suburban
1997–98 expenses: Tuition: $8,150   Room & board: $4,250
Financial aid:
% of students receiving aid: 99%   Average annual aid received: $5,565

SIMPSON COLLEGE
2211 College View Dr.
Redding, California 96003
Admissions department information:
Phone: 1-800-598-2493 or (916) 224-5606   Fax: (916) 224-5627
E-mail: admissions@simpsonca.edu   Web Site: http://www.simpsonca.edu
Founded: 1921
Affiliation: The Christian & Missionary Alliance
1996–1997 freshman admission statistics:
Number applied: 471   Number accepted: 138
Tests required: SAT or ACT
Total undergraduate enrollment: 316 men; 528 women
Faculty/student ratio: 1:21
Most popular majors: Business, education, humanities, psychology,
Christian ministries
Setting: Suburban
1997–98 expenses: Tuition: $8,200   Room & board: $4,100
Financial aid:
% of students receiving aid: 90%   Average annual aid received: $9,000

SOUTHEASTERN BAPTIST THEOLOGICAL SEMINARY AND COLLEGE

222 Wingate Dr.
Wake Forest, North Carolina 27587
Admissions department information:
    Phone: 1-800-284-6317
    Fax: (919) 556-0998
Founded: Seminary-1950   College-1995
Affiliation: Southern Baptist
Total undergraduate enrollment: 160 men; 40 women
Most popular major: Biblical studies
Setting: Urban
1997–98 expenses:
    Tuition: $70/credit hr.   Room & board: n/a
Financial aid:
    % of students receiving aid: n/a   Average annual aid received: n/a

SOUTHEASTERN BIBLE COLLEGE

3001 Highway 280 E.
Birmingham, Alabama 35216
Admissions department information:
    Phone: 1-800-749-8878
    Fax: (205) 970-9207
    E-mail: 102064.406@compuserve.com;
    Web Site: http://www.sebc.edu
Founded: 1935
Affiliation: Nondenominational
1996–1997 freshman admission statistics:
    Number applied: 105   Number accepted: 63
Tests required: SAT or ACT
Total undergraduate enrollment: 110 men; 80 women
Faculty/student ratio: 1:17
Most popular majors: Pre-seminary, elementary ed., church ed.,
    pastor's program, missions
Setting: Suburban
1997–98 expenses:
    Tuition: $5,180   Room & board: $3,040
Financial aid:
    % of students receiving aid: 85%   Average annual aid received: $3,500

SOUTHEASTERN COLLEGE OF THE ASSEMBLIES OF GOD

1000 Longfellow Blvd.
Lakeland, Florida 33801

Admissions department information:
Phone: (941) 667-5011 Fax: (941) 667-5200
E-mail: sjmarkha@secollege.edu
Web Site: http://www.secollege.edu

Founded: 1935
Affiliation: Assemblies of God
1996–1997 freshman admission statistics:
Number applied: 586 Number accepted: 439
Tests required: SAT or ACT
Total undergraduate enrollment: 562 men; 528 women
Faculty/student ratio: 1:24
Most popular majors: Church ministries, education, psychology, music
Setting: Urban
1997–98 expenses: Tuition: $4,170 Room & board: $3,226
Financial aid:
% of students receiving aid: 80% Average annual aid received: n/a

SOUTHERN CALIFORNIA COLLEGE

55 Fair Dr.
Costa Mesa, California 92626

Admissions department information
Phone: 1-800-SCC-6279 Fax: (714) 966-5471
E-mail: admissions@sccu.edu Web Site: http://www.sccu.edu

Founded: 1920
Affiliation: Assemblies of God
1996–1997 freshman admission statistics:
Number applied: 907 Number accepted: 783
Tests required: SAT or ACT
Total undergraduate enrollment: 482 men; 602 women
Faculty/student ratio: 1:16
Most popular majors: Business, education, religion, communication, psychology
Setting: Suburban
1997–98 expenses: Tuition: $11,320 Room & board: $4,860
Financial aid:
% of students receiving aid: 90% Average annual aid received: $9,932

SOUTHERN NAZARENE UNIVERSITY
6729 N.W. 39 Freeway
Bethany, Oklahoma 73008
Admissions department information:
Phone: (405) 491-6324   Fax: (405) 491-6320
Web Site: http://www@snu.edu
Founded: 1899
Affiliation: Church of the Nazarene
1996–1997 freshman admission statistics:
Number applied: 552   Number accepted: 261
Tests required: SAT or ACT
Total undergraduate enrollment: 543 men; 698 women
Faculty/student ratio: 1:17
Setting: Suburban
1997–98 expenses:
Tuition: $7,860   Room & board: $3,978
Financial aid:
% of students receiving aid: 80%   Average annual aid received: $6,100

SOUTHERN WESLEYAN UNIVERSITY
P.O. Box 1020
Central, South Carolina 29630
Admissions department information:
Phone: 1-800-282-8798   Fax: (864) 639-0826
E-mail: 103134.1317@compuserve.com
Web Site: http://www.swu.edu
Founded: 1906
Affiliation: Wesleyan Church
1996–1997 freshman admission statistics:
Number applied: 329   Number accepted: 175
Tests required: SAT or ACT
Total undergraduate enrollment: 190 men; 225 women
Faculty/student ratio: 1:11
Most popular majors: Education, business, religion, psychology, music
Setting: Rural
1997–98 expenses: Tuition: $9,980   Room & board: $3,540
Financial aid:
% of students receiving aid: 95%   Average annual aid received: $8,500

Southwest Baptist University

1600 University Ave.
Bolivar, Missouri 65613
Admissions department information:
Phone: (417) 326-1811   Fax: (417) 326-1514
E-mail: DCamtbel@bunie.edu
Web Site: http://www.sbuniv.edu
Founded: 1878
Affiliation: Southern Baptist
1996–1997 freshman admission statistics:
Number applied: 1,200   Number accepted: 1,200
Tests required: SAT or ACT
Total undergraduate enrollment: 45% men; 55% women
Faculty/student ratio: 1:17
Most popular majors: Education, business, psychology, music, science
Setting: Suburban
1997–98 expenses:
Tuition: $8,112   Room & board: $2,650
Financial aid:
% of students receiving aid: 85%   Average annual aid received: $5,000

Southwestern College

2625 E. Cactus Rd.
Phoenix, Arizona 85032
Admissions department information:
Phone: (602) 992-6101   Fax: (602) 404-2159
Founded: 1960
Affiliation: Conservative Baptist
1996–1997 freshman admission statistics:
Number applied: 134   Number accepted: 77
Tests required: SAT or ACT
Most popular majors: Elementary ed., Christian ministries, biblical studies
Setting: Urban
1997–98 expenses:
Tuition: $6,600   Room & board: $3,320
Financial aid:
% of students receiving aid: 90%   Average annual aid received: $4,400

SPRING ARBOR COLLEGE
106 E. Main St.
Spring Arbor, Michigan 49283
Admissions department information:
Phone: (517) 750-1200   Fax: (517) 750-6620
E-mail: admissions@admin.arbor.edu
Web Site: http://www.arbor.edu
Founded: 1873
Affiliation: Free Methodist Church
1996–1997 freshman admission statistics:
Number applied: 383   Number accepted: 341
Tests required: SAT or ACT
Faculty/student ratio: 1:13
Most popular majors: Education, psychology, biology, communications,
business
Setting: Rural
1997–98 expenses:
Tuition: $10,580   Room & board: $4,190
Financial aid:
% of students receiving aid: 80%   Average annual aid received: $6,500

ST. LOUIS CHRISTIAN COLLEGE
1360 Grandview Dr.
Florissant, Missouri 63031
Admissions department information
Phone: (314) 837-6777 ext. 1302
Fax: (314) 837-8291
Founded: 1956
Affiliation: Christian Churches/Churches of Christ
Tests required: SAT or ACT
Total undergraduate enrollment: 93 men; 60 women
Faculty/student ratio: 1:11
Most popular majors: Preaching, education, youth ministry, missions/inter-
cultural ministry, music
Setting: Suburban
1997–98 expenses: Tuition: $141/credit hr.   Room & board: $1,335
Financial aid:
% of students receiving aid: n/a   Average annual aid received: n/a

STEINBACH BIBLE COLLEGE

P.O. Box 1420

Steinbach, Manitoba, Canada R0A 2A0

Admissions department information:

Phone: 1-800-230-8478 or (204) 326-6451   Fax: (204) 326-6908

E-mail: pr@sbcollege.mb.ca; Web Site: http://www.sbcollege.mb.ca

Founded: 1936

Affiliation: Mennonite

1996–1997 freshman admission statistics:

Number applied: 44   Number accepted: 41

Total undergraduate enrollment: 41 men; 35 women

Faculty/student ratio: 1:9

Most popular majors: Religious studies, church ministries,
general studies, music

Setting: Rural

1997–98 expenses: Tuition: $2,900   Room & board: $3,120

Financial aid:

% of students receiving aid: 37%   Average annual aid received: $500

STERLING COLLEGE

P.O. Box 98

Sterling, Kansas 67579

Admissions department information:

Phone: (316) 278-4275   Fax: (316) 278-3690

Web Site: http://www.sterling.edu

Founded: 1887

Affiliation: Presbyterian

1996–1997 freshman admission statistics:

Number applied: 644   Number accepted: 451

Tests required: SAT or ACT

Total undergraduate enrollment: 226 men; 248 women

Faculty/student ratio: 1:12

Most popular majors: Elementary ed., biology, business, physical ed.,
behavioral science

Setting: Rural

1997–98 expenses: Tuition: $10,076   Room & board: $3,884

Financial aid:

% of students receiving aid: 96%   Average annual aid received: $10,059

STETSON UNIVERSITY

421 N. Woodland Blvd. Unit 8378

Deland, Florida 32720-3771

Admissions department information:

Phone: 1-800-688-0101   Fax: (904) 822-7112

E-mail: admissions@stetson.edu   Web Site: http://www.stetson.edu

Founded: 1883

1996–1997 freshman admission statistics:

Number applied: 1,966   Number accepted: 1,670

Tests required: SAT or ACT

Total undergraduate enrollment: 804 men; 1,047 women

Faculty/student ratio: 1:11

Most popular majors: Psychology, general business, accounting, management, elementary ed.

Setting: Suburban

1997–98 expenses: Tuition: $15,100   Room & board: $5,500

Financial aid:

% of students receiving aid: 85%   Average annual aid received: n/a

TABOR COLLEGE

400 S. Jefferson

Hillsboro, Kansas 67063

Admissions department information:

Phone: 1-800-TABOR99   Fax: (316) 947-2607

E-mail: admissions@tcnet.tabor.edu

Web Site: http://www.tabor

Founded: 1905

Affiliation: Mennonite Brethren

1996–1997 freshman admission statistics:

Number applied: 367   Number accepted: 228

Tests required: SAT or ACT

Total undergraduate enrollment: 239 men; 222 women

Faculty/student ratio: 1:13

Most popular majors: Education, pre-med, business, Bible/religion

Setting: Rural

1997–98 expenses: Tuition: $10,360   Room & board: $4,000

Financial aid:

% of students receiving aid: 100%   Average annual aid received: $5,200

TAYLOR UNIVERSITY
500 W. Reade Ave.
Upland, Indiana 46989
Admissions department information:
   Phone: 1-800-882-3456   Fax: (765) 998-4925
   E-mail: admissions_u@tayloru.edu   Web Site: http://www.tayloru.edu
Founded: 1846
1996–1997 freshman admission statistics:
   Number applied: 1,638   Number accepted: 1,019
Tests required: SAT or ACT
Total undergraduate enrollment: 856 men; 1,010 women
Faculty/student ratio: 1:17
Most popular majors: Education, business, computer science, pre-med, psychology
Setting: Rural
1997–98 expenses: Tuition: $13,270   Room & board: $4,410
Financial aid:
   % of students receiving aid: 79%   Average annual aid received: $8,000

TENNESSEE TEMPLE UNIVERSITY
1815 Union Ave.
Chattanooga, Tennessee 37404
Admissions department information:
   Phone: 1-800-553-4050   Fax: (423) 493-4497
   E-mail: ttuinfo@tntemple.edu
   Web Site: http://www.tntemple.edu
Founded: 1946
Affiliation: Baptist
1996–1997 freshman admission statistics:
   Number applied: 230   Number accepted: 220
Tests required: SAT or ACT
Total undergraduate enrollment: 254 men; 258 women
Faculty/student ratio: 1:14
Most popular majors: Bible, music, education, business, missions
Setting: Urban
1997–98 expenses: Tuition: $5,820   Room & board: $4,750
Financial aid:
   % of students receiving aid: 97%   Average annual aid received: $6,500

TOCCOA FALLS COLLEGE
Toccoa Falls, Georgia 30498
Admissions department information:
   Phone: 1-800-868-3257   Fax: (706) 886-6412
   E-mail: admissio@toccoafalls.edu
Founded: 1907
Affiliation: Interdenominational
1996–1997 freshman admission statistics:
   Number applied: 1,115   Number accepted: 773
Tests required: SAT or ACT
Total undergraduate enrollment: 411 men; 481 women
Faculty/student ratio: 1:17
Most popular majors: Bible & theology, Christian counseling,
   Christian education, world missions, teacher education
Setting: Rural
1997–98 expenses: Tuition: $7,254   Room & board: $3,708
Financial aid:
   % of students receiving aid: 85%   Average annual aid received: $7,673

TREVECCA NAZARENE UNIVERSITY
333 Murfreesboro Rd.
Nashville, Tennessee 37210
Admissions department information:
   Phone: (615) 248-1320   Fax: (615) 248-7728
   E-mail: admissions_und@trevecca.edu
   Web Site: http://www.trevecca.edu
Founded: 1901
Affiliation: Nazarene
1996–1997 freshman admission statistics:
   Number applied: 340   Number accepted: 340
Tests required: ACT
Faculty/student ratio: 1:14
Most popular majors: Education, music, allied health, business, religion
Setting: Suburban
1997–98 expenses:
   Tuition: $8,480   Room & board: $4,038
Financial aid:
   % of students receiving aid: 85%   Average annual aid received: $9,000

TRINITY BIBLE COLLEGE

50 S. Sixth Ave.
Ellendale, North Dakota 58436
Admissions department information:
 Phone: 1-888-TBC-2DAY   Fax: (701) 349-5443
 E-mail: TBC2DAY@juno.com
Founded: 1947
Affiliation: Assemblies of God
1996–1997 freshman admission statistics:
 Number applied: 206   Number accepted: 206
Tests required: SAT or ACT
Faculty/student ratio: 1:14
Most popular majors: Bible, ministerial, missions, elementary ed.
Setting: Rural
1997–98 expenses:
 Tuition: $169/credit hr.   Room & board: $1,700
Financial aid:
 % of students receiving aid: 98%   Average annual aid received: n/a

TRINITY CHRISTIAN COLLEGE

6601 W. College Dr.
Palos Heights, Illinois 60463
Admissions department information:
 Phone: 1-800-748-0085   Fax: (708) 239-3995
 E-mail: admissions@trnty.edu
 Web Site: http://www:trnty.edu
Founded: 1959
Affiliation: Interdenominational
1996–1997 freshman admission statistics:
 Number applied: 516   Number accepted: 220
Tests required: SAT or ACT
Total undergraduate enrollment: 230 men; 389 women
Faculty/student ratio: 1:12
Most popular majors: Business, education, nursing, psychology, pre-med
Setting: Suburban
1997–98 expenses: Tuition: $11,700   Room & board: $2,400
Financial aid:
 % of students receiving aid: 89%   Average annual aid received: $7,515

TRINITY COLLEGE OF FLORIDA

2430 Trinity Oaks Blvd.
New Port Richey, Florida 34655
Admissions department information:
Phone: (813) 376-6911
Founded: 1932
1996–1997 freshman admission statistics:
Number applied: 29   Number accepted: 28
Tests required: SAT or ACT
Total undergraduate enrollment: 85 men; 85 women
Faculty/student ratio: 1:11
Most popular majors: Missions, pastoral ministries, youth ministry,
counseling, Christian elementary ed.
Setting: Rural
1997–98 expenses:
Tuition: $3,250   Room & board: $2,400
Financial aid:
% of students receiving aid: 53%   Average annual aid received: $1,000

TRINITY INTERNATIONAL UNIVERSITY

2065 Half Day Rd.
Deerfield, Illinois 60015
Admissions department information
Phone: 1-800-822-3225   Fax: (847) 317-7081
E-mail: tcoadm@trin.edu
Web Site: http://www.tiu.edu
Founded: 1897
Affiliation: Evangelical Free Church
1996–1997 freshman admission statistics:
Number applied: 480   Number accepted: 313
Tests required: SAT or ACT
Total undergraduate enrollment: 400 men; 431 women
Faculty/student ratio: 1:16
Most popular majors: Education, business, youth ministry
Setting: Suburban
1997–98 expenses: Tuition: $12,630   Room & board: $4,630
Financial aid:
% of students receiving aid: 85%   Average annual aid received: $11,487

TRINITY WESTERN UNIVERSITY
7600 Glover Rd.
Langley, British Columbia, Canada U2Y 1Y1
Admissions department information:
　Phone: 1-888-GO-TO-TWU　Fax: (604) 513-2064
　E-mail: admissions@twu.ca
　Web Site: http://www.twu.ca
Founded: 1962
Affiliation: Evangelical Free Church
1996–1997 freshman admission statistics:
　Number applied: 923　Number accepted: 638
Tests required: SAT or ACT
Total undergraduate enrollment: 720 men; 1,052 women
Faculty/student ratio: 1:17
Most popular majors: Business administration, education, psychology,
　nursing, biology
Setting: Rural
1997–98 expenses:
　Tuition: $8,310　Room & board: $5,280
Financial aid:
　% of students receiving aid: 92%　Average annual aid received: $1,233

TRUETT-MCCONNELL COLLEGE
100 Alumni Dr.
Cleveland, Georgia 30528
Admissions department information:
　Phone: 1-800-226-8621　Fax: (706) 865-7615
　E-mail: penny@truett.cc.ga.us
　Web Site: http://www/truett.cc.ga.us
Affiliation: Baptist
Tests required: SAT or ACT
Total undergraduate enrollment: 1,056 men; 1,034 women
Most popular majors: Education, business, music, liberal arts, behavioral
　science
Setting: Rural
1997–98 expenses: Tuition: $1,850　Room & board: $975
Financial aid:
　% of students receiving aid: 90%　Average annual aid received: n/a

Union University
1050 University Dr.
Jackson, Tennessee 38305
Admissions department information:
Phone: (901) 661-5000   Fax: (901) 661-5187
E-mail: info@buster.uu.edu   Web Site: http://www.uu.edu
Founded: 1823
Affiliation: Southern Baptist
1996–1997 freshman admission statistics:
Number applied: 875   Number accepted: 717
Tests required: SAT or ACT
Total undergraduate enrollment: 630 men; 1,157 women
Faculty/student ratio: 1:13
Most popular majors: Business, education, nursing, Christian studies, psychology
Setting: Suburban
1997–98 expenses: Tuition: $7,990   Room & board: $3,300
Financial aid:
% of students receiving aid: 82%   Average annual aid received: $3,500

University of Sioux Falls
1101 W. 22nd St.
Sioux Falls, South Dakota 57105
Admissions department information:
Phone: 1-800-888-1047   Fax: (605) 381-6615
E-mail: admissions@thecoo.edu   Web Site: http://www.thecoo.edu
Founded: 1883
Affiliation: American Baptist
1996–1997 freshman admission statistics:
Number applied: 539   Number accepted: 502
Tests required: ACT recommended
Total undergraduate enrollment: 364 men; 465 women
Faculty/student ratio: 1:15
Most popular majors: Elementary ed., business administration,
management, wellness, religious studies
Setting: Suburban
1997–98 expenses: Tuition: $10,750   Room & board: $3,400
Financial aid:
% of students receiving aid: 83%   Average annual aid received: $8,259

The University of Mobile

P.O. Box 13220
Mobile, Alabama 36663-0220

Admissions department information:
Phone: (334) 675-5990   Fax: (334) 675-6329
E-mail: adminfo@umobile.edu   Web Site: http://www.umobile.edu/-adminfo

Founded: 1961

Affiliation: Southern Baptist

1996–1997 freshman admission statistics:
Number applied: 469   Number accepted: 385

Tests required: SAT or ACT

Total undergraduate enrollment: 673 men; 1,270 women

Faculty/student ratio: 1:22

Most popular majors: Nursing, business administration, education, religion, organizational management

Setting: Suburban

1997–98 Expenses: Tuition $7,140   Room & board $4,080

Financial aid:
% of students receiving aid: 96%   Average annual aid received: $4,625

Valley Forge Christian College

1401 Charlestown Rd.
Phoenixville, Pennsylvania 19460

Admissions department information:
Phone: (610) 917-1427   Fax: (610) 935-9353
E-mail: vfcccomp@voicenet.com

Founded: 1932

Affiliation: Assemblies of God

1996–1997 freshman admission statistics:
Number applied: 307   Number accepted: 172

Tests required: SAT or ACT

Total undergraduate enrollment: 45% men; 55% women

Faculty/student ratio: 1:20

Most popular majors: Pastoral, youth ministry, missions, early childhood ed., music

Setting: Suburban

1997–98 expenses: Tuition: $5,360   Room & board: $3,480

Financial aid:
% of students receiving aid: 80%   Average annual aid received: $3,000

VIRGINIA INTERMONT COLLEGE

1013 Moore St.
Bristol, Virginia 24201
Admissions department information:
  Phone: (540) 669-6101 Fax: (540) 669-5763
  E-mail: viadmit@vic.edu
  Web Site: http://www.vic.edu
Founded: 1884
Affiliation: Baptist
1996–1997 freshman admission statistics:
  Number applied: 449   Number accepted: 357
Tests required: SAT or ACT
Total undergraduate enrollment: 207 men; 562 women
Faculty/student ratio: 1:12
Most popular majors: Equine, photography, business, education, art
Setting: Urban
1997–98 expenses: Tuition: $10,450   Room & board: $4,250
Financial aid:
  % of students receiving aid: 86%   Average annual aid received: $10,610

WARNER PACIFIC COLLEGE

2219 S.E. 68th Ave.
Portland, Oregon 97215
Admissions department information:
  Phone: (503) 788-7495 Fax: (503) 788-7425
  E-mail: admiss@warnerpacific.edu
  Web Site: http://www.warnerpacific.edu
Founded: 1937
Affiliation: Church of God (Anderson, IN)
1996–1997 freshman admission statistics:
  Number applied: 256 Number accepted: 221
Tests required: SAT or ACT
Faculty/student ratio: 1:15
Most popular majors: Education, business, religion, science, social science
Setting: Urban
1997–98 expenses: Tuition: $10,260   Room & board: $3,890
Financial aid:
  % of students receiving aid: 81% Average annual aid received: $7,250

WARNER SOUTHERN COLLEGE

5301 U.S. 27 South
Lake Wales, Florida 33853
Admissions department information:
Phone: (941) 638-7250   Fax: (941) 638-1472
E-mail: warner@admissions.edu   Web Site: http://www.warner.edu
Founded: 1968
Affiliation: Church of God (Anderson, IN)
1996–1997 freshman admission statistics:
Number applied: 254   Number accepted: 183
Tests required: SAT or ACT
Total undergraduate enrollment: 249 men; 367 women
Faculty/student ratio: 1:14
Most popular majors: Education, business, church ministries,
music, social sciences
Setting: Rural
1997–98 expenses: Tuition: $7,560   Room & board: $1,985
Financial aid:
% of students receiving aid: 98%   Average annual aid received: $3,000

WASHINGTON BIBLE COLLEGE

6511 Princess Garden Parkway
Lanham, Maryland 20706-3599
Admissions department information:
Phone: (301) 552-1400 ext. 280   Fax: (301) 552-2775
E-mail: admiss@bible.edu   Web Site: http://www/bible.edu
Founded: 1938
Affiliation: Nondenominational
1996–1997 freshman admission statistics:
Number applied: 209   Number accepted: 121
Tests required: SAT or ACT
Total undergraduate enrollment: 177 men; 142 women
Faculty/student ratio: 1:13
Most popular majors: Biblical studies, counseling, pastoral ministries,
elementary ed., pre-seminary
Setting: Suburban
1997–98 expenses: Tuition: $5,920   Room & board: $3,990
Financial aid:
% of students receiving aid: 50%   Average annual aid received: $2,500

WESLEY COLLEGE

P.O. Box 1070, 111 Wesley Circle
Florence, Mississippi 39073
Admissions department information
Phone: (601) 845-2265   Fax: (601) 845-2266
E-mail: wesley@misnet.com
Web Site: http://www.wesleycollege.edu
Founded: 1944
Affiliation: Congregational Methodist
1996–1997 freshman admission statistics:
Number applied: 35   Number accepted: 35
Tests required: SAT or ACT
Most popular majors: Christian ed., missions, pastoral studies, Christian ministries
Setting: Rural
1997–98 expenses: Tuition: $1,920   Room & board: $4,520
Financial aid:
% of students receiving aid: 58%   Average annual aid received: $3,950

WESTERN BAPTIST COLLEGE

5000 Deer Park Dr. S.E.
Salem, Oregon 97301
Admissions department information:
Phone: 1-800-845-3005 or (503) 375-7005   Fax: (503) 585-4316
E-mail: admissions@wbc.edu   Web Site: http://www.wbc.edu
Founded: 1935
Affiliation: Independent Baptist
1996–1997 freshman admission statistics:
Number applied: 434   Number accepted: 381
Tests required: SAT or ACT
Total undergraduate enrollment: 300 men; 420 women
Faculty/student ratio: 1:16
Most popular majors: Elementary ed., secondary ed., psychology, youth work, business
Setting: Rural
1997–98 expenses: Tuition: $11,900   Room & board: $4,820
Financial aid:
% of students receiving aid: 85%   Average annual aid received: $9,500

WESTERN PENTECOSTAL BIBLE COLLEGE

Box 1700
Abbotsford, British Columbia, Canada V2S 7G7
Admissions department information:
Phone: (604) 853-7491   Fax: (604) 853-8951
Founded: 1941
Affiliation: Pentecostal Assemblies of Canada
1996–1997 freshman admission statistics:
Number applied: 76   Number accepted: 73
Total undergraduate enrollment: 106 men; 86 women
Most popular majors: Theology, religious ed., church music, discipleship
Setting: Suburban
1997–98 expenses:
Tuition: $4,386   Room & board: $3,450
Financial aid:
% of students receiving aid: 40%;
Average annual aid received: $500–$1,000

WESTMONT COLLEGE

955 La Paz Rd.
Santa Barbara, California 93108
Admissions department information:
Phone: (805) 565-6200   Fax: (805) 565-6234
E-mail: admissions@westmont.edu
Web Site: http://www.westmont.edu
Founded: 1940
Affiliation: Interdenominational
1996–1997 freshman admission statistics:
Number applied: 1,017   Number accepted: 874
Tests required: SAT or ACT
Total undergraduate enrollment: 530 men; 703 women
Faculty/student ratio: 1:16
Most popular majors: Biology, economics/business, communications,
English, education
Setting: Suburban
1997–98 expenses: Tuition: $17,486   Room & board: $6,048
Financial aid:
% of students receiving aid: 85%   Average annual aid received: $12,000

Wheaton College

501 College Ave.
Wheaton, Illinois 60187
Admissions department information:
Phone: 1-800-222-2419 or (630) 752-5005   Fax: (630) 752-5285
E-mail: admissions@wheaton.edu
Founded: 1860
Affiliation: Interdenominational
1996–1997 freshman admission statistics:
Number applied: 1,947   Number accepted: 1,022
Tests required: SAT or ACT
Total undergraduate enrollment: 1,132 men; 1,183 women
Faculty/student ratio: 1:13
Most popular majors: Literature, psychology, music, communications, biblical studies
Setting: Suburban
1997–98 expenses: Tuition: $13,780   Room & board: $4,740
Financial aid: % of students receiving aid: 60%
Average annual aid received: $6,400/scholarships & grants - $2,360/loans

Whitworth College

300 W. Hawthorne
Spokane, Washington 99251
Admissions department information:
Phone: 1-800-533-4668   Fax: (509) 777-3758
E-mail: admissions@whitworth.edu Web Site: http://www.whitworth.edu
Founded: 1890
Affiliation: Presbyterian Church (USA)
1996–1997 freshman admission statistics:
Number applied: 1,500   Number accepted: 1,200
Tests required: SAT or ACT
Total undergraduate enrollment: 654 men; 1,018 women
Faculty/student ratio: 1:16
Most popular majors: Education, communications, psychology, economics, music
Setting: Suburban
1997–98 expenses: Tuition: $14,750   Room & board: $5,200
Financial aid:
% of students receiving aid: 88%   Average annual aid received: $13,000

WILLIAM AND CATHERINE BOOTH COLLEGE

47 Webb Place
Winnipeg, Manitoba, Canada R3B 2P2
Admissions department information:
    Phone: (204) 947-6701   Fax: (204) 942-3856
    E-mail: wcbc@cc.umanitoba.ca
Founded: 1982
Affiliation: The Salvation Army
1996–1997 freshman admission statistics:
    Number applied: 37   Number accepted: 35
Tests required: SAT
Total undergraduate enrollment: 30 men; 60 women
Faculty/student ratio: 1:10
Most popular majors: Social work, biblical & theological studies,
    Christian ministries
Setting: Urban
1997–98 expenses: Tuition: $3,010
    Room & board: $3,020/single - $2,630/double
Financial aid: % of students receiving aid: 35%
    Average annual aid received: $6,000/loans

WILLIAM CAREY COLLEGE

498 Tuscan Ave.
Hattiesburg, Mississippi 39401
Admissions department information:
    Phone: (601) 582-6103   Fax: (601) 582-6454
    E-mail: admiss@mail.wmcarey.edu   Web Site: http://www.wllmcarey.edu
Founded: 1906
Affiliation: Southern Baptist
1996–1997 freshman admission statistics:
    Number applied: 409   Number accepted: 211
Tests required: SAT or ACT
Total undergraduate enrollment: 587 men; 1,175 women
Faculty/student ratio: 1:17
Most popular majors: Nursing, education, business, religion, music
1997–98 expenses: Tuition: $192/hr.   Room & board: $2,565
Financial aid:
    % of students receiving aid: 80%   Average annual aid received: $6,300

WILLIAMS BAPTIST COLLEGE

P.O. Box 3665
Walnut Ridge, Arkansas 72476
Admissions department information
Phone: (501) 886-6741   Fax: (501) 886-3924
E-mail: admissions@wbclab.wbcoll.edu   Web Site: http://www.wbc2.wbcoll.edu
Founded: 1941
Affiliation: Southern Baptist
1996–1997 freshman admission statistics:
Number applied: 190   Number accepted: 150
Tests required: SAT or ACT
Total undergraduate enrollment: 264 men; 300 women
Faculty/student ratio: 1:14
Most popular majors: Elementary ed., business administration, physical ed.,
psychology, religion
Setting: Rural
1997–98 expenses: Tuition: $2,500/semester   Room & board: $1,461/sem.
Financial aid:
% of students receiving aid: 90%   Average annual aid received: $7,000

WINGATE UNIVERSITY

Wingate, North Carolina 28174
Admissions department information:
Phone: (704) 233-8200   Fax: (704) 233-8110
E-mail: admit@wingate.edu   Web Site: http://www.wingate.edu
Founded: 1896
Affiliation: Baptist
1996–1997 freshman admission statistics:
Number applied: 1,231   Number accepted: 978
Tests required: SAT or ACT
Total undergraduate enrollment: 613 men; 568 women
Faculty/student ratio: 1:13
Most popular majors: Business, education, communication, human services,
sports medicine
Setting: Suburban
1997–98 expenses: Tuition: $11,730   Room & board: $4,100
Financial aid
% of students receiving aid: 90%   Average annual aid received: $9,500

WILLIAM JEWELL COLLEGE

500 College Hill
Liberty, Missouri 64068

Admissions department information:

Phone: 1-800-753-7009   Fax: (816) 781-7700   ext. 5540
E-mail: www.jewell.edu
Web Site: http://www.jewell.edu

Founded: 1849

Affiliation: Baptist

1996–1997 freshman admission statistics:

Number applied: 678   Number accepted: 587

Tests required: SAT or ACT

Total undergraduate enrollment: 458 men; 714 women

Faculty/student ratio: 1:12

Most popular majors: Business, education, nursing, biology, music

Setting: Suburban

1997–98 expenses:

Tuition: $11,850   Room & board: $3,560

Financial aid

% of students receiving aid: 94%   Average annual aid received: $10,600